MORNINGS with JESUS 2025

DAILY ENCOURAGEMENT *for Your* SOUL

365 DEVOTIONS

Guideposts

A Gift from Guideposts

Thank you for your purchase! We appreciate your support and want to express our gratitude with a special gift just for you.

Dive into *Spirit Lifters*, a complimentary e-book that will fortify your faith and offer solace during challenging moments. It contains 31 carefully selected verses from scripture that will soothe your soul and uplift your spirit.

Please use the QR code or go to **guideposts.org/spiritlifters** to download.

Mornings with Jesus 2025

Published by Guideposts
100 Reserve Road, Suite E200
Danbury, CT 06810
Guideposts.org

Cover design by Müllerhaus
Cover photo by Getty Images
Indexed by Frances Lennie
Typeset by Aptara, Inc.

ISBN 978-1-961126-46-6 (softcover)
ISBN 978-1-961251-91-5 (softcover large print)
ISBN 978-1-961126-47-3 (epub)

Printed and bound in the United States of America

Dear Friends,

Welcome to *Mornings with Jesus 2025*! We're excited about the 365 all-new, spirit-lifting devotions in this year's volume.

First Chronicles 16:11 (NIV) tells us, "Look to the Lord and his strength; seek his face always." In these pages, our beloved writers bring us along on their personal journeys, sharing insights as they endeavor to follow the profound directive to rely on the Lord and always seek His guidance. They share how important Jesus is to them and how their relationships with Him help them change their lives, face their trials, and deepen their faith.

We are grateful for the generosity of this year's contributors to *Mornings with Jesus:* Becky Alexander, Susanna Foth Aughtmon, Jeannie Blackmer, Isabella Campolattaro, Kristy Dewberry, Pat Butler Dyson, Gwen Ford Faulkenberry, Grace Fox, Heidi Gaul, Tricia Goyer, Jennifer Grant, Pamela Toussaint Howard, Jennie Ivey, Gloria Joyce, Jeanette Levellie, Ericka Loynes, Erin Keeley Marshall, Dianne Neal Matthews, Claire McGarry, Jennifer Anne F. Messing, Cynthia Ruchti, Emily E. Ryan, Karen Sargent, Stephanie Thompson, Cassandra Tiersma, Suzanne Davenport Tietjen, Marilyn Turk, Barbranda Lumpkins Walls, and Brenda L. Yoder.

As you read each day's scripture, followed by the writer's heartfelt devotion, we hope you will discover points of connection between the Word and the writers' experiences and your own life. We hope you will consider putting into action the "faith steps" that follow each devotion and, in doing so, move closer to Jesus. We pray that in the year ahead you know the strength, peace, and comfort that come from seeking His face always.

Faithfully yours,
Editors of Guideposts

Especially for You!

Sign up for the daily online *Mornings with Jesus* newsletter at guideposts.org/newsletter. Connect with Jesus—His teachings, love, and wisdom—featuring devotions and inspiring reflections by the contributing writers.

NEW YEAR'S DAY, WEDNESDAY, JANUARY 1

Then Moses said, "Now show me your glory."
Exodus 33:18 (NIV)

FOR THE PAST FEW YEARS, I've chosen a word that would be my focus for the year. As this year approached, I began thinking about what that word would be. Finally, one morning I woke up and *glory* came to my mind. It's a good word.

I've often thought about what God's glory is. To me, it is to feel or see His presence. Moses, the leader of the Israelites in the wilderness, was blessed to be able to meet with the Lord and talk to Him as a friend (Exodus 33:11). During one of their encounters, Moses asked God to show him His glory. The Lord granted his request and covered Moses with His own hand as He passed by. I imagine God's glory was so great that Moses wouldn't have been able to withstand it.

Like Moses, I want to see and experience the glory of God. This year I'm asking Jesus to let me be keenly aware of His presence and see His wondrous works around me. I want to hear Him loud and clear when He speaks to me. I am expecting Him to show up and show out in unmistakable ways. Even in the darkest of days, I want to know He's there. So, in the words of Moses in one of his

many conversations with God, please Lord Jesus, let me see Your glory. I am looking for You this year.
—BARBRANDA LUMPKINS WALLS

FAITH STEP: *Consider choosing a word to focus on this year. Prepare to keep a log of how Jesus shows up and shows out as you seek His face.*

THURSDAY, JANUARY 2

Restore to me the joy of your salvation and grant me a willing spirit, to sustain me. Psalm 51:12 (NIV)

MY WORD FOR THE YEAR is *restore* because we recently lost our home and all our belongings in a Colorado wildfire. The emotional and physical process of recovery has been daunting. I spent hours creating a detailed inventory for our insurance company of all our belongings, ranging from the number of spatulas in our kitchen to the cars in our garage. Most items are replaceable, but some are not, such as photos of our children through the years and our wedding album. Tears flowed as I mourned this and the loss of other precious items. This tedious process of listing all we had lost left me despondent.

Then one day my sister-in-law Liz knocked on our door. She held a silver-framed photo album with our wedding picture on the front. Turns out my other sister-in-law, Kathie, who had died a few years earlier, had taken pictures of every page of our wedding album! She also took photos at every family gathering with disposable cameras. I never knew what she did with them. Until now.

Thankfully, Liz had kept all of Kathie's albums in storage. The quality wasn't great, but I now had photos of my kids through the years, and our wedding album had been miraculously restored.

This joy-filled surprise sustained me as I continued the recovery process. Not only can Jesus unexpectedly restore lost things, but He can also restore my joy. As I worked through endless spreadsheets, I had a more willing spirit to not give up. And I expectantly keep my eyes open for joyful surprises in the midst of the loss. —JEANNIE BLACKMER

FAITH STEP: *Write about a recent time when Jesus surprised you by restoring your joy.*

FRIDAY, JANUARY 3

Then will appear the sign of the Son of Man in heaven. And then all the peoples of the earth will mourn when they see the Son of Man coming on the clouds of heaven, with power and great glory. Matthew 24:30 (NIV)

PACIFIC NORTHWEST WINTERS BRING GRAY, overcast skies. It's a glorious day when the gloom gives way to sunshine and fluffy white clouds. The rare sight compels me to set aside my work and take advantage of the opportunity to soak up the sun's rays.

On one such day, I ambled along a path parallel to the Fraser River. Sunshine warmed my face and drew my gaze heavenward. I scanned the clouds set against a backdrop of blue and imagined a future day promised to be infinitely more glorious.

The world's turmoil prompts me to pray for Jesus to come soon, to shine His light across the earth and dispel the darkness and despair. But then I think of family and friends who have not yet chosen to believe the Gospel's life-saving message, and I grieve at the thought of their hearts being unprepared for His return.

I examine my own heart and wonder how it aligns with Jesus's words about all the peoples of the earth mourning when He appears. I suspect that one glimpse of His face and the scars on His hands will leave me wishing I'd doubted Him less and loved Him more. And so, I pray, "Jesus, come soon. But until that day, have Your way in me." —GRACE FOX

FAITH STEP: *If you're able, go outside for a few minutes. Fix your gaze on the sky and ask Jesus to help you love and trust Him wholeheartedly until the day He returns.*

SATURDAY, JANUARY 4

Trust in the LORD with all thine heart; and lean not unto thine own understanding. In all thy ways acknowledge him, and he shall direct thy paths. Proverbs 3:5–6 (KJV)

WHENEVER MY COMPANY MADE ORGANIZATIONAL changes or my coworkers were leaving our team or getting promoted, I would peek at job openings. One day, a position piqued my interest. I prayed about it and applied, but the opportunity fizzled. I shared my disappointment with one of my former managers. She encouraged me not to chase titles and positions, but to ask myself if I was doing work I enjoyed. Since I loved the work I did, I took that "closed door" as a sign from Jesus to stop peeking and trust Him with my career.

Not long afterward, I received a message from a woman about an opening on her team. I was hesitant. I didn't want to entertain the thought of leaving my current job if it wasn't part of Jesus's grand plan for me, but I agreed to talk with her because a colleague referred me. The role was a great opportunity. In this case, I had several interviews take place quickly, was offered the job, and I accepted. It was the perfect position for me—and I wasn't even looking!

Sometimes when I ask Jesus to change my situation, He does. Other times when I ask Him for a change, He keeps me right where I am. I don't always understand the reason behind His plan, but I know He has one. In fact, I'd stake my job on it! —ERICKA LOYNES

FAITH STEP: *Look up synonyms for the word* trust. *Reflect on how you can demonstrate those outlooks in your life this week.*

SUNDAY, JANUARY 5

By this everyone will know that you are my disciples, if you love one another. John 13:35 (NIV)

AT THE START OF EACH new year, it feels like everywhere I look, I'm being asked to change. "New year; new you!" the message shouts. It's featured on social media, in magazines, and on podcasts and radio shows. Sometimes it feels like a kind invitation: I'm gently prompted to reflect on what matters most to me and then to prioritize these things over the course of the coming year. *Is nurturing my relationships with my husband and children a value?* I can put more family outings and dinners on the calendar. *Is spending time in prayer important to me?* I can choose to wake up a few minutes earlier than usual to pray.

Other messages I receive when a new year begins feel more guilt-inducing and like just more to put on my to-do list. Drink more water. Exercise more.

Even if these changes matter to me, such messages simply remind me of my shortcomings.

But rather than feeling guilty about what I have left undone in the past or what goal I've not yet met, I want to choose a different resolution this year. Taking Jesus's lead, I'd like to, more and more, show His love to others by seeing them with His eyes. Jesus's messages ring true, no matter what time of year it is. —JENNIFER GRANT

FAITH STEP: *Close your eyes and bring to mind three people you interact with regularly. Ask Jesus to help you see them with His eyes as you seek to show them love in the coming year.*

MONDAY, JANUARY 6

For I am not ashamed of the gospel of Christ, for it is the power of God to salvation for everyone who believes.
Romans 1:16 (NKJV)

MY NEIGHBOR PAINTS HIMSELF BLUE and gold, dons a fuzzy blue wig, and proudly wears his St. Louis Blues jersey, matching knee-high socks, and gold tennis shoes to every hockey game. When he drives to a rival city, his personalized license plate proclaims he is a Blues fan. He mows the team logo into his lawn, takes aerial photos with a drone, and posts his artwork on social media. Every conversation with him always comes back to his favorite team and their playoff chances. He is completely sold out to the St. Louis Blues.

I'm not a hockey fan, but I am Team Jesus. I wonder if people see Jesus all over my life as if I were a crazed fan. Does the joy of walking with Him reflect on my face? Does the heart beneath my faith T-shirt reflect what the writing proclaims? When I'm behind the wheel, does my driving align with my JOY FM bumper sticker other drivers see? What do my social media accounts say about my relationship with Jesus? How often do my conversations include Him and how to win eternal life?

Sometimes I flip the TV channel to the Blues game to spot my neighbor in the rowdy crowd. Yet, during Sunday worship, I cheer for Jesus quietly so no one hears me sing out of tune. Jesus doesn't expect me to paint my face and wear a fuzzy wig, but I hope others can tell I'm a sold-out fan for Team Jesus. —KAREN SARGENT

FAITH STEP: *Demonstrate you are on Team Jesus to a stranger you encounter by your actions or words.*

TUESDAY, JANUARY 7

Do not judge, or you too will be judged. Matthew 7:1 (NIV)

I WORKED FOR YEARS AS an administrator at a retirement community before I had kids. One of my responsibilities was to walk the facility and grounds once a month with a clipboard in my hand. I'd note every scuff on the wall, stain on the carpet, and lightbulb out in the parking lot. It became a to-do list for the maintenance department to address. When my husband and I bought our first home, my trained eye saw every flaw and shortcoming. That turned into a to-do list for us to address. After I had kids, that same trained eye saw every mistake they made. All my efforts were channeled into correcting and teaching them. Every. Minute. Of. Every. Day. You can only imagine how exhausting that was for them and for me.

I've decided it's time for a change. I'm now retraining my eyes. Instead of finding what's wrong, I started looking for what's right. I notice their loving and kind actions toward each other, character traits that make them unique and precious, the effort they make to do chores.

Jesus doesn't ask me to judge others. That's His Father's job (Ecclesiastes 12:14). I believe He asks me to find what's right, not just in my kids but in everyone I meet. My to-do list is complete thanks to Jesus. —CLAIRE MCGARRY

FAITH STEP: *Make a conscious effort to see what's right in every person you meet. Pray to leave your judgment in Jesus's capable hands.*

WEDNESDAY, JANUARY 8

The city had no need of the sun or of the moon to shine in it, for the glory of God illuminated it. The Lamb is its light. Revelation 21:23 (NKJV)

"OH, HALLELUJAH, THE SUN IS shining!" I say as I open my window shades on a frigid day. I can endure cold temperatures better if I can see those shimmering rays of light poking through the clouds. Sunshine gives me hope.

My circumstances remain unchanged. I still have health issues, family challenges, and work stress. My savings account hasn't tripled in size nor has my kitten quit waking me at 4:30 a.m.

But that warm, glimmering orb in the sky changes my outlook. The sunshine is a foretaste of heaven, that city of glorious light waiting for me.

How sweet to see a glimpse of our future home in the book of Revelation. No shadows or murky skies. No dark worries that hover like clouds. Only light, glowing a million times brighter than the sun. Reaching into every corner, radiating from Jesus's very being.

No matter how cold, murky, or cloudy my days on earth, I rejoice because there's a light-filled home waiting for me. The sun and the Son shine hope on every day, no matter what the weather.
—JEANETTE LEVELLIE

FAITH STEP: *Go into the darkest room of your house. Now turn the light on and thank Jesus for His promise of a bright eternity.*

THURSDAY, JANUARY 9

This is what the LORD says to Israel: "Seek me and live; do not seek Bethel, do not go to Gilgal, do not journey to Beersheba...." Seek the LORD and live. Amos 5:4–6 (NIV)

IN THE PAST, I READ the New Testament several times, though I always got bogged down somewhere in the middle of the Old Testament. To try to maintain my interest, I bounced from Bible book to Bible book and passage to passage. The random order left me wondering if I possibly missed a few pages.

So, I committed to read through the Old Testament again this year—all chapters, every verse, the entire collection of thirty-nine books—but in reverse order. I started in Malachi and set Genesis as my end goal. Today I reached Amos. And what a treasure I found there! Four simple yet profound words. I marked "Seek me and live" with a purple highlighter.

Using Amos as the mouthpiece, God pleaded for the straying Israelites to pursue Him instead of pagan religions. Idols could give them nothing; God could provide life, protection, blessings, and favor. Would they really reject an offer like that?

As I stare now at the four words in my Bible, I contemplate the massive meaning behind the short phrase. "Seek me and live." The message of mercy and grace extends across the centuries to me. My caring God sent His Son, Jesus, to offer me abundant life here on earth and eternal life in heaven. I could never turn away a love like that. —BECKY ALEXANDER

FAITH STEP: *If you haven't read the whole Bible, consider beginning this week. Create your own plan, try my backward method, or access a Bible-reading app. Exploring God's Word is an effective way to seek Jesus.*

FRIDAY, JANUARY 10

In their hearts humans plan their course, but the LORD *establishes their steps.* Proverbs 16:9 (NIV)

I START EACH WEEK WITH a nice-size to-do list. As a freelance writer with different clients, I want to make sure I have my week neatly organized. I don't like my projects to overlap. I use an online calendar and a written calendar. I add my meal planning and household chores. These are followed by the outliers on the list—oil changes, veterinary appointments, and teeth cleaning. This is my plan. And then there is the reality of what the week actually looks like.

It's more like ordered chaos. It makes me feel wild and crazy.

This week I had a last-minute deadline crop up. I took on the project not realizing how it would shift the rest of the week. Then our car started acting weird. We were down to carrots and ketchup in the fridge. And I wasn't sleeping great. I was no longer running my life. It was running me. The thing about planning is that life rarely goes as planned.

Jesus wants me to trust Him with my days (Proverbs 3:5–6). All of them. Especially the ones that don't go as planned. I want to feel like I am in control. He reminds me that abundant life is not found in my well-meaning expectations and calendar dates, but in Him (John 10:10). I'm grateful that in those wild and crazy moments of life, Jesus is establishing my steps. —SUSANNA FOTH AUGHTMON

FAITH STEP: *Look at your to-do list today. Pencil in time with Jesus and ask Him to establish your steps, even when things get wild and crazy.*

SATURDAY, JANUARY 11

God saw all that he had made, and it was very good. And there was evening, and there was morning— the sixth day. Genesis 1:31 (NIV)

ANOTHER GRAY MORNING. The sky hung like a slate curtain, the atmosphere almost dripping with gloom. I looked across the table at my husband, David, his expression a dogged impersonation of contentment, and I knew my face held that same resolve. Would winter never end?

Then I reached for the Bible and devotional, a discipline David and I have held for more than 30 years. The day's verse came from Genesis, and it seeped into me as if Jesus had spoken it, His voice loving and words gentle. "God saw all that He had made, and it was very good." Not just good, but *very* good. My gaze rose from the page. I wanted to discover this world Jesus had created, the one I'd lost track of. Where could I find the good in this day?

As I washed the breakfast dishes, I prayed for Jesus to help change my bitter heart to a grateful one. I reminded myself that the dark skies bring rain for farmers. I noticed how soothing the sudsy dish water was on my skin. Our old cat, Julie, sashayed in figure eights around my ankles, a furry testimony to love. In the next room, the phone rang. My sister's voice greeted me from hundreds of miles away. As the morning turned to afternoon, blessings popped into my awareness. My health, home, marriage...and my Jesus. I gave thanks. Yes, this life and world are very, very good.
—HEIDI GAUL

FAITH STEP: *Make a list of your blessings, large and small. You'll be surprised—it's easy once you start. Then give Jesus praise.*

SUNDAY, JANUARY 12

And call on Me in the day of trouble; I will deliver you, and you shall honor and glorify Me. Psalm 50:15 (AMPC)

THAT JANUARY, I HAD CABIN FEVER, so even though the temperature had dropped to zero overnight and fog covered the frozen pavement, I had to get out. Of course, this was the perfect recipe for black ice, but I was experienced in these conditions. Driving slowly, I figured I could control what Mother Nature created. When I entered the last curve on the deserted highway, my wheels hit black ice and the car spun counterclockwise. I steered into the curve without success. My tires couldn't get traction.

"Jesus, help!" I prayed as I skidded across the two-way road, took out a blizzard marker, and ended up perched precariously over an irrigation ditch. It seemed like everything had happened in slow motion, but thankfully I was safe. It also seemed like a good time to pray. "Thank You, Jesus."

The car and I were undamaged. I had cell service, and my husband came, as did the sheriff and, eventually, a tow truck. Having worked in an emergency room, I knew events like this don't always end well. I live my life as if I am in control, but my slip on the winter road let me know who was really in control. And I'm so glad He came to my rescue when I cried out. —SUZANNE DAVENPORT TIETJEN

FAITH STEP: *In what area are you trusting your own wisdom? Cry out to Jesus to save you from potential harm.*

MONDAY, JANUARY 13

Therefore comfort each other and edify one another, just as you also are doing. 1 Thessalonians 5:11 (NKJV)

I OFTEN SETTLE ON A word of the year, something I sense Jesus wants me to focus on or pursue. In past years, it's been a word like *peace, hope, courage, linger, pilgrimage* (that was interesting), *strength* . . .

One year, I thought I should choose *diligence. Diligence?* "Jesus, haven't we been over that before?" I wasn't waiting for Jesus to audibly reply to me, but I did sense that I should hold on a little longer, seek a little stronger for whatever it was He wanted me to make a priority that year.

I discovered the answer in a most curious way. I hadn't been flipping through my Bible or spending time deep in prayer. Although I wouldn't recommend the method, I firmly believe Jesus answered me through a social media ad. The word *solace* jumped out at me. Instantly peace settled over me. My word of the year was *solace.*

Whatever that meant.

I generally knew the definition, but even as I sensed Jesus calling me to devote myself to solace in a more intentional way than I had before, I also had a feeling I knew too little. The dictionary told me solace is comfort and consolation offered during a time of distress or sadness. Another source included both giving and receiving consolation.

A whole year devoted to practicing solace, Jesus? I'd sought Him. He'd answered. So I embarked. And it led to a year of diligently seeking Jesus for words of comfort for others. —CYNTHIA RUCHTI

FAITH STEP: *You may have sought Jesus for a particular focus word. Tell someone what you discovered and how it changed you.*

TUESDAY, JANUARY 14

When you call to me, I will answer you. Psalm 91:15 (GW)

LAST YEAR MY MOM TRADED in her landline for phone service based on Wi-Fi. She faced a learning curve with so many new features, but eventually, all the kinks seemed to be worked out. Then suddenly, my calls stopped going through. Since I lived several hundred miles away, our long-distance chats were especially important. My mom could call me, but when I punched in her number, I received an unsettling message: "This customer has blocked your number. Please hang up." Instead of being hurt, I knew there had to be some explanation. The woman who had loved me unselfishly for seven decades would never do such a thing intentionally. Sure enough, my younger brother discovered that Mom had accidentally hit the block button during one of our phone conversations.

To be honest, there are times when I wonder if my prayers have been blocked. Maybe I've prayed for the same need so long that it seems as though Jesus is ignoring my request. Or I'm pouring out my heart but don't sense a closeness to Him. In those moments, my response should be similar to how I reacted when my calls to Mom were rejected. How can I think that the One who loves me unconditionally and sacrificially would cut off communication with me? The explanation might be an unconfessed sin or my disobedience to some instruction He's given me. He may be helping my patience and faith grow. Or I might be letting my emotions control my attitude. Regardless of how I feel, I can trust that with Jesus, the line is always open. —DIANNE NEAL MATTHEWS

FAITH STEP: *Do you ever feel as though Jesus isn't taking your calls? Search the Psalms or other scriptures that promise He always hears and underline them in your Bible.*

WEDNESDAY, JANUARY 15

But now the Lord who created you, O Israel, says: Don't be afraid, for I have ransomed you; I have called you by name; you are mine. Isaiah 43:1 (TLB)

MY NIECE, CORI, IS A self-taught cake artist. She can create fabulous baked goods that not only taste great but look like works of art. Cori often texts me and her mom photos of her latest creations. Recently she sent us pictures of some amazing cake pops that she was experimenting with—one looked like a slice of cake and the other was an ice cream cone, both seemingly suspended in thin air on a stick!

Cori said she didn't know how much to charge for them. Her mom and I immediately told her she needed to price them above her regular cake pops because of the increased time invested in them and the sheer artistry involved. "Don't underestimate your work or your worth," I texted. As soon as I wrote it, I knew that was a word for me too.

Just as the Lord told the Israelites that He had redeemed them and "you are mine," I should never

underestimate my worth to Jesus either. He paid a great price with His life to ransom me from sin. Jesus's love for me and all those who seek Him runs deep and is everlasting (Jeremiah 31:3). I am among His greatest creations. Through His grace, mercy, and countless blessings, Jesus constantly tells me that I'm worth it. And so are you.
—BARBRANDA LUMPKINS WALLS

FAITH STEP: *What do you value most in your life? Your family? Your job? Your health? Whatever it is, think about how much Jesus loves you—certainly more than anything you value.*

THURSDAY, JANUARY 16

He has always been! It is His hand that holds everything together. Colossians 1:17 (VOICE)

WHEN A CASE OF SHINGLES caused ongoing pain, I whined that I couldn't help our daughter Marie's family as much as I wanted to. Jesus had answered my twenty-year-long prayer to move Marie and her three teenagers near us. I was disappointed I wasn't able to be there for them.

At every turn, Jesus had someone waiting to give Marie exactly what she needed. Her youth pastor's wife made a meal and delivered it when our grandson,

Dan, had surgery. My close friend and her daughter helped Marie and her family unpack after they moved into a new house. An entire family from our church assembled a storage shed for them (something I couldn't do even when I was feeling well!).

I know Jesus didn't cause my shingles outbreak, but He used it to show me how capable He is of managing everything. When I read it in black on white, it seems laughable that I need proof of Jesus's proficiency. But it appears I do because on a fairly regular basis, the Lord needs to remind me that I'm not the center of the universe. I want to be the fixer, the hero. Which boils down to the fact that I want to be in charge. There, I said it.

But I know I'm never really in charge, and it took feeling unwell for me to remember—again—that only Jesus is. No matter what the need is, Jesus has it covered. —JEANETTE LEVELLIE

FAITH STEP: *Think of a situation in which you can't do anything and give it to Jesus. Know He has it covered. Then sit back and watch the miracle unfold.*

FRIDAY, JANUARY 17

Carry each other's burdens, and in this way you will fulfill the law of Christ. Galatians 6:2 (NIV)

"CAN YOU HELP ME?" I texted my sister Meghan after I'd been staring at my computer for an entire evening without making any progress. "I don't even know where to begin." We met at a local cafe the following week and settled into a cozy spot near the fireplace. As the warmth from the fire spread to my bones, I unloaded my concerns over coffee and pastries.

Three hours later, I had a plan and a smile. Meghan had been just the sounding board I needed, and her calm presence helped settle my heart so I could focus more clearly. She pointed me back to Jesus and reminded me that He had already promised me the strength I needed to complete the project He'd called me to pursue. As long as I turned to Him daily, the long-term goal would fall into place.

I could also count on her, she said, and she promised to check in with me regularly along the way. We set up a weekly accountability template that I updated and sent to her every Sunday night for 4 months. Each time I did, I thanked Jesus for the blessing of a sister and sister-in-Christ with whom I could share my burdens. —EMILY E. RYAN

FAITH STEP: *Who do you have in your life who can hold you accountable with the big and little things you're doing for Jesus? Set up a regular meeting with that person, and be honest about your struggles when they come up.*

SATURDAY, JANUARY 18

Do everything without complaining and arguing, so that no one can criticize you. Live clean, innocent lives as children of God, shining like bright lights in a world . . .
Philippians 2:14–15 (NLT)

EACH NEW YEAR, I SPEND time reflecting on the past year. One question I ask is, "What is something I'm doing that I don't want to do?" The first thought that came to me this year was, *I don't like going to the grocery store.* I procrastinated and complained every time I went. As a mom of three boys, I've spent countless hours perusing the grocery store aisles and filling up a shopping cart to keep my always-hungry boys healthy, happy, and full. Now, with the boys gone from our home, I still needed to keep our pantry and fridge supplied, although with much less food. So I decided to try Instacart and have our groceries delivered to our home. It's fantastic! I'm not very techy, but this service provided a simple solution to help me change my attitude and actions.

As a Jesus follower, I hope to be more like Him, and I don't think Jesus ever complained. Yet to continue doing something I didn't like to do didn't seem right either. I knew bitterness would grow. So using Instacart actually helped me to do the task and not complain.

If I can approach disliked tasks differently, strive to do all things without complaining, and find creative solutions to help stop my grumbling, then I know I will be a brighter light in the world, giving hope to all those around me. —JEANNIE BLACKMER

FAITH STEP: *Write down one thing you complain about. Brainstorm how you can stop grumbling by changing your attitude and actions and following Jesus's example of being a light in this world.*

SUNDAY, JANUARY 19

If we confess our sins, he is faithful and just and will forgive us our sins and purify us from all unrighteousness.
1 John 1:9 (NIV)

MY MORNINGS SEEM INCOMPLETE WITHOUT coffee, so I knew I was in trouble on the day my coffee maker failed. I flicked the off/on switch several times, and it lit up as it always had, but nothing else happened.

Checking the machine's various parts led me to the root issue: the pod I'd inserted had broken and spilled grounds everywhere they didn't belong. I could have tried to fix the problem by polishing the machine's exterior, but, of course, that wouldn't have worked. I had to address the real issue and resolve it with a thorough cleaning. Within minutes my coffee maker was restored and brewing a cup of my favorite drink.

I savored my coffee that morning with new appreciation and thought about my relationship with Jesus. He is my everything—my source of strength, peace, hope, and joy. Allowing sin to creep into my life restricts those blessings. Gossip, envy, ingratitude, and unforgiveness jam my connection with Jesus and diminish my effectiveness as a reflector of His love and light.

I could try to resolve the problem by increasing my God-honoring activities to make myself look good on the outside, but that doesn't work. Sin is the root issue, and only one solution fixes it: confession. True to His Word, Jesus forgives and cleanses me. He restores me to a right relationship with Him so I can once again live to please Him and fulfill my potential as a Kingdom-builder. —GRACE FOX

FAITH STEP: *Sip a cup of your favorite hot drink and invite Jesus to show you if anything is hindering your relationship with Him.*

MARTIN LUTHER KING JR. DAY, MONDAY, JANUARY 20

For even the Son of Man did not come to be served, but to serve, and to give his life as a ransom for many.
Mark 10:45 (NIV)

As A CHILD, I HAD no understanding of the bravery and righteousness of minister and activist Martin Luther King Jr. I'd never heard of a Nobel Peace Prize or racial inequality. Then as a young adult, I regarded this holiday commemorating his birthday and life as just another day off from work.

It took some growing up to learn the value of this man's wisdom. His goal was equality for all races and relief for the poor through nonviolent resistance. He spent his time serving God and others right up until his assassination. He prayed, "Use me, God. Show me how to take who I am, who I want to be, and what I can do, and use it for a purpose greater than myself." That sounds a lot like Jesus.

I want to live a life of service as Dr. King and Jesus did. My community is small, and I don't have influence over millions of people, but I want to help those in need as much as possible. I pray to be the hands and feet of Jesus. Whether I do it in a one-on-one manner or join in an organized effort, it's time to make my mark. And the best way to do that is to pray like Dr. Martin Luther King Jr.: "Use me, God, for a purpose greater than myself." —HEIDI GAUL

FAITH STEP: *Pray Dr. Martin Luther King Jr.'s prayer: "Use me, God. Show me how to take who I am, who I want to be, and what I can do, and use it for a purpose greater than myself." Ask Jesus where and how you can serve.*

Tuesday, January 21

But without faith it is impossible to please him: for
he that cometh to God must believe that he is, and
that he is a rewarder of them that diligently seek him.
Hebrews 11:6 (KJV)

I don't make New Year's resolutions. Initially, I didn't because they weren't something we did in my family when I was growing up. Eventually, I made the decision on my own not to make them. I've read many articles explaining that people set goals incorrectly. Some are idealistic, lacking the smaller, realistic actions that need to be taken to achieve the desired results. Other goals are uninspiring and void of the motivation needed to pursue them, leaving people to ditch resolutions after only a few months.

Though I don't make official resolutions, I do have my own New Year's tradition. I love to pull out my prayer lists at the beginning of January and review the items I set for my spiritual and personal growth from the previous year. When I review my prayer requests from the past, I realize some of them also lack true action steps or the inspiration needed to achieve them. At times, I find myself missing the mark and feeling discouraged and disappointed.

Failure does not have the final say. Like the disciple Peter, I can come back from a setback. Peter failed in his resolve to acknowledge Christ at all costs, but he returned to Jesus even more committed than before (John 21:15–19). I, too, through the help of Jesus can persevere and do the same in this new year. —ERICKA LOYNES

FAITH STEP: *Dust off your old resolutions or prayer requests. Focus on the top one you want to achieve and write at least three actionable steps that will help get you there.*

WEDNESDAY, JANUARY 22

And the God of all grace, who called you to his eternal glory in Christ, after you have suffered a little while, will himself restore you and make you strong, firm and steadfast. 1 Peter 5:10 (NIV)

HAVE YOU DISCOVERED THE LITTLE miracle called mushroom popcorn? Shaped like a mushroom top, it's regular popcorn, only bigger and better. My husband recently purchased a bag, and it forever changed our TV snacking experience. How could one tiny kernel produce such a huge puff? I had to find out.

Apparently, inside the protective hull of the corn kernel is a small amount of water. When heated, the water turns to steam, causing the inside to soften and expand. The pressure breaks the hull and reveals fluffy popped goodness waiting to be buttered. While the result is delightful, the process, for the kernel, is not.

I've felt the heat many times in my life. You too? A scary diagnosis, a financial crisis, a struggling relationship, or a career failure. With pressure on all sides, I attempt to control things beyond my ability until I feel like I will pop.

But just like that little kernel of corn has water inside it, I have Living Water inside of me (John 7:37–39). Jesus is with me through the heat of every trial, softening and expanding my heart. I lean into Him as I face another doctor appointment. When the bills keep coming, I watch Him provide. The fires I endured have changed me. Stronger and firmer in Jesus, my faith becomes bigger and better, just like mushroom popcorn. —KAREN SARGENT

FAITH STEP: *Treat yourself to some mushroom popcorn and think about your faith. If it's like a hard kernel at the bottom of the bowl that didn't have enough water inside to pop, claim Jesus's promise to restore you and make you strong.*

THURSDAY, JANUARY 23

After Job had prayed for his friends, the LORD restored his fortunes and gave him twice as much as he had before.
Job 42:10 (NIV)

IT'S NOT UNCOMMON FOR ME to seek the Lord for everyday advice or wisdom. "Jesus, where did I put my shoes?" But many times, my prayers are for far more weighty requests than shoes. Answers for grown children or growing grandchildren. Spiritual renewal. Minutes ago, a dear friend asked me to pray as she meets with a daughter who has been estranged for 2 years. Weighty.

This week I lingered over a phrase I'd overlooked in the Bible. Job suffered misery upon misery, trial upon trial, worst-case scenarios that grew even worse. Weighty things. And his "friends" proved to be accusatory, fed him only half-truths, or drove him crazy with their misguided chatter.

But when Job began to pray for his friends, his fortunes were restored. The tide turned. All he'd lost was replaced and then some when he began to pray for those not-much-help friends.

With my multitude of prayer needs brought to Jesus, I'm adding the practice of praying for the troublemakers or those who are unkind who surround those I'm praying for. Like Job, I won't pray for their demise but rather for good to fall upon them and divine wisdom to guide them. —CYNTHIA RUCHTI

FAITH STEP: *Have you exhausted yourself in prayer over a pressing concern? Consider following Job's breakthrough moment and pray for those "friends" who surround and speak untruth into that concern.*

FRIDAY, JANUARY 24

Sing to the LORD a new song; sing to the LORD, all the earth. Psalm 96:1 (NIV)

I SAT IN THE DINING ROOM at my daughter's house coloring with my middle granddaughter. I thought we were alone until a little voice from under the table startled me by singing the first lines of one of my favorite hymns. When I expressed surprise that three-year-old Leo knew "Be Thou My Vision," Lilah joined in with her sister. The beautiful sound of those two little girls singing an old song based on an ancient Irish poem represents a moment of pure happiness that I will treasure forever.

Growing up, I mainly knew the songs from our church's hymnal and an occasional visiting Southern gospel quartet. As a young adult, I discovered contemporary Christian artists and modern praise music. But I enjoy a wide range of music styles—from simple childhood tunes like "Jesus Loves Me" to majestic hymns like "Immortal, Invisible, God Only Wise" and everything (almost) in between.

I'm glad we have so many different types of musical styles for worship and praise because no music is beautiful enough to fully convey our Savior's majesty and worth. Even the most gifted orchestra and choir cannot adequately express the honor due Him. Thankfully, Jesus is more interested in

the condition of my heart than in my skill. That motivates me to sing praises to Him even more.
—DIANNE NEAL MATTHEWS

FAITH STEP: *Why not sing a "new song" to Jesus today? Revisit an old, cherished verse or hymn from your childhood, go online to sample a new music style, make up your own tune to a favorite Scripture passage, or simply sing the words that are in your heart.*

SATURDAY, JANUARY 25

Finally, brothers and sisters, rejoice, mend your ways, be comforted, be like-minded, live in peace; and the God of love and peace will be with you.
2 Corinthians 13:11 (NASB)

THIS COLD MORNING, I DUG in the drawer for my favorite socks and put them on. Two steps later, I couldn't help but notice that my bare heel touched the chilly tile. The bad thing about thick woolen socks is their propensity for wearing through at the heel.

Too often I live like much of our throw-away society. But instead of taking the easy way out and throwing away holey socks, I've started darning them. If I don't have matching yarn, I spin some or tell myself darning can be decorative.

Grandma May, who raised four boys during the Depression (and darned a lot of socks in her day), taught me how. You put the heel over a darning egg (any ball that fits will do) and sew a circle as a boundary around the hole. Then make long vertical stitches advancing from one side of the circle to the other. It'll look like the bars of a cage. Then weave the needle sideways over and under the "bars" to the other side, anchoring the needle into the circle. Repeat side-to-side, weaving and anchoring until the resulting patch covers the circle.

Jesus fixed things too. In His ministry, He healed people and repaired their bodies. He cared for the poor and restored their lives. He valued them and loved them, no matter who they were or where they were from. And far from taking the easy way out, Jesus fixed the sin problem by dying for us. Darning holey socks reminds me that Jesus, the Ultimate Fixer, values and loves me too. —SUZANNE DAVENPORT TIETJEN

FAITH STEP: *Fix something instead of throwing it away. As you do, ask Jesus to show you where your personal restoration is needed.*

SUNDAY, JANUARY 26

Whoever conceals their sins does not prosper, but the one who confesses and renounces them finds mercy.
Proverbs 28:13 (NIV)

I WENT TO THE DENTIST last week for the first time in 6 years. I knew things were bad but hoped that ignoring them would make them go away. I was also avoiding the dentist's reaction, thinking she'd shame me for taking the coward's way out by burying my head in the sand.

The bad news is I've done so much damage from grinding my teeth at night that I need four crowns. I almost fell off the dentist chair when she told me how much that's going to cost. The good news? There was no shaming at all, only understanding and support. The hygienist and the dentist care about teeth. They only want what's good for mine.

I avoid more than the dentist. I also avoid bringing my sins to Jesus. Once again, I fear the shame I'll feel laying all my sins at His feet. So I bury my head in the sand and hope ignoring them will make them go away.

The bad news? Unconfessed sins fester, eroding my soul and creating a barrier to Jesus's grace. The good news, though, is that shaming isn't a tactic Jesus ever uses. He extends love and mercy. He cares about my soul and only wants what's good for it.

I mustered the courage to go to the dentist to get back on track with my teeth. And it's time to seek out Jesus's forgiveness so He can remove the barrier I created and get me back on track for the good of my soul. —CLAIRE MCGARRY

FAITH STEP: *Take stock of the health of your soul, bringing any unconfessed sins to the feet of Jesus.*

MONDAY, JANUARY 27

The LORD is my shepherd, I lack nothing. Psalm 23:1 (NIV)

I FEEL MOST CONNECTED AND loved when I'm personally interacting with others, which made my job as a counselor during the pandemic difficult. All therapy sessions had to be online in the early weeks. When an opportunity arose to work in a school, I made an intentional job change to have daily face-to-face interactions.

Likewise, my relationship with Jesus can sometimes feel challenging. I can't touch or see His face as I do others. I must be deliberately creative to feel connected to Him.

Recently, I discovered a spiritual practice that made me feel more connected to Jesus. Reflecting on Psalm 23, I visualized Jesus as a shepherd. I closed my eyes and envisioned us sitting together on a hillside overlooking mountains. I pictured talking to Him about my worries and cares.

Then I imagined what it would sound like for Jesus to respond to me. I waited. His voice was gentle. It was not harsh or uncaring. In His quiet presence, we talked back and forth, as if He were with me. I felt connected to Jesus in a way I had not experienced before.

Now when I need to hear from Jesus or want to be in His presence, I quiet myself and picture us sitting on a hillside. I'm beside the Good Shepherd through this intentional pursuit and can connect with Him anytime. He's with me at school or online, anywhere I go. —BRENDA L. YODER

FAITH STEP: *Picture yourself in Jesus's presence for a few minutes. Where is He? Where are you in proximity to Him? Visualize yourself with the Good Shepherd or use another scriptural image.*

TUESDAY, JANUARY 28

The third time he said to him, "Simon son of John, do you love me?" John 21:17 (NIV)

A FEW MONTHS AGO, I started seeing an assortment of recurring numbers. At first, I thought it was just a weird coincidence, but it got consistent enough for me to take notice. I asked Jesus, "What is this about, Lord? Is it You?"

I didn't get a clear reply but started researching biblical numerology and soon found a reputable teacher with this area of expertise. I discovered a whole new, amazing world of insight into God's Word and how He communicates with us.

I soon learned the numbers I was seeing did have compelling meaning, though I still didn't really understand how they applied to me. I read my Bible, researched references, took notes, and prayed again: "Jesus, what are You trying to tell me?"

Though I didn't get a memo with detailed instructions, I did get a strong sense that Jesus wanted me to connect with Him more and with greater intention. Now when I see the recurring numbers, I make it a point to pause and briefly pray the relevant topic or simply turn my thoughts to Jesus, many times per day. I don't know if this will lead anywhere specific, but I am grateful for the recurring prompt to connect with Jesus. —ISABELLA CAMPOLATTARO

FAITH STEP: *Whether you see recurring numbers or not, look for a prompt to pray more often, if only for a moment—for instance, when you see signs like a red car, hear a siren, or when the phone rings.*

WEDNESDAY, JANUARY 29

Christ Jesus who died—more than that, who was raised to life—is at the right hand of God and is also interceding for us. Romans 8:34 (NIV)

ONE JANUARY DAY, FOUR OUT of five of my family members had health issues. Our oldest son, Josh, had a cyst removed from his eye that was sent for testing. I had a mole removed on my leg that was also biopsied. Jordan, our middle son, had an accident and separated his rib from his sternum during a recent trip to Mexico. Our youngest son, Jake, was driving across the country in a two-wheel-drive truck filled with his belongings to move home with a 103-degree fever. Driving through Colorado, he had to put chains on the tires due to a recent snowstorm. I felt overwhelmed and battled the worst-case scenarios running through my mind. I didn't even know what to pray.

I found comfort knowing that Jesus intercedes for me. More than that, He knows exactly what to pray. Yet I still needed to do something about those negative thoughts swirling through my mind. So, in conjunction with knowing my risen Jesus was sitting at the right hand of God, I began reciting the Lord's Prayer found in Matthew 6:9–13. This allowed me to take control of my thoughts and redirect them in a positive direction.

Thankfully, Josh's cyst was not cancer, Jordan's rib healed, Jake made it home safely, and I had a larger area of atypical tissue removed from my leg. The promise that Jesus is praying for me and my reciting of the Lord's Prayer helped me through this difficult day. —JEANNIE BLACKMER

FAITH STEP: *Write out the Lord's Prayer and recite it several times today.*

THURSDAY, JANUARY 30

Taste and see that the LORD is good; blessed is the one who takes refuge in him. Psalm 34:8 (NIV)

MY NEW FRIEND NICOLE AND I are on a quest to find good tacos. We both moved from the San Francisco Bay Area to Idaho. We were chatting after church a month ago and realized we shared an affinity for Mexican food. The number of delicious taquerias in the Bay Area is significant. Finding a good street taco up here would be like a little taste of home.

We met at a local taqueria a few weeks ago. It had delicious tacos, guacamole, and sopes (thick corn tortillas with yummy toppings). It was our first time getting together and talking. We found out about each other's lives. We talked about careers and kids and husbands. We chatted about how glad we are that Jesus had opened the door for new opportunities in our lives. Who would have thought that two California girls would be meeting up for chips and salsa in the Boise foothills? We left feeling filled up in body, mind, and spirit.

Jesus has an amazing way of leading me to unexpected places. He has shown His goodness to me over and over again in thoughtful and creative ways. The Psalmist says He delights in the details of our lives (Psalm 37:23, NLT). From new friendships to career shifts, in life's different seasons, Jesus is constantly looking for ways to show me His delight and goodness. I can trust Him with my life. He fills me up body, mind, and spirit.
—SUSANNA FOTH AUGHTMON

FAITH STEP: *Throughout your day, make it a point to look for ways that Jesus is showing you His goodness. When you notice Him at work, thank Him for it.*

FRIDAY, JANUARY 31

Even when you're old, I'll take care of you. Even when your hair turns gray, I'll support you. I made you and will continue to care for you. I'll support you and save you.
Isaiah 46:4 (GW)

SEEING EVERYTHING BLANKETED IN A white winter snowfall brings to mind reassuring verses about having my sins washed away, being made white as snow (Psalm 51:7). But winter snow can also cast shadows of concern. Concern for the welfare of family, friends, neighbors. *Do they have sufficient firewood or heating fuel to keep warm? Enough food to last while housebound during these snow days?*

This winter my eighty-year-old mother's heating fuel was stolen. We immediately filed a sheriff's report, ordered new security lighting, and installed a stout padlock on Mom's fuel tank—preventative measures to deter future theft. And, fortunately, Mom's fuel tank was refilled promptly.

However, there's no secure padlock to prevent worry or fear of future theft (or worse). It's been a challenging season, learning to trust Jesus to take care of Mom since Dad died. To trust Jesus as her Protector and Provider. Unable to fulfill the role of my father, I have to rely on my Heavenly Father for that. Jesus whispers to me that He is Mom's Heavenly Husband. Jesus assures me He'll continue to care for Mom in Dad's absence.

With His help, I'm learning to trust Jesus to take care of Mom, as well as me, my husband, family, friends, and neighbors. So I needn't worry when it snows... because Jesus is taking care of us.

—CASSANDRA TIERSMA

FAITH STEP: *Write out Isaiah 46:4, inserting your name (or that of an elderly loved one) instead of the word "you." Thank Jesus for caring for you and your elderly loved ones.*

SATURDAY, FEBRUARY 1

---

*"Come now, let us settle the matter," says the LORD.
"Though your sins are like scarlet, they shall be as white
as snow; though they are red as crimson, they shall be like
wool." Isaiah 1:18 (NIV)*

ROAD CONDITIONS WERE LESS THAN ideal when
my husband and I left the Des Moines, Iowa, airport in a rental car. We were headed for a Bible
camp approximately 90 miles away—an easy trip
we'd made several times in the past. But this time,
we suspected, would be different because a blizzard
had blown through the area earlier that day.

Our suspicions proved correct. The farther we
drove from the city, the more snow we encountered
on the road. Nearly 4 hours later, we turned onto
the final 3-mile stretch leading to our destination.

The country road and adjacent fields lay before
us like a seamless white blanket, unmarred by vehicle, human, or animal tracks. Amazed at the white
expanse, we stopped the car and gazed at the scene in
silence. God's words about snow came to mind, and
gratitude welled within me.

I recalled how my sinful thoughts, words, and
actions had stained my heart in God's eyes, but Jesus
removed that stain when I placed my faith in Him for
salvation. He washed my sins as white as snow the
moment I chose to follow Him, and He continues

to cleanse me every time I confess my wrongdoing to Him (1 John 1:9).

With a fresh appreciation for what forgiveness looks like, we started the car and resumed our journey. "Thank You, Jesus," I whispered, as I snapped a picture to immortalize the moment. —GRACE FOX

FAITH STEP: *Google "best snow photos" and enjoy the pictures while thanking Jesus for making your scarlet sins as white as snow.*

SUNDAY, FEBRUARY 2

God is our refuge and strength, an ever-present help in trouble. Therefore we will not fear, though the earth give way and the mountains fall into the heart of the sea, though its waters roar and foam and the mountains quake with their surging. Psalm 46:1–3 (NIV)

A FEW YEARS AGO, I was diagnosed with an autoimmune disease. It has greatly affected my energy levels. I have been looking for ways to nurture my body. My vitamin game is strong. And I have been asking Jesus to heal me.

Slowly but surely, my body is responding. But the amount of blood draws, shots, and tests I have endured is substantial. Last month, my doctor sent me ten diagnostic tests from different labs to complete. I have taken two.

This morning, I was talking with my friend Jane, who lives in California. She has been full of empathy and deep wisdom and a great encouragement to me during this process. I told her about the unfinished tests. Jane asked, "Sue, would you like me to sit with you on the phone while you complete them?" That made me cry. She knew I was overwhelmed. Her love for me was palpable at that moment. She lives more than 600 miles away, but she wanted me to know I could count on her.

Jesus is with me no matter what I am going through. He is my refuge and strength. He's the place I find comfort when I am afraid. He's my source of power when I am weak. I love that in any circumstance, Jesus is my ever-present help.

—SUSANNA FOTH AUGHTMON

FAITH STEP: *Are you feeling alone or overwhelmed? Meditate on Psalm 46:1 today and reach out to Jesus, the friend you can always count on.*

MONDAY, FEBRUARY 3

But seek first His kingdom and His righteousness, and all these things will be provided to you. So do not worry about tomorrow; for tomorrow will worry about itself. Each day has enough trouble of its own. Matthew 6:33–34 (NASB)

BEING A MOM WAS EASIER when my son was young. I was in control of directing his choices for everything. Now that he is a young adult making his own decisions, my current role in his life requires me to listen and advise more than to tell. From time to time, I get nervous about the number of choices he has to make. This change has not been easy for me.

I remember being on the other side of this parent-child relationship when I was a young adult, and it was an adjustment. My mother had a strong presence in my life. When she told me what to do, I did it whether I agreed with the decision or not. When our relationship shifted from her telling me what to do to her asking me what I was going to do, it caught me off guard. Though I was eager to make my own choices, actually doing so was at times frightening.

Even though my relationship with my son is changing, I am so grateful that my relationship with Jesus remains the same. Our Jesus is the same yesterday, today, and forever. Because He was able to sustain me through the shift with my mother back then, I know He is able to sustain me through this shift with my son now. Whatever life stage I'm in, with Jesus I need not worry. —ERICKA LOYNES

FAITH STEP: *On one Post-it note, write down a worry. On another, write, "Don't worry, Matthew 6:34." Post both where you can see them.*

TUESDAY, FEBRUARY 4

Give thanks to the LORD, for he is good; his love endures forever. Psalm 118:29 (NIV)

TWO MONTHS AGO, MY HUSBAND, Kevin, and I traveled from Illinois to Ohio on a speaking trip. Halfway there, a dump truck rear-ended our SUV. The car was still drivable, so we continued our trip, thanking Jesus all the way for His protection.

I wasn't thankful, though, when Kevin and I had to share a car for 2 weeks to get the bodywork on the SUV done.

We live in the country, 7 miles from my workplace. We transport our two teenage grandkids, who live 6 miles away, to and from the school bus stop and to various appointments. And Kevin conducts a Thursday afternoon worship service at a nursing home 20 miles from home.

After whining, sighing, and some serious complaining, I realized no one in our family was hungry, thirsty, or in danger. My brilliant conclusion? We were experiencing a first-world problem. This was merely an inconvenience. I didn't jump up and down in glee, but I did begin to search for the gold flakes in this mud puddle. We have a car. *Thank You, Jesus.* We live in a state that paves its roads. *Praise You, Lord.* We have insurance that paid $4,000 to fix my car. *A huge blessing from above.*

Praising Jesus for the good in every trying circumstance is to my advantage. It's much more fun to live being grateful than groaning. —JEANETTE LEVELLIE

FAITH STEP: *If you're in a circumstance that forces you to wait, find three things to thank Jesus for and be grateful.*

WEDNESDAY, FEBRUARY 5

The third time he said to him, "Simon son of John, do you love me?" Peter was hurt because Jesus asked him the third time, "Do you love me?" He said, "Lord, you know all things; you know that I love you." Jesus said, "Feed my sheep." John 21:17 (NIV)

I RUN A NONPROFIT, NONPARTISAN organization called Arkansas Strong. We seek to amplify stories of everyday Arkansans doing good things. We also try to bring people together over shared values to work on solutions to problems everyday Arkansans face. Because of this work, I meet people from all over the state whom I would never otherwise know.

I was asked to speak about our work at a church in Little Rock and planned to talk on the topic of hope. Days before the engagement, a giant tornado swept through the city and my speech was canceled.

I would be rescheduled because the congregation was going to make sandwiches and hand them out to those affected by the tornado instead of having church service.

I felt a nudge, as if the hand of Jesus was on my shoulder, as if His gentle breath blew the dust out of my eyes. Instead of talking about hope, I had the chance to put my words into action. Hope as a verb instead of a noun. So I went to Little Rock and joined the church members in their efforts, which felt, in some ways, better than a regular church service. It was a chance to feed His sheep.
—GWEN FORD FAULKENBERRY

FAITH STEP: *How can you turn the love you have for Jesus into an action? Find one specific need you can meet for His sheep.*

THURSDAY, FEBRUARY 6

Depend on the LORD and his strength; always go to him for help. 1 Chronicles 16:11 (NCV)

I WOKE UP THIS MORNING to a winter snowstorm power outage. The house was cold, dark, and silent except for the sound of snowplows scraping the roads outside. Judging by the discrepancy between my electric clocks and battery-operated clocks, the power had been out for 3 hours. I bundled up in extra layers over my pajamas—wool sweater, coat, scarf, fingerless gloves, thick socks, knee-high sweater-knit slippers—grabbed the emergency flashlight, and telephoned my hubby, who was already at work, to indulge in a little pity party. I had no way to heat the house, no way to cook, and no way to power my computer.

Every time the power goes out, I'm reminded how energy-dependent I am. I almost feel silly, shallow even, fretting about it. Regardless of whether the electricity is on, the power source I need to be most dependent upon is Jesus. He's an infinitely greater source of power than that supplied by my local electric company.

Despite my temporary inconvenience as I seek the face of Jesus on this cold, wintry morning, I'm praying that I'll always remember Jesus is the true source of power. Regardless of my temporal outer circumstances, I want to be energy-dependent on Jesus. —CASSANDRA TIERSMA

FAITH STEP: *Check the battery on your emergency flashlight to make sure it's working and replace it, if needed. While you're doing that, check in with Jesus to thank Him for being your true source of power.*

FRIDAY, FEBRUARY 7

Remember those who led you, who spoke the word of God to you; and considering the result of their way of life, imitate their faith. Hebrews 13:7 (NASB)

I'VE BEEN AN OLD SOUL since childhood and felt displaced among my peers. Pop culture fads held no allure, and I preferred being with older people. I sometimes wondered if I was born in the wrong era. Even now, I seek wisdom from Christian mentors and authors from the past. Their sustainable faith is empowering amidst today's news reports and complex situations with my work as a public school counselor.

One devotional book I use is *Streams in the Desert* by L. B. Cowman, published in 1925. It's an original copy that belonged to my husband's grandmother, Ola. The yellowed pages and penciled notes make me feel that Ola and the author are personally mentoring me.

One day when I needed encouragement, I read that the world needs more people who have seen Jesus. It surprised me that those saints of old also needed positive influences. I assumed life was more serene in past generations when compared to today, but apparently, people in days gone by also needed mentors with exemplary faith.

I realized that while I have looked to older people as an influence in my life, younger generations also need mentors. I considered people I could encourage—former students who are new moms, current elementary students, or younger teachers at my school. I was comforted that Jesus didn't misplace me in the twenty-first century. He purposed me in today's culture to reach the souls of another generation for Him. —BRENDA L. YODER

FAITH STEP: *Draw a large circle on a sheet of paper. Pray to Jesus, asking Him to inspire you with people you can mentor or influence for Him. Write their names inside the circle.*

SATURDAY, FEBRUARY 8

How good and pleasant it is when God's people live together in unity! Psalm 133:1 (NIV)

LAST CHRISTMAS, I PURCHASED TICKETS for our family to go to an escape room. This is a business that locks willing participants in a room to play a game. The group is required to solve a series of puzzles within a certain amount of time to accomplish a goal. You have to race against the clock and decipher clues to solve a mystery. Our challenge was to figure out how to steal a fake diamond locked behind iron bars. I wasn't sure if this was going to be a good family experience or a disaster. We all like to lead and have strong opinions. Let's say good communication and working together have not been words to describe us in the past.

The clock started ticking, and everyone went into action. We found locked briefcases, clues, codes, and a secret room, and we successfully "stole" the diamond within the hour. It was gratifying to watch each family member step into different roles and work together to accomplish the goal.

Reflecting on the game, I think I had a taste of how Jesus feels when we as believers are unified. Jesus prayed we would "be perfected in unity" (John 17:23, NASB). And the purpose of this unity was so the world would know Jesus was sent from God because He loves us so much.

Working together as a family, each operating in our unique giftedness, was more than good and pleasant. The escape room experience bonded us. May we as believers never escape opportunities to work side by side and grow tighter together in love as a huge, united family of Christ. —JEANNIE BLACKMER

FAITH STEP: *Pray for unity today for Jesus followers around the world. Think of an activity you can do with someone else to share Jesus's love.*

SUNDAY, FEBRUARY 9

He rained down manna for the people to eat, he gave them the grain of heaven. Psalm 78:24 (NIV)

ONE SUNDAY MORNING, I WATCHED big snow-flakes softly fall to the ground. They were lovely to see. The whole scene is how I envision God sending provision for the Israelites as they made their way through the wilderness to the Promised Land in Canaan.

I've long been fascinated by the story in the book of Exodus in which the Israelites complained to Moses about the lack of food while they wandered in the wilderness after they departed Egypt. Some even said they regretted leaving Egypt—where they had been enslaved! The people weren't thrilled to be in the desert without the food they had once enjoyed. God heard their grumbling but still came through. He gave them quail to eat in the evening and "bread from heaven" that fell from the sky in the morning. God's chosen people were blessed and sustained in an unusual and unexpected way.

Many of God's blessings in my life fall upon me in unexpected ways too. A gift from a colleague left on my doorstep. An unforeseen refund shows up in the mail. A long-ago friend calls out of nowhere. Each one is like manna from heaven. God's compassion, grace, and provision rain down upon me. Like those falling snowflakes I watched, each blessing is unique and beautiful. And collectively they are real, relevant, and tangible gifts from Jesus, my Provider and Sustainer. —BARBRANDA LUMPKINS WALLS

FAITH STEP: *What blessings has Jesus recently rained upon you? Pause right now and give Him thanks.*

MONDAY, FEBRUARY 10

Create in me a pure heart, O God, and renew a steadfast spirit within me. Psalm 51:10 (NIV)

LAST YEAR, A SERIOUS CONFLICT with a friend surfaced and we sat down to clear the air. Initially I felt OK, but I soon realized I had lingering discomfort I sensed was all mine. My emotional pain threshold is low, and my spirit was unsettled within me. I wanted to address it as soon as possible. I added this person to my prayer list and asked Jesus what was going on with me. My thoughts and feelings were muddy, but I persisted in prayer, motivated by the dull ache in my heart that I feared might harden into resentment.

I knew I was finding fault with the other person and on some level still blaming her for the tension between us. I knew better than to indulge that line of thinking or to talk with my friend again. I just *knew* it was something inside me. I persevered in prayer as my pain persisted. It took some time, but finally the answer came.

I saw my part in stark relief and felt an avalanche of sorrow at my sin. A pattern of unhealthy thinking and behaving badly had contributed to my malaise. As I suspected, it wasn't about the other person at all. She was just a mirror.

I was led to Psalm 51. I copied it into my prayer journal and highlighted the verses that stood out. I prayed, meditated, and journaled insights until I felt my serenity restored, my spirit renewed. I could let the person and myself off the hook. I was free.
—Isabella Campolattaro

Faith Step: *Are you struggling with a bad feeling or even clear conviction about a sin? Consider praying, meditating, and journaling on Psalm 51 until your spirit is renewed.*

TUESDAY, FEBRUARY 11

For this is the message you heard from the beginning: We should love one another. 1 John 3:11 (NIV)

SOME OF MY BEST IDEAS come while I'm driving. I keep index cards in my car so I can jot down and capture the inspirations for later. My kids have seen me in action as I cart them around town for their various activities. When an idea hit the other day, the card I grabbed already had something written on it. At the next red light, I took a closer look and read: "Have a great day. Love you!" I recognized my daughter, Jocelyn's, handwriting. It was a small gesture, but the sentiment behind it was huge. She knew exactly where I'd find her message. She also has such a pure heart I knew those six words were packed with an immense amount of love.

The experience reminded me that Jesus leaves me messages all the time too. The difference is He uses the world as His index card and solutions to my circumstances as His pen. That parking spot that opens up near the front of the grocery store when I'm in a hurry? That's Him. That five-dollar bill I find in my car when I'm desperate for coffee at the drive-thru? That's Him. That flower that grows through the crack in the pavement that gives me hope during an impossible situation? That's Him.

Jesus knows me and tailors His love notes specifically to me. I recognize His handwriting and His pure messages packed with an immense amount of love. —CLAIRE MCGARRY

FAITH STEP: *Take a moment to text a message or leave a note for someone. Let them know you and Jesus love them.*

WEDNESDAY, FEBRUARY 12

And let us consider how we may spur one another on toward love and good deeds. Hebrews 10:24 (NIV)

NOT TOO LONG AGO, WHEN our family was going through an emotionally challenging time, I opened the front door and found a half-dozen bags of groceries on our porch. A smile tugged at the corners of my mouth, and tears filled my eyes. I was overwhelmed by the anonymous random act of kindness.

As Christians, we are called to love one another and to show kindness to those around us. Simple things make a big difference, such as writing a thank-you note to someone who has made a difference in our lives, paying for a stranger's coffee or meal, leaving a positive message for someone to find, donating to a charity or cause that is important to us, and performing a small act of service for someone in need. By performing these acts of kindness, our actions can transform someone's day, maybe even their life. When we love as Jesus does, our small acts of kindness can make a significant impact. Our small actions can help others during hard times and bring smiles to their faces. And I should know; my pantry was filled when I least expected it.

—TRICIA GOYER

FAITH STEP: *Ask Jesus to inspire you with a specific, anonymous gesture that shows kindness to someone and do it today.*

THURSDAY, FEBRUARY 13

I no longer call you servants, because a servant does not know his master's business. Instead, I have called you friends, for everything that I learned from my Father I have made known to you. John 15:15 (NIV)

I AM THE OFFICIAL DRIVEWAY shoveler in our household. My husband, Scott, tried it a few times and wanted to move back to California, but I enjoy the organizational challenge—figuring out where to put the snow over the course of the winter season is a puzzle. What I like best about shoveling my driveway is that my neighbors are out doing the same thing. We wave to each other. Sometimes we cross the street and help each other finish up our sidewalks. It's a time of community bonding.

The other day while I was shoveling, one of our neighbors came out with his two little boys and their small snow shovels. The three-year- old didn't recognize me all bundled up. I heard him ask his dad as he pointed at me, "Is she our friend?" His dad laughed and told him that I was a friend. At that, the boy crossed the street and started trying to help me shovel my driveway. He thought I needed help. Best shoveling experience ever. I loved being his friend.

Jesus wants to be my friend. It is the reason He came down from heaven and gave His life for me. He knows that I can't navigate this life on my own. I need His strength, mercy, and unending grace to flood my days. He crossed the street for me, and because of His deep love, I can become the person He created me to be. —SUSANNA FOTH AUGHTMON

FAITH STEP: *Jesus has called you a friend. List five ways that Jesus has been your friend this year and why you are grateful for His friendship.*

VALENTINE'S DAY, FRIDAY, FEBRUARY 14

"I have loved you, my people, with an everlasting love. With unfailing love I have drawn you to myself."
Jeremiah 31:3 (NLT)

THIS MORNING, I CAUGHT MYSELF entertaining a ridiculous thought. For weeks, I'd been caregiving for my husband after a mishap that landed him writhing on the ground instead of where he'd been on the roof of our house, repairing rain gutters.

The caregiving included my taking on all his chores as well as mine as he healed from what turned out to be minor repercussions that still necessitated long hours in his recliner.

Two days earlier, I'd "encouragingly" said, "Your goal today, should you choose to accept it, is to become self-sufficient." This morning, my mind prepared to say, "Honey, you can't have all five love languages every single day. That's just not possible." Good thing Jesus stopped my mouth from saying what my mind was thinking.

When I consider the divine love I'm shown on good or bad days, when I'm self-sufficient and when I'm excessively needy, when my pain is my own doing and when it's due to someone else's actions or words, I'm speechless. Jesus's unfailing love can be counted on daily. Everlasting. Faultless. Never keeping score.

And whose example should motivate me in my love relationships on this earth? Love isn't expressed with candy hearts that say "Be mine" or with an even exchange of "I showed you this much love today, so tomorrow you're making breakfast for me, right?"

No. It's loving like Jesus. My ridiculous thought became a plan to show my husband all five love languages every single day. —Cynthia Ruchti

---

FAITH STEP: *Look up the five love languages online. Think of a way you can express Jesus's amazing, unfailing love using one or all of them to someone today.*

SATURDAY, FEBRUARY 15

The tempter came to him and said, "If you are the Son of God, tell these stones to become bread." Jesus answered, "It is written: 'Man shall not live on bread alone, but on every word that comes from the mouth of God.'"
Matthew 4:3–4 (NIV)

THE LETTER ARRIVED ON SATURDAY afternoon and wrecked the rest of my day. "The Alabama Law Enforcement Agency has learned that you have a debilitating medical condition which may affect safe driving. The enclosed form must be completed by your doctor and returned by the date above. Otherwise, your driving privilege will be suspended."

What? I didn't have a medical condition! I sat stunned at my desk, spinning from dismay to confusion to fear. I couldn't contact the agency during the weekend. So, I fretted and fumed for hours before taking a break to pray.

In rapid succession, one scripture after another arose from my memory. "You intended to harm me, but God intended it for good…" (Genesis 50:20, NIV). "…All things work together for good to those who love God…" (Romans 8:28, NKJV). "No weapon formed against you shall prosper…" (Isaiah 54:17, NKJV). "…If God is for us, who can be against us?" (Romans 8:31, NIV). Jesus settled my spirit and showed me how to battle a problem with Bible verses, like He did Himself while on earth.

I learned later that an agency employee had noticed my prosthetic arm when renewing my driver's license. Without informing me, she initiated the medical review, though I'd been driving with one arm for 45 years. Thankfully, my doctor resolved the issue quickly, and I was cruising around town in my little red Beetle in no time. —BECKY ALEXANDER

FAITH STEP: *Memorize a Bible verse that can encourage you in the future.*

SUNDAY, FEBRUARY 16

He also said, "This is what the kingdom of God is like. A man scatters seed on the ground. Night and day, whether he sleeps or gets up, the seed sprouts and grows, though he does not know how." Mark 4:26–27 (NIV)

MY WINDOWSILL SEEDS ARE STARTED. Every winter, I plant seeds in miniature compost pots along with enough quality soil to help the fledgling veggies survive. Come summer, melon, squash, and heirloom tomatoes will take their places in our raised planters. For now, I water and wait, watching for the first sprouts. As snow dances just outside the window, my dreams take root indoors.

I've heard it said that to plant a tree is to believe in tomorrow. To seed growers, that saying holds true for every flower and vegetable seed they place in the ground. Gardening is hope and dirt and God's promises all mixed together. Jesus compared God's kingdom to a seed growing. It's not necessary for me to understand how He will make it grow or when He will deem the right time for harvest. My job is simple. I need only to plant the seeds. Living out my faith in an open and inclusive way, I spread my love for Jesus everywhere I go. Sometimes I use words, but more often my actions bear witness for Him. Many of the people I encounter, I'll never meet again, and that's OK. Jesus will nurture their faith from planting to harvest. All I need to do is plant seeds. —HEIDI GAUL

FAITH STEP: *Pick up a packet of seeds to start in the warmth of your home. Watch as the magic of creation fills you with hope for the Kingdom of Heaven.*

PRESIDENTS' DAY, MONDAY, FEBRUARY 17

When he takes the throne of his kingdom, he is to write for himself on a scroll a copy of this law, taken from that of the Levitical priests. Deuteronomy 17:18 (NIV)

IN HIGH SCHOOL, I CREATED a lot of flash cards. Making them helped me to learn vocabulary words, science facts, and math equations. I wrote important information on one side of the small card and a related question or cue on the other. Once, one of my classmates commented on how much work went into making them. Yet for me, creating these cards helped me to actively engage with the material and break it into small manageable chunks. The actual writing helped me learn.

This memory from more than three decades ago came to mind during my recent Bible reading. At the end of his life, Moses reminded the Israelites of their escape from bondage. Moses wanted this chosen nation to pass on this message to generations. Because Moses wanted any future king of Israel to know God's law, Moses instructed him to copy the law in the priest's presence. Moses knew that writing the law would guide the king in remembering the law. Moses also desired that the king sit with the priests to learn the ways of the Lord.

This directive from Deuteronomy was long ago, but it's a message for me in the twenty-first century too. In high school, I used flash cards, but now I use them too. Writing down scripture verses is a great way to memorize the words of Jesus. —TRICIA GOYER

FAITH STEP: *Choose a few favorite scriptures to write out on note cards. Ask Jesus to hide His Word in your heart as you set out to memorize them.*

TUESDAY, FEBRUARY 18

Do not be afraid; you will not be put to shame. Do not fear disgrace; you will not be humiliated. You will forget the shame of your youth and remember no more . . .
Isaiah 54:4 (NIV)

I DRESSED AND LOOKED IN the mirror at my curvier midlife body. I took a deep breath and smiled. I felt a new feeling of being OK with myself.

Since childhood, I wanted everything about me to be smaller—my personality, my size, and the space I occupied. I struggled with an eating disorder as a teen and young adult. I worked hard as a young mom to have a healthier lifestyle by eating better and being physically active. Thankfully, food and body issues weren't as prevalent in the busy years of raising a family.

But midlife was different. Metabolism decreased. I ate out of boredom or to soothe my emotions. I lacked the motivation to exercise. My menopausal body was more padded than ever.

Thoughts and feelings from the past resurfaced. I felt shame in my appearance, my personality, and my presence. I was too old to struggle with this!

When listening to a podcast one day, the host said, "You have permission to take up space." Wow! It was as if Jesus directly spoke to me, addressing the disproportionate shame and insecurities I had felt since my youth.

I realized I had lacked permission to be myself all these years. As I embraced this mindset of acceptance, I prayed that Jesus would help me be gentler with myself and help me embrace who I am and how I look. —BRENDA L. YODER

FAITH STEP: *Envision yourself sitting beside Jesus as you share your insecurities and shame. Imagine Him saying, "You have permission to take up space."*

WEDNESDAY, FEBRUARY 19

Jesus said, "Let the little children come to me, and do not hinder them, for the kingdom of heaven belongs to such as these." Matthew 19:14 (NIV)

MY TWO-YEAR-OLD NEIGHBOR, LILY, IS just beginning to talk. After a few months of mostly indecipherable requests, silent pointing, or speaking a single word ("doggie" and "more" are two of her favorites), she now speaks in short sentences.

A few days after Valentine's Day, I received a text from her mother. Lily made a craft at daycare and kept pointing at my door, wanting to bring it over. For my husband and me—people who love the company of young children and are not yet grandparents—her visits are delightful.

"Of course!" I texted back. "Come anytime."

A few minutes later, Lily and her mom were at our front door. Lily gave me a little red valentine heart decorated with scribbled lines and googly eyes. "For Jen," she says, handing it to me. Then Lily ran to our kitchen and we hung the valentine on the refrigerator.

When Jesus's disciples scolded the adults who brought children to Him for a blessing and for prayer, He not only welcomed them but said that the Kingdom of Heaven actually *belonged* to little children.

What is it about young children that would prompt Jesus to say that? Is it their open, trusting hearts? Their generous proclamations of love? Their uncomplicated faith? Sense of wonder? Valentine's Day has come and gone, but each time I see Lily's heartfelt gift on the fridge, I'm reminded to come to Jesus like a child. —JENNIFER GRANT

FAITH STEP: *Find one tangible way to express your love to another person today. Send a note, make a phone call, or drop off something sweet to a neighbor or friend. Your act of love may remind them that Jesus loves them too.*

THURSDAY, FEBRUARY 20

He is like the light of morning at sunrise on a cloudless morning, like the brightness after rain that brings grass from the earth. 2 Samuel 23:4 (NIV)

THE DOOR TO MY FOURTEEN-YEAR-OLD daughter's bedroom slammed, and I plopped down onto the sofa. Both of us needed to cool off after a difficult homeschool morning. I closed my eyes and prayed, "Lord, show me how to reach Cassidy."

Opening them again, my gaze shifted to the framed print by Jack Vettriano hanging across from me. The simple scene of a man and woman, dressed in their finest, dancing at sunset on a rainy beach, is my favorite. Trying to shield them from the weather with umbrellas are their two servants, but despite how hard they try, the couple is obliviously happy and wet. Art critics disparage it for its uneven finishing, inconsistent lighting, and the odd position of the dancers. Maybe that is why I am drawn to it. Life can be like that at times— gloomy, cheerful, uneven, optimistic, and inconsistent.

My mind refocused on my child and not the schoolwork dampening our spirits. A creative lesson plan came to mind, then Cassidy and I shared a midday picnic lunch, lingering and laughing. Under the umbrella of Jesus's perfect balance, we hit the books later that afternoon with gusto. —GLORIA JOYCE

FAITH STEP: *Look up the Jack Vettriano print called "The Singing Butler" online. Think of a rainy place in your life and pray for Jesus to shelter you and teach you to find balance in the rain.*

Friday, February 21

With my whole heart I have sought You; Oh, let me not wander from Your commandments! Psalm 119:10 (NKJV)

THE WORD *HEART* IS MENTIONED more than five hundred times in the Bible. I keep a "Heart List," regularly jotting down verses as I discover them. I write the word *heart* in capital letters and red ink.

Perhaps my interest in the heart developed during Dad's four decades of procedures—two open-heart surgeries, a pacemaker, twenty-eight stents, and a defibrillator. Each time, the doctor drew a diagram to explain the plan for repair. I learned about the four chambers of the heart and asked questions about the atria, the aorta, and the pulmonary artery. I added the "V" terms to my vocabulary: ventricle, vein, valve, and vessel.

When I think of seeking Jesus with my whole spiritual heart, I like to picture the parts of my physical heart. The right atrium takes in oxygen-poor blood; I tell Jesus I am depleted of energy, direction, patience, and love. The right ventricle forces the blood into the lungs to receive oxygen; I ask Jesus to replenish me with those things that I need. The left atrium, like a reservoir, holds the oxygen-rich blood; I thank Jesus for refreshing me and sheltering me in His care. And finally, the left ventricle pumps the blood throughout the body; I pray for

Jesus to send me out in His name, sharing His offer of rescue, proclaiming His restoring love.

Someday, my Heart List may inspire me to write a heart devotional book. But for now, I'll continue adding scriptures and following Jesus with all my heart. —BECKY ALEXANDER

FAITH STEP: *Grab a red pen and begin a Heart List with Psalm 119:10. Find two more heart verses today. Then watch for others in the future.*

SATURDAY, FEBRUARY 22

Whether you turn to the right or to the left, your ears will hear a voice behind you, saying, "This is the way; walk in it." Isaiah 30:21 (NIV)

AFTER LOSING OUR HOUSE TO the Marshall Fire in Boulder, Colorado, we faced uncertainty. We'd not only lost all our possessions—we also had no home. We did have insurance, but like most everyone else, we were underinsured. We didn't know if we could rebuild or if we should sell our lot and find a new place. Should we stay in Boulder or move somewhere else? We had so many questions. I prayed constantly for God to give us direction.

Our friends and family also asked us loads of questions about our future. Every time I said, "I don't know," I felt more anxious.

To have peace, I had to figure out how to trust Jesus and believe He would show us the way to go. The Bible states He will guide us on right paths (Psalm 23:3), direct our steps (Proverbs 16:9), and assure us of His leading (Psalm 32:8). I started answering the questions from others with "I don't know, yet." *Yet* is a powerful little word that quelled my anxiety and infused hope into my answer. I may not have known His plan at that moment, but I believed He would reveal it to me eventually. It kept me hopeful in awaiting the unfolding of His plan.

I believe if I keep seeking Jesus rather than answers to my questions, He will say, "This is the way, walk in it." —JEANNIE BLACKMER

FAITH STEP: *For what current circumstances in your life are you seeking direction from Jesus? Do a Google search on "Bible verses promising God will direct you." Write your favorites on note cards and keep them handy for reference when uncertainty sneaks up on you.*

SUNDAY, FEBRUARY 23

Be still before the LORD, all mankind, because he has roused himself from his holy dwelling. Zechariah 2:13 (NIV)

I FIND IT CHALLENGING TO be still when friends or family are visiting. I want those I love to feel comfortable and appreciated. I engage with my grandchildren by playing games and reading books. I offer refreshments and snacks. I prepare and serve elaborate dinners. When I finally sit, I remember something else to do.

My busyness in caring for our guests was especially true when my husband's parents were in town. No sooner would we sit down to talk than I'd be back on my feet. After all, I wanted to show them how much I care by making sure they had everything they needed.

As I made my way toward the dining room in search of a board game, my father-in-law grabbed my hand. I stopped mid-step. When I looked down, I noticed a sparkle in his eyes. Pause and listen, his gaze seemed to say. My father-in-law held my hand gently as he spoke. He wanted to bless me, thank me for my hospitality, and encourage me. My father-in-law needed me to pause long enough to hear what he had to say.

The interaction with my father-in-law reminded me that Jesus also wants me to stop and listen. Jesus is always speaking to my heart, but sometimes I get too busy to listen to what He's saying. Even though I cannot physically grasp His hand, I can pause throughout the day to reconnect with Him. Spending time with Jesus is worth sitting still for.

—TRICIA GOYER

FAITH STEP: *Pause right now. Envision Jesus reaching out to take your hand as He gives you words of affirmation that bless you and encourage you. Sit still and hear what He has to say.*

MONDAY, FEBRUARY 24

. . . for the happy heart, life is a continual feast.
Proverbs 15:15 (NLT)

I'M A BELIEVER IN THE lesser-known sixth love language: food. I learned about the original five love languages as taught by Gary Chapman (quality time, physical touch, acts of service, gifts, and words of affirmation) when my husband and I attended marriage enrichment classes. But I've since come to recognize that *food* is another powerful love language. Preparing food for someone demonstrates our love; receiving food prepared for us, we feel loved.

Food motivates me. I shamelessly admit I'm more inclined to attend a meeting, seminar, or other event if food will be provided. Wanting to bless our congregation through this biblically demonstrated love language, my women's ministry group and I hosted a Valentine dinner with delicious food, homemade desserts, and heartwarming fellowship. Gathered together, we celebrated brotherly love for one another and Jesus's love for us.

Jesus demonstrated His love for others with food by feeding the multitudes (Mark 8:1–8) and cooking fish on the beach for His disciples after they'd had an unsuccessful night of fishing (John 21:9). Jesus called Himself the bread of life and said anyone who comes to Him will hunger no more (John 6:35). The way I see it, that's another vote for the sixth love language of food.

I'm sure Gary Chapman would agree that regardless of whether there are five or six love languages, Jesus shows the greatest love of all. —CASSANDRA TIERSMA

FAITH STEP: *Express the love of Jesus by sharing food with someone in your life today.*

TUESDAY, FEBRUARY 25

Truly I tell you, you will not get out until you have paid the last penny. Matthew 5:26 (NIV)

THE CHIROPRACTOR PLACED A DIME on the back of my hand and asked if I could feel the weight of the coin. I could not. He explained a straight spine protects the central nervous system, but a misaligned spine applies pressure, interfering with communication between the nerves and the rest of the body. On a diagram, he pointed out each vertebra and the organs, systems, and muscles it affects. Then he asked if I could feel the dime on my hand. I did! He explained that, like the dime, the slightest pressure on the nervous system increases over time.

I wish I had a dime for every time I've been bent out of shape because someone struck a nerve and I refused to straighten myself out. Instead, I focused on my hurt feelings or how I had been wronged. I recall a toxic coworker who told half-truths and enjoyed pitting one person against another, and an extended family member who made sure I knew I was a stepchild. I carried one grudge for years, the other for decades. I spent emotional currency avoiding my coworker and certain family functions. I lay awake at night, taking both adversaries to court in my mind.

Jesus instructs us to make peace with our adversaries and avoid court where conflicts can grow out of control and we could be thrown into prison (Matthew 5:25). As my grudges grew heavier, I sentenced myself to solitary confinement in my own misery. With Jesus's help, I paid my last emotional dime, forgave my adversaries, and embraced freedom. —KAREN SARGENT

FAITH STEP: *Read Matthew 5:25–26. Ask Jesus to reveal the cost of a grudge you hold and to help you embrace forgiveness.*

WEDNESDAY, FEBRUARY 26

As a result of the apostles' work, sick people were brought out into the streets on beds and mats so that Peter's shadow might fall across some of them as he went by. Crowds came from the villages around Jerusalem, bringing their sick and those possessed by evil spirits, and they were all healed.
Acts 5:15–16 (NLT)

IT SEEMED NO MATTER HOW many foods I eliminated or how many pills I toted around, the irritable bowel syndrome (IBS) I was diagnosed with at age sixteen had no mercy. It caused painful abdominal cramps after I ate and lots of embarrassing moments rushing into public restrooms. Doctors said there was no cure.

One evening at a Bible study with friends, the young pastor preached: "God wants us well!" He called out various illnesses and invited people to come for prayer. I didn't go forward, but I felt a stirring in my spirit.

I sat amazed as miracles happened right around me! Two girls who had carpal tunnel syndrome were prayed for and walked back to their seats rotating their wrists in awe. I was happy for them—but I wanted healing too. Jesus simply prompted me to "catch it!" as the girls walked by me. Desperate but hopeful, I grabbed at the air, essentially, at their shadows. I chose to believe I was healed that night and celebrated it with my friends.

The next day, Jesus led me to eat three meals that contained the worst things for a person with IBS to consume and I had no symptoms! It's been 28 years and the debilitating illness I wrestled with has never returned. —Pamela Toussaint Howard

FAITH STEP: *Do you believe in Jesus's miraculous power? Write down any pain or illness you are suffering with and ask Jesus how you can catch His healing.*

THURSDAY, FEBRUARY 27

I love those who love me, and those who seek me find me.
Proverbs 8:17 (NIV)

ALTHOUGH I VISIT MY DENTIST faithfully, twice a year, each time I go, I discover I need some major procedure—a root canal, a crown, an implant. I am vigilant about caring for my teeth, but I still get decay. My dentist recommended a pricey water flosser/brush, and since I was desperate, I ordered it.

When it arrived, I removed it from the box, intimidated by the puzzling parts. My husband put it together for me and plugged it in on my bathroom counter. Not decorative in any way, it also consumed a good deal of space. I rarely read directions, but I studied these, and they thoroughly confused me. To prepare the unit, I had to fill the reservoir with water. There were three buttons on the power handle, one for brushing, one for flossing, and the third remained a mystery. Finally, after eyeballing my expensive new wonder gadget for a week, I decided to try it. I put the power handle in my mouth and pressed FLOSS. My mouth filled with water, I choked, and I let go of the power handle. It leaped out of my hand, spewing water on me, the mirror, and my cat.

How relieved I am that a relationship with Jesus is not mysterious. It doesn't require assembly or complicated directions. I can always find Him. If I whisper His name, He's there. I don't have to figure out how He works. He *always* works! He doesn't spew anything. He's faithful, user-friendly, always at hand. He may not prevent tooth decay, but He soothes my soul. —PAT BUTLER DYSON

FAITH STEP: *List five advantages to having a relationship with Jesus. Thank Him for being easy to find.*

FRIDAY, FEBRUARY 28

Some of you were once like that. But you were cleansed; you were made holy; you were made right with God by calling on the name of the Lord Jesus Christ and by the Spirit of our God. 1 Corinthians 6:11 (NLT)

MOMENTS AGO, I WAS METAPHORICALLY on my face before Jesus on behalf of all who will read this devotion. The young mom creatively sneaking time for Jesus between myriad tasks. The older couple who always start their day here, in these pages. The businessperson who can't imagine skipping this time of focus on what matters most. The retired teacher, the retired pastor, the college student, the farmer, the gardener, the computer programmer, the childcare provider, the doctor, the baker, the sustainably resourced candlestick maker.

Seeking requires listening. If I ask for Jesus's help but then write what I think instead of quieting myself to hear what He might say—in His Word, impressions on my spirit, the counsel of godly friends—I've wasted the seeking.

Today as I quieted myself, I was reminded of a troubled friend who agonized over the consequences of bad decisions. She was mired in regret. The solace I gave her was "Temporarily. You're temporarily mired, stuck, frustrated with yourself. It won't always be this way. Jesus offers all of us the opportunity to grab His hand so He can pull us out of our stuck place and we can move forward."

As always, what Jesus gave *through* me He intended to be *for* me as well. What a wonder that He allows all of us to rewrite the stories we've been stuck in and step into a fresh chapter with Him.
—CYNTHIA RUCHTI

FAITH STEP: *Where have you felt stuck or mired in regret? Imagine Jesus stamping the word* **temporarily** *over your circumstances.*

SATURDAY, MARCH 1

Do not be conformed to this age, but be transformed by
the renewing of your mind, so that you may discern
what is the good, pleasing, and perfect will of God.
Romans 12:2 (HCSB)

I RECENTLY LOOKED THROUGH MY reading list and
was surprised at how many World War II–era novels
I've read in recent years. Some of them focused on
organized resistance movements by people whose
country had been invaded by Germany. A few told
the stories of British and American citizens who willingly risked their lives by going to France to serve
as spies or help sabotage the Nazi army's attacks on
Allied forces. These stories of courage in the face of
extreme danger made me wonder if I could be that
brave and self-sacrificing if I were called to step up
in such a time.

The next week I read a quote from *Mere Christianity* by C. S. Lewis that helped me understand that this
is such a time: "Enemy-occupied territory—that is
what this world is. Christianity is the story of how
the rightful king has landed, you might say landed
in disguise, and is calling us all to take part in a great
campaign of sabotage."

As a follower of Jesus, I'm called to become like
Him (1 John 2:6). That means I have to resist letting
other people or our culture influence me in ways that

go against my King's instructions and example. This perspective has made me more committed to prayer, Bible study, and obedience. My mission as a resistance fighter in Christ's kingdom is to follow His example as summed up in Romans 12:21 (NET): "Do not be overcome by evil, but overcome evil with good." —DIANNE NEAL MATTHEWS

FAITH STEP: *Make your own personalized resistance plan to help you live more like Jesus.*

SUNDAY, MARCH 2

Ask and it will be given to you; seek and you will find; knock and the door will be opened to you. Matthew 7:7 (NIV)

"WHAT WILL WE DO IF we can't resolve this?"

My husband stared at the highway from his position behind the steering wheel. I stared at the same scene from the passenger side. But I might as well have been turned to face out the back window for all the distance between our opinions on the topic. Funny, now I can't remember the issue, but what came out of that seemingly impossible impasse changed me.

I turned my attention to the road's shoulders and ditches we passed in miles of silence. And I turned my heart in a better direction—to seek Jesus.

In the quiet of my soul, I sought His wisdom. The situation wasn't impossible to Him. He didn't see our disagreement as an impasse. I let my emotions step back. *Jesus, what do You want me to do?*

Moments later, I swiveled toward my husband. "I think Jesus wants me to encourage you more," I said gently. *What?* No defending my position? No three-point plan explaining how right I was? No "and another thing..."?

As the Jesus-breathed sentence was spoken, peace settled deep in my heart. And the vehicle. I saw a similar peace rest on my husband's shoulders as they relaxed.

All I did was seek Jesus in a moment that seemed answerless. The solution wasn't what I expected, planned, or created. It startled me. But it perfectly fit the situation because it came from the Jesus wisdom I sought. —CYNTHIA RUCHTI

FAITH STEP: *Before you speak today, seek Jesus. Listen. Wait. Act upon His wisdom.*

MONDAY, MARCH 3

Therefore, there is now no condemnation for those who are in Christ Jesus, because through Christ Jesus the law of the Spirit who gives life has set you free from the law of sin and death. Romans 8:1–2 (NIV)

I COULD TELL SOMETHING WAS wrong when my youngest son, Solomon, asked to talk to me before bedtime. When we sat down on the couch, tears welled up in his eyes as he began his story. Earlier that day, he had used his school computer to search for a phrase he'd overheard online. He told me the words he typed into the search bar, and my heart sank. I knew he had stumbled upon information too mature for a ten-year-old. He said he immediately closed the browser after scanning the search results and realizing the information wasn't appropriate for him, but he was sick with guilt and worried he'd be in trouble at school and at home.

After a long hug, I smiled and told him I was proud of him. Though he had walked blindly into temptation, he had not fallen to it. Instead, he had escaped it as quickly as possible and confessed the situation to someone who could help him. The fact that he refused to keep his close call with temptation a secret showed sensitivity to the Holy Spirit and evidence of Jesus's reign over his young life. The more I reminded him of the unconditional love of Jesus, the more his whole countenance brightened.

I've had moments like Solomon when I've felt guilt from my mistakes and have been tempted to turn away from Jesus in my shame. I am so thankful He gives grace, not condemnation, when I stumble.
—EMILY E. RYAN

FAITH STEP: *Read Romans 8. Highlight verses that reflect the grace of Jesus.*

TUESDAY, MARCH 4

But the king answered, "No, I will pay you for it. I will not offer to the LORD my God sacrifices that have cost me nothing." 2 Samuel 24:24 (GNT)

I'D BEEN PRAYING ABOUT WHAT to give up for Lent. During my morning quiet time the Tuesday before Ash Wednesday, I sensed Jesus telling me to give up social media. *What?* For 40 whole days? I loved scrolling through my feeds, and this Lent sacrifice seemed extreme to me. I boldly asked for three confirmations and got them in quick succession. *OK, Jesus, if You insist!*

I posted a note on social media that I was giving it up for Lent, let folks know they could text and email me, and deleted all the social apps off my phone. I suddenly felt alone, vulnerable, and kind of cast adrift. That certainly seemed telling, underscoring my unhealthy attachment. *Jesus, help me*, a simple prayer I use often.

I caught myself picking up my phone a lot and switching screens on my laptop, remembering my resolve. Boy, did I have it bad, but I was committed.

I quickly found healthy alternatives to fill my free time. I read a couple of books, including one with a friend, meeting regularly to discuss it. I prayed and read Scripture more. I took an online class. But mostly I just sat still more, listening for the gentle voice of Jesus—a voice I usually silenced with online activity. In general, I was more serene, present, and attuned to the Holy Spirit.

Lent has come and gone. While I posted an Easter greeting, I'm not sure I want to get back into the social media scene. For now, I feel called deeper into the quiet stillness after giving up something I loved for the Lover of my Soul. —ISABELLA CAMPOLATTARO

FAITH STEP: *Prayerfully ask Jesus about giving up social media for a time. Take note of how you feel.*

ASH WEDNESDAY, MARCH 5

. . . to bestow on them a crown of beauty instead of ashes, the oil of joy instead of mourning, and a garment of praise instead of a spirit of despair. Isaiah 61:3 (NIV)

THE DAY WE FLED OUR home from a raging wildfire, ashes rained down on us. We drove to a parking lot and watched our house burn to the ground. Thankful to be alive yet devastated at the loss, we then drove to our son's condo. When I looked in the mirror, I had black smudges on my face and ash pooled in the corner of my eyes.

One gift I received after the fire from a friend was a T-shirt that said: Beauty from Ashes. I'd heard that phrase before, but it had never resonated with me until then. Slowly, I've seen our property come back to life—beauty literally replaced ashes. And we've had a caring community uphold us with their generosity and kindness. After a season of sorrow, my joy has returned and my despair turned to praise as we dream and plan on rebuilding our home.

As I reflect on this past year, a year of cleaning up ash from our land, mourning the loss of our home, and feeling despair in that moment, Ash Wednesday has new meaning for me. I possess a deeper appreciation of Jesus's resurrection power. He specializes in resurrecting the dead and giving life. I can't help but recall that day I had ashes in my eyes and sorrow in my heart. Yet beauty is coming. And when Easter morning comes, along with declaring, "He is risen," I'll confidently proclaim He creates beauty from ashes. —JEANNIE BLACKMER

FAITH STEP: *How have you experienced Jesus creating beauty from ashes? Make a post online or share your experience with someone today.*

THURSDAY, MARCH 6

A time to search and a time to give up . . .
Ecclesiastes 3:6 (NIV)

AS A COUNSELOR, I CAN drive myself crazy, talking myself through my feelings. I need trustworthy people with whom to process my thoughts. One day, I struggled with control over a situation with one of my children. I was frustrated as I searched for a solution, knowing I couldn't fix things.

I stopped by my friend Debbie's house on my way home from work. She thoughtfully listened as I shared my problem. "Most parents struggle with control at some time," she said. Then, she gently suggested *I* might be the obstacle to Jesus working in the situation. She wanted me to consider two responses to the problem: stepping aside or stepping away.

That sounded like giving up! I wrestled with these concepts. Could I be a hindrance to Jesus's work? I knew it wasn't my role to find the answer to my child's problem. It was time to step aside and let Jesus work His plan in my child's life.

Lying in bed that night, I pictured giving up control and fear to Jesus using Debbie's metaphors. I imagined walking beside my child. I stepped aside. Then I stepped away. The image helped me to see Jesus on the path with my child. Rather than being in the way, I turned my worry into prayer and control into trust, confidently envisioning Jesus caring for my child. The surprising lesson was that it was just the two of them. Jesus was there instead of me. —BRENDA L. YODER

FAITH STEP: *Is there a situation where you need to search for answers or where Jesus is asking you to give up control? Sit with Him and ask Him to show you what to do.*

FRIDAY, MARCH 7

Heaven and earth will pass away, but my words will never pass away. Mark 13:31 (NIV)

THE CROCUSES ARE BLOOMING. EVERY year, these small flowers rise up through the frost and snow to brighten our yard. Their petals open to the elements, braving—and seemingly enjoying—the cold and wet weather. They spread the good news: spring is coming. Looking at them, I smile. They know something I tend to forget during the dead of winter. The temperatures will warm. Birds will nest. The seasons will change just as they always have.

How can these tiny purple blooms make such a difference in my attitude? They arrive when I need them most and stay until other flowers make their appearance. Spring and summer come, and the garden explodes with color. But as autumn passes and the trees cast off their leaves, I remember my crocuses and what they mean to me.

Like the crocus corms hidden under the soil, waiting for the right time to cheer me, Jesus's words come to mind when I need them most. Jesus will return in His chosen time, when the world's seasons have all run their course. For now, I remember Him, the words He spoke, and the promises He made. How could one man make such a difference in my life? Like the crocus that spreads the good news, Jesus is the good news. But unlike those little flowers, Jesus and His Word are more than seasonal; they're with me for eternity. —HEIDI GAUL

FAITH STEP: *Next fall, plant a corm or bulb. When tending it, remember that Jesus's words, like the bulb, are hidden inside of you and available when you need them.*

SATURDAY, MARCH 8

Then he said, "Jesus, remember me when you come into your kingdom." Jesus answered him, "Truly I tell you, today you will be with me in paradise."
Luke 23:42–43 (NIV)

A POWERFUL CROSS DISPLAY STANDS along Interstate 75 in Chattanooga, Tennessee. Three colossal steel crosses reach 100 feet into the air, the center one a bit higher than the others. The sight proclaims the message of Jesus to millions of passersby each year.

I literally gasped the first time I saw the crosses, traveling with my daughter and two little granddaughters. I shared the whole story with the girls—Jesus in the middle, a criminal on one side saying mean things to Him, a criminal on the other side being kind to Jesus and asking Him for help. I concluded, "Jesus told the second man he would be in heaven that same day."

The car grew quiet for a while. Five-year-old Sadie sketched in her art kit. When we got home, she handed me a sheet of paper. "This is for you."

I looked at her picture—three big crosses made with uneven lines, colored with a brown marker, the center cross much taller than the other two. "Oh!" I blinked back tears. "I love this, Sadie!"

Jesus's gentle words to the thief on the cross bring peace to my heart. They assure me of a place called paradise, which is heaven. Jesus's Words also promise I'll be in His presence when I die, on the very day I breathe my last breath.

I hope you get to see the three crosses in Chattanooga someday. If not, you can still proclaim their meaning. —BECKY ALEXANDER

FAITH STEP: *Draw three crosses. Write "peace" above the middle one. Consider the precious peace that Jesus provides.*

SUNDAY, MARCH 9

Jesus also used this illustration: "The Kingdom of Heaven is like the yeast a woman used in making bread. Even though she put only a little yeast in three measures of flour, it permeated every part of the dough." Matthew 13:33 (NLT)

I THOUGHT ABOUT SKIPPING LYDIA CIRCLE, my volunteer group at church. I'd neglected my to-do list and needed to catch up. The 45-minute round trip and the hour-plus meeting would take up a big chunk of time, but I decided to go anyway.

It was my baking day, so on my way out the door, I fed the sourdough starter its breakfast of hard red wheat and water. I stirred the additions in and checked for signs of life. Tiny bubbles broke the surface of the dough, quickly popped, then disappeared. Yeast spores give off carbon dioxide that would raise the loaf. Invisibly.

Sometimes I think the things I do are invisible, small, and mostly unseen. Does it matter if I gather with my Christian sisters to study God's Word, sign cards to shut-ins, and bake cookies for funerals?

Jesus, largely unrecognized as the Messiah by many people in His day, used yeast to describe how the Kingdom of Heaven would arrive, small and mostly unrecognized, like a woman's yeast that penetrates every part of the dough. Yeast is often associated with sin in the Bible because of its tendency to spread and take over, but not in this case. Small enough to be almost invisible, the yeast expands the loaf, just like the good news of Jesus would grow and penetrate the whole world.

When I got home from Lydia Circle, the dough was ready. What was little became large indeed.
—SUZANNE DAVENPORT TIETJEN

FAITH STEP: *Do a small action today that will make a big impact for Jesus. Cook a meal, donate household items, babysit, or run an errand.*

MONDAY, MARCH 10

My sheep listen to my voice; I know them, and they follow me. I give them eternal life, and they shall never perish; no one will snatch them out of my hand.
John 10:27–28 (NIV)

OUR SON WILL IS A MUSICIAN. Ever since he was a tiny boy, he has loved to sing. In junior high, he began playing guitar and piano. In high school, he began writing and producing his own music. Now, he is a music and worship major in college. Every once in a while, Will emails us a new song he is working on. I pass the link along to all of our family members. I want them to get in on the joy.

The latest video Will sent us was his first time performing with his worship studio class. They were leading the music for an event and the students took turns. When Will stepped up to the microphone to lead worship, I teared up a bit. A little because I am his mom and a little because it was beautiful. I really love the sound of his voice. I would know his voice anywhere, on any song, at any time. Probably because I have spent 20 years listening to it. It's the best voice. Of course, I'm not biased at all!

Jesus wants me to know His voice. He wants me to recognize His direction and guidance. And He wants me to listen for His truth. When I hear Jesus's voice, I can know that I am safe and loved. It's the best voice—I'm not biased at all.
—SUSANNA FOTH AUGHTMON

FAITH STEP: *Do you know the sound of Jesus's voice? Read John 10 and invite Jesus to help you listen to His words and understand their meaning.*

TUESDAY, MARCH 11

By faith Moses, when he had grown up, refused to be known as the son of Pharaoh's daughter. He chose to be mistreated along with the people of God rather than to enjoy the fleeting pleasures of sin.
Hebrews 11:24–25 (NIV)

LAST WEEK AT OUR LADIES' Bible study, I commented that Jesus has set us free from the condemnation of our past sins, whether we sinned 40 years or 40 minutes ago. "You know how a little devil sits on your shoulder and says, 'You call yourself a Christian, and look what you did. You should be ashamed.'"

One of the women interrupted. "That's not what my devil says. He says, 'That was fun. Let's do that again!'"

All twelve of us laughed. I imagine because we each remembered a time when sin felt good, even though our conscience told us it was wrong.

Like Moses, Jesus had the choice to enjoy the "fleeting pleasures of sin." Instead, He obeyed His Father to the end and suffered a horrible death by crucifixion. Why would someone choose torture and shame over pleasure?

Jesus saw beyond the temporary fun that sin could provide. He saw beyond the shame of the cross (Hebrews 12:2). Jesus saw you and me and everyone who would one day say yes to His invitation to join Him as one of God's children. Jesus chose obedience and gives us, through His Spirit, the power to obey. —JEANETTE LEVELLIE

FAITH STEP: *Next time you're tempted to sin, think of Jesus laying down His life for you and say yes to obedience.*

WEDNESDAY, MARCH 12

While Jesus was still speaking, some people came from the house of Jairus, the synagogue leader. "Your daughter is dead," they said. "Why bother the teacher anymore?" Overhearing what they said, Jesus told him, "Don't be afraid; just believe." Mark 5:35–36 (NIV)

WHEN MY HUSBAND AND I sensed the Holy Spirit leading us toward living full-time aboard a sailboat, we faced the task of finding suitable moorage. The challenge caught us off guard: every yacht broker within a 200-mile radius warned of a seven-year waiting list for liveaboard space in our area. Several marina managers laughed aloud when we asked about availability.

Perhaps the nautical professionals were right. Maybe we'd embarked on a dead-end path. Why waste Jesus's time and attention by asking Him to provide moorage when there was none available?

Our situation reminded me of Jairus's story. The desperate father sought Jesus's help to save his twelve-year-old daughter from death, but all too soon his friends came bearing bad news: the girl had died. Why bother asking Jesus to heal her when she'd already passed away?

Jesus overheard the conversation between Jairus and his friends, and He overheard ours. He responded by giving us an inner peace to pursue the path before us. He also gave us specific scripture verses that reassured us to trust Him, to not be afraid, and to believe in His ability to do the impossible.

We trusted, prayed, and moved forward in faith. Sure enough, Jesus provided suitable moorage, and He did so within 2 months. Negative voices and impossible circumstances could not stop Him from doing a miracle. —GRACE FOX

FAITH STEP: *Are you facing an impossible situation? Complete the sentence: "Don't be afraid. Just believe that Jesus can _____."*

THURSDAY, MARCH 13

Be patient, then, brothers and sisters, until the Lord's coming. See how the farmer waits for the land to yield its valuable crop, patiently waiting for the autumn and spring rains. James 5:7 (NIV)

IT'S THE SAME EVERY SINGLE YEAR, yet somehow the succession of bleak, gray days in March in Chicago always takes me by surprise. Hardware stores and garden centers begin to arrange wooden pallets and tables in their parking lots. In a few months, they'll hold a beautiful array of tomato plants, rose bushes, and herbs. In Zone 5, where I live, often the first flowers to be set out for sale are impatiens or hanging baskets of pink or purple petunias. But now the parking lot, like the sky, is a dull gray, the tables dolefully empty.

Like me, they long for spring.

Stopped at a red light, looking at those empty tables, I bring to mind the fact that all of the plants that will fill those spaces are already sprouted, growing stronger in their little trays and pots elsewhere. They exist, but I just can't see them yet.

Similarly, when I am going through a spiritual "winter," one when I don't feel a sense of joy or of God's presence, when my mood feels as colorless as the gray sky, Jesus is still at work in me.

He is with me—even when I can't see new growth in me or hopeful signs of spring in my heart. And, as it always does, spring will come. —JENNIFER GRANT

FAITH STEP: *Today, sketch your life as an empty garden patch where Jesus is planning to bring new life. Draw what He might bring forth. Maybe new friendships that might be planted in your life? Ideas that will take root and grow in you? Volunteer opportunities?*

FRIDAY, MARCH 14

The eternal God is your refuge, and underneath are the everlasting arms. Deuteronomy 33:27 (NIV)

MY HUSBAND'S AUNT SARA PASSED away recently, just shy of her 102nd birthday. A few weeks before, Hal and I had dinner with her and her daughter at a restaurant while we were visiting in their city. The four of us chatted and laughed as we caught up with each other, and Aunt Sara recounted a story or two about things that had happened long ago.

When we prepared to leave, Aunt Sara held on to her trusty walker/chair combo, which her daughter, Bertrice, had dubbed Ruby the Rollator. The walker traveled with Aunt Sara, giving her support and a place to sit whenever she needed to rest. Aunt Sara even tricked out her walker with a horn and would sometimes add streamers and bells, any decorations that matched the season or holidays throughout the year. Ruby was like Aunt Sara's faithful friend and protector, something that she leaned on till the very end.

I'm not quite ready for a walker like Aunt Sara's, but I do lean on Jesus for support every day. I depend on Him to keep me from falling to temptations and from stumbling down the wrong path. I look to Jesus when I need a place to rest from life's demands and challenges. And when I don't have the strength to go another step, I look to Him for refuge.

Aunt Sara was doubly blessed in her life. She had Jesus for support, and He provided Ruby to assist her. Jesus is also the One who props me up with His everlasting arms. —BARBRANDA LUMPKINS WALLS

FAITH STEP: *What or who do you hold on to when you need support? Jesus is always available.*

SATURDAY, MARCH 15

But love your enemies, do good to them, and lend to them without expecting to get anything back. Then your reward will be great, and you will be children of the Most High, because he is kind to the ungrateful and wicked.
Luke 6:35 (NIV)

MY DAUGHTER'S NEW JOB REQUIRES frequent travel and extended stays in posh resorts. Like good parents, we decided to book a flight to Arizona and crash her swanky hotel room.

While she worked, my husband and I took in the sights. The arid desert, rocky terrain, and scattered vegetation contrasted sharply with the lush green Ozark Mountains where we live. I marveled at the Creator's artistic imagination.

I especially appreciated the iconic saguaro cacti standing guard. Some were 40 feet tall with many arms reaching toward the azure sky. Others had only a few prickly appendages. I was shocked when a local told me the saguaros are dying. She explained the cacti may look healthy, but many were diseased by bacteria rotting them from inside. Injury allows the bacteria to enter a cactus. Left untreated, the cactus splits, oozes black liquid, and dies. How sad!

As I contemplate the saguaro, I consider prickly people who ooze their disease onto others. A few faces come into view. Do I have as much compassion for them as I do the cactus? Have I considered a wound might be hidden beneath their exterior? How can I treat them differently, knowing what I see on the outside may reflect something hurtful is eating them on the inside?

Answering these questions honestly isn't easy because sometimes my own heart can be a little prickly. It's hard to love the unlovable. But Jesus did. That answers all my questions. —KAREN SARGENT

FAITH STEP: *Send a thinking-of-you card to a prickly person in your life. Express something specific you appreciate about him or her.*

SUNDAY, MARCH 16

Then he said, "I tell you the truth, you must change and become like little children. Otherwise, you will never enter the kingdom of heaven." Matthew 18:3 (NCV)

I ONCE HAD A PASTOR who'd often say, "I want to be like Stu when I grow up." Stu was an elderly retired minister who was a quiet, soft-spoken spiritual mentor to many. The Lord has put this memory on my heart, prompting me to consider who is my inspirational role model. I know I need to become more like Jesus, but I've also been asking Jesus who else in my life I should aspire to become more like.

He showed me. It wasn't someone I would've expected. Unlike that pastor's role model who was a senior citizen named Stu, my role model is a high school senior named Hunter. My husband and I are blessed to have this special friend in our life. Not only is this young man remarkably considerate, thoughtful, and social, but he's also refreshingly positive, upbeat, and enthusiastic. Hunter inspires me. He's brimming with what the French call *joie de vivre* (joy of life). Barely able to contain his *joie de vivre,* he beams with delight in whatever moment he's enjoying, whether it's riding the bus, going to church, drinking coffee, raking leaves for an elderly neighbor, playing Ping-Pong, or pounding out self-taught boogie-woogie piano music. Such unadulterated *joie de vivre* is a joy to be around.

I want to be like Hunter when I grow up—radiating childlike joy in Jesus and my daily interactions. Jesus answered my prayer by bringing Hunter to my attention. Now I hope, pray, and trust Jesus will help me radiate joy to others. —CASSANDRA TIERSMA

FAITH STEP: *If you don't have an inspirational role model, ask Jesus to show you a person who could be your mentor.*

MONDAY, MARCH 17

I will build you up again, and you, Virgin Israel, will be rebuilt. Jeremiah 31:4 (NIV)

THERE USED TO BE A racetrack in the next town that shut down 15 years ago. Five years later, as it sat empty, crews began expanding the road eight lanes wide. It didn't make sense. When I drove by, I wondered if it was necessary to have such a wide stretch of road when there was absolutely nothing there. Until a few years ago. All of a sudden, that area became a beehive of activity with construction vehicles and personnel going in and out. In no time at all, they built store after restaurant after condo. It's now a mini-city in and of itself that needs eight lanes to get in and out of.

Jesus has shut down some things in my life. Even more painful is how He broke down certain parts of me and then expanded me in ways I didn't think possible. During those years of difficulty, it didn't make sense. The stretching seemed fruitless and an exercise in futility. Until now. Looking around at what Jesus has built in my life, I understand. The old me wasn't equipped for this new chapter of life filled with challenging teenagers, a thriving writing career, and the plethora of other things I have going on.

Jesus is the architect and carpenter (Hebrews 3:4) who knows the master plan for my life (Jeremiah 29:11). Even if I don't understand what He's constructing in me, I need to trust that He's always building for my good. —CLAIRE MCGARRY

FAITH STEP: *Write down what doesn't make sense in your life right now. Date it and tuck it in your Bible. Every now and then, read it until it makes perfect sense.*

TUESDAY, MARCH 18

I prayed for this child, and the LORD has granted me what I asked of him. 1 Samuel 1:27 (NIV)

THE NUMBER ROSE TO SEVEN pregnancies—but only one living child. Years of jubilant highs and devastating lows left me emotionally exhausted. The physical part hadn't been easy either—doctors, specialists, procedures, surgeries. Each pregnancy brought fatigue and nausea in the first trimester, followed by the painful process of miscarriage. And it was occurring again. No heartbeat. Pregnancy hormone levels decreasing.

"Let's wait one more week and see what happens," my doctor said.

Heaviness overshadowed the next few days. I believed Jesus could give me a second child, but would He choose to do so? I prayed for a miracle yet braced for another loss.

Before my return appointment, my sister called. "I have something to tell you." She hesitated. "I've been praying specifically for the baby's heart to beat. In the middle of the night, Jesus told me in my spirit the baby's heart is beating."

Could it be? I pondered my sister's bold words during the drive to the medical center. My feelings jumped from hope to fear to joy to dread. By the time I reached the all-too-familiar exam table, I just wanted to cry.

The doctor placed the cold ultrasound probe on my abdomen and gently glided it across. Then I heard the sound I had longed for. *Thump-thump, thump-thump, thump-thump.* "There it is!" he exclaimed. "Strong and steady."

Twenty-nine years later, that thumping can still be heard if I lay an ear on my son's chest. We'd prayed for him to live, and the Giver of heartbeats graciously granted what we had asked. —BECKY ALEXANDER

FAITH STEP: *Seek Jesus on behalf of someone who is struggling to have a child or who needs a boost of faith. Send an encouraging card.*

WEDNESDAY, MARCH 19

And I shall walk in a wide place, for I have sought your precepts. Psalm 119:45 (ESV)

I VISITED SOME FRIENDS RECENTLY who are going through a very hard time. I consider them both mentors as I spent many hours as a younger woman learning to trust Jesus through a Bible study they led in their home. Now in their eighties, the husband had a stroke and the wife has Parkinson's disease, which has progressed to a point that she cannot do many daily-living activities. They are totally dependent on others to help with basic needs.

It had been some years since I'd seen my friends. As I comprehended their changed state, I fought back tears. I listened as they told me about their declining health issues. Grief for their physical losses was evident. The husband said he even woke up crying in the middle of the night because he was no longer able to care for his wife.

And yet, amid this difficulty, a theme emerged. They were taking the same approach to life they had when they led Bible study: trust Jesus. The wife said she felt Jesus's nearness as He ministered to her when her body was restless and shaking. Sometimes all she could do was walk around the house, but she felt Jesus walking with her. And the husband said He relies on Jesus to be strong now that he is weak.

I went to see my friends to encourage them, but I left inspired. The couple who mentored me to trust Jesus when I was younger is teaching me how to trust Jesus in aging too. —GWEN FORD FAULKENBERRY

FAITH STEP: *Send a card to someone today who needs to be reminded that Jesus is near those who seek Him.*

THURSDAY, MARCH 20

But the one who stands firm to the end will be saved.
Matthew 24:13 (NIV)

MY OLDER SON, PIERCE, GUEST played baseball for a travel team for a weekend of preseason games. He only knew a few of the players and barely knew the coach. During the games, the coach moved the players around to several positions. I think he was experimenting with the optimal combination and the best player for each position.

Most of the kids hadn't played with the others. Some hadn't played their particular positions before. To make matters worse, our team roster was composed of sixteen-year-old players, while the other team was made up of eighteen-year-olds who'd been practicing together for weeks.

Our team lost big, but I was struck by how those boys did the best they could, even as they were being totally trounced. I was impressed and humbled. Even with all the various obstacles and disadvantages, they suited up, showed up, and stood firm.

I confess that more than a few times I've let my failures or frustrations—or those of others—cause me to quit. If not literally, then definitely mentally. In sports, there's no margin for recovery time to nurse an ego, blame someone else, or have a pity party. The game must go on!

Jesus exhorts us to do life this way too—stand firm no matter what the circumstances. With Jesus as my coach, I strive to shake off adversity, suit up, show up, and stand firm for Him. —ISABELLA CAMPOLATTARO

FAITH STEP: *Check a favorite sports team or athlete's track record. Informally chart their trajectory with a line graph. Can you relate?*

FRIDAY, MARCH 21

I will give them a heart to know me, that I am the LORD. They will be my people, and I will be their God, for they will return to me with all their heart.
Jeremiah 24:7 (NIV)

MY PHONE ALARM SOUNDED AT 5 a.m. and I popped right up. That was a good sign since I am not a morning person. I was looking forward to dialing in to the 6 a.m. prayer call that would begin my church's 40 days of sacred time of prayer and fasting, which we call Seek.

I knew my prayer and devotional life had grown weak over the last several months. As a result, I felt restless, overwhelmed, and dispassionate. I needed a jump-start, so I committed to reconnecting with Jesus. I wanted to feel His presence again. I plunged right in. Each morning I listened to the morning prayer call, read a couple of devotionals and Scripture, and talked to Jesus. I was amazed at how what I read all tied together. I sat quietly and waited to hear from Him. I bared my soul to the Lord in my journal and wrote down what He said to me. My effort made all the difference.

I had entered the Seek fast with a heavy heart. By the end, I felt much calmer, lighter, and optimistic. Jesus had taken care of the burdens that had weighed me down. He honored my efforts, despite my fasting stumbles, and extended me grace. I'm so glad I have a closer walk with Him again. I had wandered, but now I have returned.
—BARBRANDA LUMPKINS WALLS

FAITH STEP: *Are you feeling a little distant from Jesus? Commit to spending 20 minutes a day with Him and watch what a difference it makes.*

SATURDAY, MARCH 22

I thank God, whom I serve, as my ancestors did, with a clear conscience, as night and day I constantly remember you in my prayers. 2 Timothy 1:3 (NIV)

DRIVING OFF TO GROCERY SHOP, I switched the radio on and caught a breaking news alert. "One dead and many injured in a shooting at Sam Houston University." *No, Jesus!* My eighteen-year-old grandson, Ty, was a freshman at Sam Houston! I pulled over and texted Ty. The news report continued, and I learned the shooting had occurred the night before. Intellectually, I knew that if Ty had been hurt, I'd have heard by now. But I was desperate to know he was OK.

Finally, Ty texted me. "I'm fine, Honey. Thanks for your prayers." *Thank YOU, Jesus!*

I was relieved but puzzled. I didn't know about the shooting so how could I have been praying? I decided to call Ty.

"You told me when I left for college that you and G-Dogg would pray for me every day," Ty said. "So I knew you were praying for me."

Oh, Jesus, how could I forget? My husband, G-Dogg to the grandchildren, and I had prayed for Ty even before he was born. Prayers for each family member were part of our morning devotional time with Jesus. Of course, we had prayed for Ty, covering him for whatever he would encounter. I wanted to chat with Ty, to hear his sweet voice, but knowing he wasn't into phone conversations, I told him I loved him and wished him a good week ahead.

"Thanks, Honey," Ty said. "Keep praying for me."

Jesus, our faithful prayer partner, would see to that! —PAT BUTLER DYSON

FAITH STEP: *Pray daily for loved ones and for others who need prayer. Tell them you are praying for them.*

SUNDAY, MARCH 23

The thief comes only to steal and kill and destroy; I have come that they may have life, and have it to the full.
John 10:10 (NIV)

ZANE AND I BOUGHT NEW alpine touring equipment. It's ski gear that allows us to hike up the mountain and ski down in fresh powder. Excited, we planned our first outing to use our new gear. But the night before we were to set out, our dog, Ody, barked a few times to be let outside after we were already in bed. We had a hard time falling back to sleep. We woke up tired and cranky. We almost gave up going. We were short with each other and had lost some of our enthusiasm to make the effort.

I've always loved Jesus's promise in John 10:10. Jesus came to give us abundant life. But the thief comes to kill, steal, and destroy. I mentioned this to Zane and suggested we not let our joy be stolen, even if the effort to get to the mountain felt like a lot of work. He agreed.

We drove to the ski area. It was windy, cold, and icy. We pushed through the negativity. We put on our skis and started hiking up the mountain. Once we entered the pine forest, the wind lessened and the sun came out. Despite our rough night, we had a fantastic day together enjoying the outdoors, exercising, and having meaningful conversation. Persevering when we wanted to give up reminded us of the abundant life Jesus gives us. —JEANNIE BLACKMER

FAITH STEP: *If you feel like giving up today, pray for strength to persevere and call a trusted friend to encourage you. Don't let Satan steal the abundant life Jesus promises!*

MONDAY, MARCH 24

Therefore do not worry about tomorrow, for tomorrow will worry about itself. Each day has enough trouble of its own. Matthew 6:34 (NIV)

DURING A UNIT ON ARGUMENTATIVE TEXTS, I taught my students how to spot common logical fallacies in print and video advertisements. After analyzing the breakdown in logic, they created their own ads using one of the fallacies we'd studied. Their favorite was the slippery slope fallacy. It assumes that one small event now will lead to a catastrophic future. For example, if you fail one test in high school, you won't get into college and will end up unemployed, living in a tent under a bridge in winter.

The students caught on quickly, and the ease with which they were able to take one insignificant moment and follow it to ridiculous consequences both amused and impressed me. However, it wasn't long before I began to see the breakdown of my own illogical thoughts reflected in their assignments. How often do I allow a slippery slope of worry to paralyze me with fear? I fixate on the false reality that my entire future depends on my success or failure in one particular moment and allow my imagination to create a story that ignores Jesus and forgets His divine power and presence in my life. As a result, I ruin today with worry over tomorrow.

That realization stuck with me as I navigated big changes in my life over the next several months. Instead of letting worry create worst-case scenarios in my mind, I reminded myself that no matter what my future held, Jesus would be with me. —EMILY E. RYAN

FAITH STEP: *Use your imagination to picture Jesus standing by your side in the future. When worry sneaks in, remind yourself of that image.*

TUESDAY, MARCH 25

The king said, "Now I know that your God is above all other gods and kings, because he gave you the power to explain this mystery." Daniel 2:47 (CEV)

COZY WHODUNIT MYSTERIES ARE MY go-to for relaxing bedtime reading. Interesting enough to keep me turning pages but not too scary or over-stimulating to prevent me from being able to sleep. The perfect balance of suspense and comfort for unwinding at day's end. In contrast, daily life's rarely intriguing, let alone mysterious. Mine's rather predictable, with its ordinary rhythms and routines.

Except for one tiny, perplexing unsolved case. Last summer I found a perfect large white strawberry neatly tucked into the crotch of two slender branches of my dogwood tree. A flawless specimen that had been plucked before ripened from one of my straw-berry plants. The mystery of who'd placed it there piqued my curiosity for months. *How did it get there?*

Still puzzled about the case of the misplaced strawberry two seasons later, I saw the famous 1883 textile design by William Morris, called "Strawberry Thief," featuring birds with strawberries in their beaks. A clue! A quick internet search revealed our native blue jays loved strawberries. Mystery solved.

Was it silly of me to have kept wondering about such a tiny caper? Questioning myself, I sensed Jesus remind me that He gave me an inquisitive mind and appetite for truth. No mystery about it, Jesus made me curious about the mysteries of life, including my native blue jays. —CASSANDRA TIERSMA

FAITH STEP: *If there's something you don't understand, ask Jesus, the revealer of mysteries. Praise Him for the intriguing, mysterious ways of the world He created.*

WEDNESDAY, MARCH 26

When they had sung a hymn, they went out to the Mount of Olives. Matthew 26:30 (NIV)

SINGING ISN'T MY NATURAL RESPONSE when I've had a bad day. I'm more prone to go for a walk, seek solitude to process my thoughts, or tell my woes to my husband. Sometimes I'll listen to a playlist of worship songs to focus my mind on all things good, but that's not the same as bursting into song myself.

Seeking Jesus's example about how to respond well on difficult days leads me to the story of the Last Supper. Picture this: on the evening of the Last Supper, Jesus said that, in less than 24 hours, one of His disciples would betray Him, Peter would deny Him three times, all would desert Him, and He would die. Clearly, Jesus had seen better days, but He let neither circumstances nor emotions dictate

His response. Amid a no-good, very bad day, Jesus chose to sing.

Jews traditionally ended the Passover meal by singing the Hallel— Psalms 113–118. It's likely, then, that Jesus sang lyrics such as these: "When hard pressed, I cried to the LORD; he brought me into a spacious place. The LORD is with me; I will not be afraid. What can mere mortals do to me? The LORD is with me; he is my helper. I look in triumph on my enemies" (Psalm 118:5–7, NIV).

Despite knowing that the cross awaited, Jesus worshipped God in song. Discovering His response to difficult days challenges me to do likewise. —GRACE FOX

FAITH STEP: *Read several verses from Psalm 118 aloud while envisioning Jesus as worship leader en route to the Mount of Olives with His disciples.*

THURSDAY, MARCH 27

Let the peace of Christ rule in your hearts, since as members of one body you were called to peace. And be thankful. Colossians 3:15 (NIV)

THE LIST WAS LONG. Check prices at the building-supply store. Purchase fabric. Drop off books at the library. And groceries—the refrigerator nearly echoed it was so empty. So much to do and so little time. I hadn't left the house and already felt frazzled.

I got in the car and turned the key. Nothing. Maybe the engine was cold. I tried again. Silence. The dashboard lights remained dark. The battery was dead, the cable broken. I headed indoors to arrange a tow and schedule an appointment at the auto repair shop. Any plans for the day were ruined.

My mind filled with dread as I contemplated what I could throw together for dinner. But when I searched the freezer, I found one last protein—a small turkey. Resting beside it was a bag of cranberries. I grabbed the items and laid them on the counter. I rifled the pantry's dark corners and discovered enough sides to fabricate a unique but tasty holiday-style dinner. I shrugged. *Thanksgiving in March.*

Hours later, I surveyed the feast spread across our table and smiled. Once again, I had the opportunity to slow down and be reminded of the peace and abundance Jesus provides. The day wasn't ruined. The errands could wait. I bowed my head and folded my hands. There was plenty to be thankful for. Thanksgiving in March? Why not! —HEIDI GAUL

FAITH STEP: *Collect and donate the items necessary for a holiday dinner to a food bank, even if that holiday is out of season. Give thanks for your abundance.*

FRIDAY, MARCH 28

The LORD is good to those who wait for him, to the person who seeks him. It is good to wait quietly for salvation from the LORD. Lamentations 3:25–26 (CSB)

WHILE I WAS ON MY way to work one day, it seemed like every person on the road decided to drive the minimum speed limit. That would be commendable, of course, if I wasn't running late. Whether I sped up, slowed down, or changed lanes, I only got a few feet before approaching another driver who seemed to be on the road for a casual cruise.

Every fiber in my being wanted to zoom ahead and zip past these slowpokes to avoid being late, but I had a gnawing feeling I shouldn't speed up and push my way through. Sometimes when that feeling arises, I'll see a patrol car a few moments later and feel relieved that I didn't disregard the speed limit. But that was not the feeling this time. There was something deeper.

Too often I zip through the day trying to finish my to-do list of household responsibilities, work tasks, or passion projects. I accept the false belief that some days there's not enough time to slow down and sit with Jesus before rushing off to work. I think that arriving at my destination quickly is more important than experiencing what's happening along the journey.

Instead of a patrol car with flashing lights trying to get my attention, Jesus was signaling me. I needed to slow down and enjoy the ride with Him.
—Ericka Loynes

FAITH STEP: *Be a slowpoke as you walk or drive down a familiar street. Take note of what you haven't noticed before, thanking Jesus as you enjoy the journey with Him.*

SATURDAY, MARCH 29

For we are taking pains to do what is right, not only in the eyes of the Lord but also in the eyes of man.
2 Corinthians 8:21 (NIV)

WHEN I WALKED INTO CVS, a petite older woman, wearing a threadbare blue dress and flip-flops, approached me. "Did you lose this?" she asked me, holding up a five-dollar bill.

I shook my head.

"Well, I need to find the owner and return it."

Cynically, I figured *anybody* could tell this woman they'd lost the five dollars and she'd be none the wiser. It looked to me as though *she* could have used that money herself, but Jesus must have prompted her in her quest.

While I was in the drugstore, I noticed her approaching customers, asking if they'd lost the bill.

To the credit of my fellow shoppers, no one claimed the money.

As I was leaving, the woman brushed past me, clutching the bill. "Checking the parking lot now," she murmured. When I left, she was still making her rounds, despite the cold drizzle. I'll never know if the woman found the person who'd lost the money, but the fact that she was so persistent about finding the rightful owner must have pleased Jesus. I hoped that after all her efforts, no one claimed the money and she would keep it. It looked to me as though she could have used a burger. But that was *my* wish. I think the woman's greatest desire was to please Jesus with her honesty.

Diogenes, the Greek philosopher who conducted a fruitless search for an honest man, could have found that (wo)man at the CVS on College Street in Beaumont. —PAT BUTLER DYSON

FAITH STEP: *Make a list of three recent times when you have witnessed someone being honest.*

SUNDAY, MARCH 30

What grieved them most was his statement that they would never see his face again. Then they accompanied him to the ship. Acts 20:38 (NIV)

I COUNTED ON SEEING MY FRIEND at an annual Christ-centered retreat we both attended. Many miles separated us the rest of the year. That January, I couldn't help but notice Lucinda struggled to be her exuberant self. She still poured herself into the tasks assigned to her. She still made sure everyone's needs were met. But something wasn't quite right. What she considered a disturbing but likely minor physical distress sometimes brought her to tears that weekend. But she soldiered on and promised to keep us informed in the weeks after the retreat ended.

In March, we heard the doctor's report. Nothing about her condition was minor. She was gone within 2 weeks of receiving her diagnosis. Her goal in those final weeks? To honor Jesus in dying as she had in living.

Jesus invites me to seek Him always. When life is good. When it's fading. When I'm minutes away from seeing Him face-to-face. With the loss of my friend, I find myself praying: "Lord Jesus, don't let me have to learn in heaven what I should have learned on earth." Like Lucinda, I want to stay exuberant, serve well, and meet the needs of others. I want to seek to honor Jesus in everything I do. I want a life that will encourage others to kneel with me, pray with me, and be willing to accompany me to the ship when that time comes. —CYNTHIA RUCHTI

FAITH STEP: *Look up the lyrics to or a video of "I Then Shall Live." Make it your prayer.*

MONDAY, MARCH 31

My flesh and my heart may fail, but God is the strength of my heart and my portion forever. Psalm 73:26 (NIV)

A NURSE WELCOMED MY HUSBAND to a private room on the leukemia floor that would be his home-away-from-home for the next month. We were still in shock from the diagnosis he'd received only hours before, trying to imagine what 7 days of round-the-clock chemo would do to his body that required a month-long stay.

"You must get out of bed and walk the halls," the nurse instructed. She told us how many laps equaled a mile and said being active builds strength. "Every day you lie in bed, you lose 3 percent of your muscle mass."

It's been several years since my husband's diagnosis, but I often recall the nurse's warning about how quickly muscle deteriorates from inactivity. I think the same is true for the heart muscle. My heart needs a daily workout. But I admit, now that I'm retired, sometimes my heart wants to be a bit lazy.

Donating money to a young missionary is easier than attending her fundraiser at church. Keeping a coffee date with a mother of little ones means I can't wear my all-day pj's. Agreeing to pull weeds for a widow makes me think of my own overgrown flower beds.

But I attended the fundraiser, reconnected with a friend I hadn't seen in years, and received a sincere hug from the missionary. Over coffee, I shared words of encouragement with a weary mama who needed a morning out. Watching my friend admire her flowers when she can no longer kneel to weed them herself fills me up.

Jesus's command was clear: love others. It's a daily activity that keeps my heart muscle strong. —KAREN SARGENT

FAITH STEP: *Exercise your heart today by doing a good deed for someone.*

TUESDAY, APRIL 1

*Open my eyes that I may see wonderful things in
your law. Psalm 119:18 (NIV)*

ONE OF MY MOST SIGNIFICANT steps of faith this
year was starting a daily Bible podcast with my friend
Michelle. I love reading Jesus's Word—it has truly
transformed my life. As we prepared to launch our
podcast, worries filled my mind: I didn't have a semi-
nary degree. I can't read Hebrew or Greek. Did I have
what it takes? Would I be able to join Michelle every
day to talk about Jesus's Word and what we learned as
we read? Thankfully, I didn't let those worries stop me.

We've recorded over one hundred podcasts
already, and I understand Jesus's Word more than
ever. I didn't need prior knowledge before opening the Bible. Instead, Jesus has given me wisdom.
Every single day I discover something I hadn't realized before. It's not because I'm brilliant. It's because
Jesus is faithful to meet me.

Drawing near to Jesus, I grow in wisdom as I
focus on the verses, ponder them, and ask Jesus
to open my mind to understand them. It's incredible how Jesus can speak and nourish my heart,
even with the little I know. I don't have to try
to figure it all out. Instead, I can turn to Him
and seek to understand one small truth. Because
of my willingness to step out, I now realize each

day of seeking Jesus is a significant step of faith.
—Tricia Goyer

FAITH STEP: *Find a friend to read through the Bible with you—someone with the same goal of drawing closer to Jesus through His Word. Set up a time to daily share thoughts and insights together.*

WEDNESDAY, APRIL 2

Whatever you have learned or received or heard from me, or seen in me—put it into practice. And the God of peace will be with you. Philippians 4:9 (NIV)

I LOVE A GOOD CORNED-BEEF sandwich. So whenever I'm in my hometown, I try to stop by my favorite spot to get the mile-high sandwich that the restaurant is famous for. The place is usually packed with folks, waiting patiently in line to place their orders.

During a visit home, I walked into the restaurant and noticed an open Bible and some Christian books on a table near the entrance. I thought such a display said a lot about the restaurant's owners. One thing I had always liked about the place (besides the food) is that the employees cheerfully greeted customers, whether they were construction workers or people dressed in business suits. They also called them by their names or "honey" and "dear," thanked them, and wished each person a blessed day. It was good to see the character of Christ displayed by the owners and their employees.

In his letter to the church at Philippi, the Apostle Paul encourages the people to imitate Jesus's life and follow His teachings. In other words, practice what Jesus preached and have the same mindset as Christ (Philippians 2:5). That's my prayer every day—to be a little bit more like Jesus in the way I treat others and to be a walking, talking billboard for Him. I strive to not only be a hearer of the Word but also a doer. Just like my friends at my favorite sandwich shop. —BARBRANDA LUMPKINS WALLS

FAITH STEP: *Identify one character trait of Jesus and put it into practice today. Show others you know Him by the way you act.*

THURSDAY, APRIL 3

Let the message of Christ dwell among you richly as you teach and admonish one another with all wisdom through psalms, hymns, and songs from the Spirit, singing to God with gratitude in your hearts. Colossians 3:16 (NIV)

I CAME HOME FROM A long day at work feeling worn out and short-tempered. My students had been unruly and disrespectful. The traffic on the way home had been slow and awful, and I still had an evening of chores ahead of me. I silently gave myself a pep talk to prepare me for the hard work of keeping my emotions in check as I greeted my family and started a load of laundry while we waited for supper to be ready.

I didn't notice the exact moment when my mind and body began to relax, but slowly I became aware that I felt calm rather than anxious. I paused to evaluate. Tension had left my shoulders. My head didn't ache. My heartbeat was steady. The realization was comforting but confusing. What had changed that had somehow given me peace?

That's when I noticed the music coming from upstairs. My daughter Adelle was at the piano, practicing hymns for her weekly lesson. The songs were new to her, and her false starts and missed notes resulted in choppy rhythms and interrupted melodies. But the essence of the hymns was clear. Without realizing it, my heart had begun to echo the familiar messages of grace and peace. I stopped and listened more closely, thanking Jesus for His gift of music and for its lasting effect on my soul. —EMILY E. RYAN

FAITH STEP: *Play instrumental hymns or praise music softly in the background of your home. Let your soul fill in the words as prayers to Jesus.*

FRIDAY, APRIL 4

Many plans are in a man's heart, but the counsel of the LORD will stand. Proverbs 19:21 (NASB1995)

SPONTANEITY IS NOT PART OF MY DNA, especially on weekends or vacation days. I like surprises after they happen—I don't handle the initial unknown or suspense well. I also struggle when my day doesn't go as planned after having envisioned all the tasks I would accomplish or all the leisurely activities I would enjoy. This (not-so) internal battle has been going on for years.

I remember my sixteenth birthday. Birthdays were a big deal in my household growing up. I woke up that morning with limitless ideas for celebrating, but all of them were rejected by my parents. I was livid. Well, hurt, really. That evening, they finally suggested picking up a pizza. When I stepped inside to pick up our order, I ran into several of my friends hanging out at the pizza place. Forcing a smile on my face, I spoke but was shocked they didn't invite me to join them, especially on my birthday. What slowly became apparent was that my parents had planned something special all along. I had just walked into my own surprise party.

When I respond to surprises as interruptions to my schedule or plans, I won't see them as invitations to rest, celebrate, or experience new things. Just as I trusted my parents, I need to trust that

Jesus has wonderful surprises in store for me too, better than anything I could ever plan for myself. —ERICKA LOYNES

FAITH STEP: *Abandon your original plans for one day this week. Pay close attention to how Jesus decides to surprise and delight you.*

SATURDAY, APRIL 5

The twelve gates were twelve pearls, each gate made of a single pearl. The great street of the city was of gold, as pure as transparent glass. Revelation 21:21 (NIV)

BOBBIE AND I ENJOYED A common interest—a love for travel. During eight decades of life, my friend pulled a camper across most of the fifty states and parts of Canada. I loved hearing about her adventures, and she loved hearing about mine. Wherever my tour director job took me, she followed along through my online posts, revisiting the towns tucked in her memories.

I spoke at her celebration of life yesterday. "Bobbie has now traveled somewhere I've never been, a place I've only read about. But I want to go there. It's on my list."

When a loved one dies, we seek comfort from Jesus, perhaps more than any other time in our earthly experience. And His Word doesn't fail us. The descriptions of heaven in Revelation 21 and 22 fill us with hope and peace and joy, even amid our sorrow. A destination with no tears, no death, no mourning, no pain. A city of light with walls of jasper, sapphires, emeralds, rubies, and amethysts. A river of life flowing from the thrones of God and Jesus, shaded on both banks by the tree of life.

I shared those beautiful truths and then ended with a testimony from Bobbie herself. "Each of the twelve gates in heaven is made of a single, giant pearl," I said. "Bobbie told us about them a few days ago. So very sick and confined to bed, she proclaimed in a loud voice, 'I see the pearly gates!'" —BECKY ALEXANDER

FAITH STEP: *Read Revelation 21 and 22. Lift a prayer of praise for Jesus, naming some wonderful details of heaven.*

SUNDAY, APRIL 6

Heaven and earth will pass away, but my words will never pass away. Matthew 24:35 (NIV)

WHILE I WAS SITTING AROUND talking to family members, the conversation turned to favorite clothing and shoes. My brother-in-law told a story about his wife's favorite pair of shoes, which she rarely wore. Linda decided to put them on for a special affair she was attending. As she walked through the house, she started to leave a trail of bits and pieces of the shoes' soles, a sure sign that age and heat had gotten the best of them. We all collapsed with laughter. I could relate. The same thing happened to me with some old boots. After years in the closet, they simply began to disintegrate with each step that I took after I finally put them on.

Thinking about our family chat later, I recalled that the Israelites wandered through the wilderness for 40 years without their clothes and sandals wearing out (Deuteronomy 29:5). Wow. Talk about durable and supernatural. Like the Israelites' attire, Jesus tells His disciples that His Word will stand the test of time and never pass away. He will return and they can count on it.

I can count on that too. Jesus and His promises are everlasting. They are the same yesterday, today, and forever (Hebrews 13:8). Nothing can or will destroy the Eternal One (Daniel 6:26). While my shoes won't last forever, I know that as I continually seek Jesus, I can confidently walk with Him and be assured that He will hold me together.
—BARBRANDA LUMPKINS WALLS

FAITH STEP: *What do you feel is falling apart in your life right now? Ask Jesus to give you strength as He helps you pick up the pieces and find your way.*

MONDAY, APRIL 7

Peace I leave with you; my peace I give you. I do not give to you as the world gives. Do not let your hearts be troubled and do not be afraid. John 14:27 (NIV)

AFTER SEVERAL JOB RELOCATIONS through the years, my husband and I have been impacted by some severe weather events in different states: tornadoes, blizzards, ice storms, flooding, earth tremors, and a major hurricane. Last weekend, we listened to warnings and reports about a system of destructive storms and tornadoes moving through our new area. It reminded me that no matter where we live, we will always face the possibility of some type of dangerous weather.

Matthew 14:22–33 tells how Jesus's disciples found themselves in a boat buffeted by fierce winds. Jesus had sent them ahead, knowing the storm they would face. He did not show up until the boat was far from land; they'd already battled the wind for hours. But when Jesus did appear shortly before dawn, He came displaying His power and sovereignty, walking on top of the waves. After He climbed into the boat, the wind finally died down.

Thankfully, severe weather events are normally few and far between, but there is the possibility for inner storms on any given day. The way I respond to unexpected or frightening life events can create inner turmoil that may lead to destructive consequences. Dwelling on current world events may cause constant anxiety and fear. But I can trust Jesus to help me battle negative emotions. Once He displays His power and sovereignty, any turbulence will die down. —DIANNE NEAL MATTHEWS

FAITH STEP: *Memorize John 14:27 to help you prepare for any type of storm. Ask Jesus to help you choose His peace over fear and a troubled heart.*

TUESDAY, APRIL 8

Every good and perfect gift is from above, coming down from the Father of the heavenly lights, who does not change like shifting shadows. James 1:17 (NIV)

MY TEENAGE SON, MASON, WAS in a play this past weekend. Right before the curtain went up on opening night, I needed to use the restroom. On my way back into the theater, I snuck in through a side door knowing it was closer to my seat. Lo and behold, I stumbled upon Mason, who was waiting in the wings for his entrance. It felt like such a gift to get to see him right before he went on stage, give him a quick hug, and tell him to "break a leg." I went back to my seat feeling so fortunate for that precious moment. I made sure I did the same thing for each performance of the weekend.

I've had similar experiences with Jesus. Right in the middle of a busy day I've rounded a corner and stumbled right into Him. It might be that glimpse of a fox trotting through my backyard, a text that drops into my phone from the exact person I was just thinking about, or a song that plays on the radio that perfectly matches my situation. They may not be evident to an outsider, but those moments are gifts that strike a chord deep in my heart, making them holy. After that pause of recognizing Him, I usually go on with my day. Yet I do so feeling so fortunate for the gift of a precious moment I shared with Him. —CLAIRE McGARRY

FAITH STEP: *The next time something strikes a chord in your heart, stop and see if you can recognize a gift from Jesus in that precious moment.*

WEDNESDAY, APRIL 9

Are you tired? Worn out? Burned out...? Come to me. ... I won't lay anything heavy or ill-fitting on you. Keep company with me and you'll learn to live freely and lightly. Matthew 11:28–30 (MSG)

I'D NEVER BEEN MUCH INTO weightlifting. But now I have a whole new appreciation for it.

When trying to cope with all the things that needed to be done after my father died, I didn't realize how much extra emotional weight I was carrying. It just piled on, virtually overnight. I didn't sleep for the entire first 2 weeks after Dad died. Yet, in spite of the heaviness weighing me down, every day required doing unfamiliar tasks while negotiating a minefield of emotions, delicate dealings with family members, hard conversations, difficult decisions, and multiple meetings with the funeral director.

Which is why I'll never forget the day Mom and I met with the pastor who would be officiating Dad's funeral service. Bearing up under a heavy yoke of responsibilities that needed to be planned and arranged, we went into the meeting laden with questions and concerns. But, one by one, Pastor Brandon handled each of our worries and inquiries, bringing order to the overwhelming array of details that needed to be addressed. He gently assured us that he would take care of everything.

Sometimes Jesus uses others to lighten the load. Through Pastor Brandon, Jesus lifted all that weight I'd been carrying off of my shoulders. Exhaling with a huge sigh of relief, I marveled at how much lighter I felt after that weightlifting session.
—CASSANDRA TIERSMA

FAITH STEP: *Are you carrying a heavy burden? Get a hand weight or heavy object and label it with your concern. Carry it with you until you are ready to surrender it to Jesus. Ask Him to lift the weight from your spirit as well.*

THURSDAY, APRIL 10

*This also cometh forth from the LORD of hosts,
which is wonderful in counsel, and excellent in working.
Isaiah 28:29 (KJV)*

I LET THE PHONE CALL go to voicemail. I didn't answer an email from the same person moments later, although I did skim to make sure it was an "emergency" only in the mind of the sender, not truly urgent. She needed guidance. Happy to offer it, I couldn't at that moment. Other priorities consumed me.

I shot up a quick prayer, then attended to the needs in front of me.

Guilt? Sure. It was easy to let the guilt of putting off my friend, even temporarily, slide its smelly foot into where my focus had to be. But I recognized the odor of guilt and refused to let it linger. Trusting Jesus to see to the concerns of my friend, I applied myself to the task at hand.

It was hours before I could get back to the voicemail. When I did, an important life lesson waited for me.

My friend who had often leaned on me for counsel said, "It's OK. When I couldn't get you, I just took it to Jesus. I should have done that in the first place."

The needs that kept me from responding gave my friend a far more perfect answer than I could have offered because she was pressed to go to the ultimate Counselor—Jesus.

How often have I phoned a friend, cried on someone's shoulder, or run to the internet when a smarter first move would have been to seek Jesus on the subject? Thankfully, He always takes my call. —CYNTHIA RUCHTI

FAITH STEP: *The next time you're tempted to text or phone a friend for advice, call on Jesus instead.*

FRIDAY, APRIL 11

But the fruit of the Spirit is love, joy, peace, forbearance, kindness, goodness, faithfulness, gentleness and self-control. Against such things there is no law. Galatians 5:22–23 (NIV)

FLIPPING THROUGH MY RECIPE BOX, I recognized Mom's handwriting and pulled out the yellow, tattered index card for her perfect cheesecake. Instead of imagining her decadent dessert, I recalled a time when Mom's cheesecake wasn't so perfect.

Our family was gathered around the table. Dessert had been served, but an awkward silence lingered. Mom was the last to help herself to a piece and take a bite. All eyes were on her. Finally, realization dawned on her face. "I forgot to add the sugar." Sighs of relief followed because no one wanted to insult the chef.

Mom's cheesecake has a gazillion ingredients, but omitting just one turned her dessert into a disaster. She could have forgotten the eggs or the cream cheese or the milk, and the result would have been unsavory. All of the ingredients were necessary to produce her perfect cheesecake.

Like Mom, the Bible has a pretty good recipe with a list of vital ingredients. If I want to be more like Jesus, I need love, joy, peace, patience, kindness, goodness, faith, gentleness, and self-control. I don't get to pick and choose ingredients. Love, joy, and peace come naturally to me. But patience—more specifically my attitude while I'm trying to be patient—is a work in progress. And self-control? Not around the clearance rack at my favorite department store. Or cheesecake. Omitting one fruit of the Spirit bruises all the others.

Unlike Mom's cheesecake, I will never be perfect on earth. But I can try to be more like Jesus by perfecting my own fruit of the Spirit salad.
—KAREN SARGENT

FAITH STEP: *Read Galatians 5:22—23 and list the fruits that challenge you. Choose one to perfect today.*

SATURDAY, APRIL 12

God is not unjust; he will not forget your work and the love you have shown him as you have helped his people and continue to help them. Hebrews 6:10 (NIV)

I PLOPPED DOWN IN THE CORNER of our dining room, our "camping corner." My husband, Ron, and I wanted to replicate the feeling we had when we spent time in nature, so I created an indoor space to mimic camping by arranging plants and chairs by our picture window. I hoped the area would be relaxing and worshipful. Most often, it's simply where I land exhausted after the school day.

My job as an elementary school counselor is rewarding but challenging. A first grader cries because his mom is going to jail. A fourth grader is anxious about her dad's cancer. Helping kids with their problems is often draining. I often don't connect with Jesus as I intend throughout the week. Today, like most days, worship is the last thing on my mind.

Sitting in the camping corner, I received a Facebook message. A former student thanked me for being a kind presence when she was young. I was surprised because I didn't recall a significant inter-action with this student. She was one of many I'd encountered over the years. A conversation here, a word of encouragement there.

Suddenly, my exhaustion evaporated and the camping corner felt worshipful. I was refreshed as I felt Jesus's favor for how I cared for His children. Funny, I went to the camping corner looking to worship Jesus, but Jesus showed me true worship happens when I tend to those He places in my care.
—BRENDA L. YODER

FAITH STEP: *List acts of kindness you do for others in your home, community, or workplace. Offer them to Jesus as an act of worship.*

PALM SUNDAY, APRIL 13

Suppose one of you has a hundred sheep and loses one of them. Doesn't he leave the ninety-nine in the open country and go after the lost sheep until he finds it?
Luke 15:4 (NIV)

PALM SUNDAY DAWNED OVER JERUSALEM and ush-ered in the week leading to the cross.

The scene began with Jesus's humble entrance into Jerusalem, as King on a donkey while people laid out a processional of palm fronds. The masses cheered, but Jesus knew what was to come.

Some in that crowd would soon shout for His death.

The religious leaders would act on their jealousy, ruthlessly and lawlessly.

His own followers would desert Him.

And He knew all of this ahead of time.

As Jesus rode through the city, He saw people who would sin terribly against Him. And He kept going. For them.

Recently I was awake late, unable to sleep as an old struggle replayed in my mind. Jesus and I had dealt with this issue, but there it was again, toying with the freedom I'd fought hard to accept from Him. I was weary of this cycle and wished for the escape of slumber.

Thankfully, Jesus, the One who never sleeps (Psalm 121:3–4), reminded me what His salvation meant for me. It was today, Palm Sunday, when He continued into Jerusalem, all the while knowing what the week would bring.

When I'm tempted to doubt how much He loves me, I remember how Jesus put aside His human emotions, stayed the course, did the will of His Father, and kept going. Not only for them but also for you and me. —ERIN KEELEY MARSHALL

FAITH STEP: *Draw a palm branch on a sheet of paper. Write areas you struggle with or cycles of sin on the leaves. As you gaze at the drawing each day during Holy Week, ponder the perseverance of Jesus and know He made this journey for you.*

MONDAY, APRIL 14

I am sending you out like sheep among wolves. Therefore be as shrewd as snakes and as innocent as doves. Be on your guard . . . Matthew 10:16–17 (NIV)

OUR FAMILY WATCHED, SHAKING OUR heads, as all three dogs maneuvered for each other's food bowls. Why all the jockeying? Every bowl had the same kibble mix. The dogs' selfish positioning at mealtime is comical, ridiculous, and humbly humanlike. Even usually docile members of the animal kingdom struggle for power as they feel threatened by what someone else has.

The Monday after Palm Sunday, Jesus dealt with the deceitful power plays of the Jewish leaders. They could have had the salvation Jesus offered. Instead, they manipulated at every turn, struggling for power to secure their uncertain standing.

Their first recorded questions to Him in Matthew 21:23 (NIV) reek of cowardly bullying: "By what authority are you doing these things? And who gave you this authority?" Can you picture them, puffed up by their self-righteous bellowing?

Yet Jesus did not submit to the leaders. Instead, He used parables to expose the hatred of the religious leaders in contrast to those who humbled themselves before God. His teachings to the disciples modeled how to be shrewd as snakes and innocent as doves. Jesus gave them, and us, the tools to deal wisely with arrogant power players.

Not everyone lives rightly or even fairly, but Jesus showed how to blend gentleness with courageous strength. When I'm tempted to selfishly maneuver, like our dogs, for what I see as mine, I remember Jesus's teaching: healthy innocence is also strong and shrewd. —ERIN KEELEY MARSHALL

FAITH STEP: *Is there an area in your life needing more innocence or more shrewdness? Ask Jesus to build in you a pure heart that models His behavior in blending gentleness with courageous strength.*

TUESDAY, APRIL 15

Do not be anxious beforehand what you are to say, but say whatever is given you in that hour, for it is not you who speak, but the Holy Spirit. . . . And what I say to you I say to all: Stay awake. Mark 13:11, 37 (ESV)

I FIND SMALL TALK STRESSFUL. I love having deep conversations, and when I feel out of my lane, words often fail. Although some public speaking coaching has helped in these situations, I want nothing more than to walk away from interactions outside my comfort zone.

These verses in Mark 13 offer empowerment for knowing what to say. Jesus assures His disciples that the Holy Spirit will provide the right words when they're confronted for their faith. I believe a similar heart applies for all situations when we need wise words.

Scriptures detailing the events on the Tuesday before Easter are loaded with Jesus revealing the truth of people's hearts, from the Pharisees, whose darkened hearts opposed His spiritual authority by trying to trap Him with words, to Judas setting in motion his betrayal of Jesus. Yet Jesus responded with two wise words that are effective even when offered in silence: "Stay awake" (Mark 13:37, ESV).

Stay awake. A directive that carries no emotion yet is full of deep meaning.

This command empowers us to see through deception. It's practical and unapologetic about its boundaries. It's responsible and employs common sense. It's respectful and assumes we're capable of obeying it.

It tells us that Jesus will provide, even in the most difficult and stressful situations.

So today, I stay awake so I can discern the Holy Spirit's words, even when my own won't come. As I recognize His voice, I trust Him to cover the rest of the conversation. —ERIN KEELEY MARSHALL

FAITH STEP: *What do you need today to stay awake? What situation needs wise words of response or initiation? Meditate on Mark 13:11, 37 and listen for the Holy Spirit.*

WEDNESDAY, APRIL 16

Yes, my soul, find rest in God; my hope comes from him. Psalm 62:5 (NIV)

I SLIPPED ON MY RUNNING shoes, grabbed my phone, and headed outside for a walk. Soon I was deep in conversation with a friend.

When COVID-19 was in full swing, those long talk-walks became lifelines of sanity, breathing spaces to clear my head and find joy in the uncertainty. Those ventures created the quiet space I needed.

Wednesday of Easter week is quiet in Scripture. Some scholars suggest Jesus spent the day in Bethany at the home of his friends Lazarus, Mary, and Martha. I imagine He probably felt safe surrounded by people who loved Him and who let Him rest as He gathered strength for what was to come. This day makes me consider how Jesus prepares us before launching us into what's next. How He recognizes the importance of rest and peace in the midst of turmoil.

As a writer, I've been taught to vary action scenes with breather scenes to offer readers calming equilibrium. I read Wednesday as a breather scene, a steadying silence.

Some weeks during COVID-19 were like that for me. Days of near isolation lent themselves to a calming of thoughts and time to connect with family at home and with friends by phone. Those deep conversation walks that spanned 2 hours and several miles likely would not have happened in more normal circumstances.

Many people experienced a new normal when the world opened up post-pandemic. Thanks to Jesus's lesson, my new normal includes what only He can provide: breathing space to calm, restore, and prepare us, including long walks. —ERIN KEELEY MARSHALL

FAITH STEP: *Work a breather scene into your week. As you become more accustomed to one a week, start building in one a day, even if only for a few minutes.*

MAUNDY THURSDAY, APRIL 17

A new command I give you: Love one another. As I have loved you, so you must love one another. John 13:34 (NIV)

Maundy Thursday. The day when Jesus experienced the sting of betrayal and the tender ache of painful goodbyes at the Last Supper. Jesus's heartache is evident in John 13:21, 27 (NIV): "Jesus was troubled in spirit and testified, 'Very truly I tell you, one of you is going to betray me.' As soon as Judas took the bread, Satan entered into him. So Jesus told him, 'What you are about to do, do quickly.'"

Jesus's anguish is clear. *Just get it done. Don't delay the pain.*

And in spite of those feelings, Jesus did something remarkable. He poured water into a basin, took a towel, and began washing the disciples' feet. After kneeling before each of His disciples, including Judas, who would betray Him, and taking on the role of a humble servant, Jesus gave His final instructions before He would go to the cross: "Love one another."

I, too, have experienced the heartache of betrayal by someone I thought was a loyal friend. I grieved what I had believed about that friendship and the loss of connection. Healing took time, and I struggled to focus on love as Jesus did with His disciples on Maundy Thursday.

Jesus wasn't forced to love us any more than He was forced to love the disciples. Yet He chose to love us with His life, and He commands us to love others as He has loved us.

Today, as I remember Jesus's suffering, I also remember that I have a duty to love as He loves me.

And as I recall my own suffering from betrayal and heartache, I'm better able to forgive and love others as He taught me. —ERIN KEELEY MARSHALL

FAITH STEP: *Ask Jesus to bring to mind someone you need to forgive and love. Write a card, send a text, or extend an act of mercy to that person today in an effort to love like Jesus.*

GOOD FRIDAY, APRIL 18

Simon, Simon, Satan has asked to sift all of you as wheat. But I have prayed for you, Simon, that your faith may not fail. And when you have turned back, strengthen your brothers. Luke 22:31–32 (NIV)

A WHILE BACK, I KEPT HEARING about God "sifting" His people. It was a message in church, on Christian radio, and in blogs I read.

When Jesus spoke of sifting, He was referring to separating the valuable portion of us from the worthless portion, shaking out what doesn't serve His purposes. Sifting can come from crisis. It can be the result of our actions or the actions of others. God allows sifting, with revealing effects.

I've felt that sifting in my life and family, in our community, and in the world. My faith has been tested, stretched, and refined. Jesus has been close and patient with my questions. But sifting need not result in discord or discarding faith.

Luke 22:31–32 contains a game-changing discovery when Jesus prayed over the sifting of His followers, that their faith would remain intact. As Good Friday dawned, they would need their Savior's prayers.

Being sifted within the guard of Jesus's prayers can cleanse, grow, and strengthen us. The fact that He spoke of it to Peter before heading to the cross leaves me speechless for how Jesus loves. As He faced death, He prayed for His followers.

God allows us to be sifted to prepare us for His purposes. His sifting strengthens us when we are weak, discouraged, or feeling hopeless, leaving behind His grace and love. Jesus's prayers yielded victory that day so long ago, and they do the same for us today as He calls us to consider His eternal plan on this Good Friday. —Erin Keeley Marshall

FAITH STEP: *Journal about your own sifting season and how it grew your faith. Thank Jesus for His prayers.*

SATURDAY, APRIL 19

And these are but the outer fringe of his works; how faint the whisper we hear of him! Who then can understand the thunder of his power? Job 26:14 (NIV)

ON THE SATURDAY AFTER CRUCIFIXION, heaven's whisper may have been lost on those who'd followed Jesus. After darkness fell, the earth rumbled, and the curtain closed on the previous day, I imagine the landscape echoed the deafening silence of hope lost.

Considering the atrocities done against Jesus, it's hard to fathom His followers' trauma and heartache that Saturday. Although no trauma and heartache in my life compare to what Jesus's followers must have experienced, I, too, have lost hope at times.

Many generations earlier, Job wrote of how we can miss the ways God whispers (26:7–10, NIV): "He spreads out the northern skies over empty space; he suspends the earth over nothing. He wraps up the waters in his clouds, yet the clouds do not burst under their weight. He covers the face of the full moon, spreading his clouds over it. He marks out the horizon on the face of the waters for a boundary between light and darkness."

God's actions have always whispered hope to creation. While Jesus was in the grave, hope's life-changing promise whispered across the landscape that all was not lost.

When my heart hurts from loss or an unmet longing or the sorrows of someone I love, the waiting time between the crucifixion and resurrection reminds me all still is not lost. I'm learning to trust more deeply that Jesus is quietly doing more than I can see. I can imagine Him saying, "I am working. Learn to hope with Me in the quiet." —ERIN KEELEY MARSHALL

FAITH STEP: *Read Job 26 and hear beyond the whispers from heaven. Let them boost your hope.*

EASTER SUNDAY, APRIL 20

God is in the midst of her, she shall not be moved;
God shall help her, just at the break of dawn.
Psalm 46:5 (NKJV)

FOR THE PAST WEEK, I'VE dealt with physical aches and stiffness. My body is good at letting me know when it's suffering—that's my positive spin on a chronic but manageable condition I have. This week my body has felt out of balance.

Psalm 46:5 feels like an empowering yet calming balm. It reminds me that God is in my midst, in my very core—watching over and readjusting me, and not just physically. His Spirit flows within me too.

This verse also brings to mind the women who walked with Jesus through His darkest days. They had awakened on Good Friday to horrors descending on Jesus. Yet even then, God was in the midst of each woman. And while they were shaken, they remained unmoved in their faith in Him. On

Resurrection Day, they were the first to see the resurrected Christ, "just at the break of dawn," as the Psalmist declared centuries earlier.

Jesus was with those women, and He replaced their pain with joy. They were tasked with telling the apostles that the Jesus who died was in their midst, interceding for them and offering hope.

Today my pain is lightened knowing that Jesus is in my midst. Before the break of dawn, He is already with me. I never wake to a circumstance that is unknown to Him. And I can have faith He will replace my distress with joy and hope.
—ERIN KEELEY MARSHALL

FAITH STEP: *What is making you ache today? Ask Jesus to replace your pain with joy, happiness, and hope.*

MONDAY, APRIL 21

The King will reply, "Truly I tell you, whatever you did for one of the least of these brothers and sisters of mine, you did for me." Matthew 25:40 (NIV)

OUR CHURCH HOSTS A VOLUNTEER appreciation event each year. I attend because I'm part of the worship team, but I am always astounded at the volume of people who serve in the parking lot, those who help keep the grounds nicely landscaped and the flower beds weeded, those caring for kids in children's church, those who provide transportation for people who can't drive, and those who aid the church staff in innumerable and often unseen ways.

I greeted a young woman at our latest appreciation event, someone I didn't know well. She expressed my heart when she said, "I had no idea how many would be here. And it makes me wonder why I was invited. I do so little. I kept the infused water dispensers filled during the women's gathering. Is that why I'm here?"

That same week, I came across the verse in Matthew where Jesus reassured His followers regarding their service for Him. That verse is preceded by the ones where the disciples ask, "Lord, when did we see you hungry and feed you, or thirsty and give you something to drink? When did we see you sick or in prison and go to visit you?" (Matthew 25:37, 39, NIV).

My heart swelled with new appreciation for the kinds of serving and volunteering that move Jesus. He applauded that they hadn't even been aware that their small acts of kindness or meeting the needs of others had been credited to them as if they'd personally handed Him a glass of infused water. Thanks for the reminder, Jesus. —CYNTHIA RUCHTI

FAITH STEP: *As you serve others today, allow yourself a silent, "This is for You, Jesus."*

TUESDAY, APRIL 22

*Jesus said to her, "I am the resurrection and the life.
He who believes in Me, though he may die, he shall live."*
John 11:25 (NKJV)

I CONNECTED WITH A FORMER high school class-mate on social media shortly before he retired as a riverboat captain. Sadly, Lanny passed away a couple of years later. I will never forget a memory he shared online from one of his trips down the Mississippi River. Lanny had reached his destination after dark. The next morning, on Easter Sunday, he woke up to discover the boat docked next to his was named *The Resurrection.*

I normally think about the term *resurrection* either in the past tense, as in Jesus rose from the dead on the third day after His Crucifixion (Luke 24:46), or in the future tense, the promise that believers in Christ will receive new, eternal life after physical death (John 10: 27–28). But before Jesus called Lazarus from the tomb, He spoke of it in the present tense: "I am the resurrection and the life."

The same power that raised Jesus from the dead is available through Him (Galatians 2:20). When I choose to follow Jesus, I am identified with His death, burial, and resurrection. My old self has been crucified; I've been raised to walk in a new way of life—resisting sinful temptations, following

God's will instead of my personal desires, becoming more like Jesus. I can only live this new life through His power. The first step is to open my eyes and recognize His resurrection power is alive inside my heart and He is beside me every day. —DIANNE NEAL MATTHEWS

FAITH STEP: *Think about an area of your life where you sometimes feel weak or inadequate. Ask Jesus to open your eyes to see how His resurrection power can help you walk in a new way of life.*

WEDNESDAY, APRIL 23

For he will command his angels concerning you to guard you in all your ways; they will lift you up in their hands, so that you will not strike your foot against a stone.
Psalm 91:11–12 (NIV)

MY FOUR CHILDREN ARE YOUNG adults and no longer live at home. I pray for them every day, asking that angels will keep them safe, but I rarely have confirmation that my prayer is being answered.

Early one morning, my son Ian's name popped up on my phone screen. When I answered, he spoke evenly.

"Mom, I'm fine, but I've been in an accident," he said. "I think my right hand might be broken."

He had been riding his bike to work and a car had hit him. I drove to the hospital, expecting he'd be dressed and ready to leave, but instead he was in an emergency room cubicle hooked up to an IV and a series of other machines. He'd underplayed the seriousness of the accident, not wanting me to panic.

Over the next hours, X-rays, ultrasounds, bloodwork, and other tests showed that he had been miraculously protected. After he was treated and released, I drove him home with a broken hand, a fractured foot, minor lacerations, and a few stitches. In my car, Ian told me about the accident and how passersby stayed with him as he lay under the car and waited for the ambulance.

"One woman just sat down on the street, right beside me. She didn't say much, but I felt like I was being wrapped in peace."

A knowing washed over me. Thank You, Jesus, for protecting Ian and sending an angel to watch over him. My prayer had been answered. —JENNIFER GRANT

FAITH STEP: *Ask Jesus to send an angel to protect someone who is vulnerable as they go about their day.*

THURSDAY, APRIL 24

I know every bird in the mountains, and the insects in the fields are mine. Psalm 50:11 (NIV)

I HAVE ALWAYS LOVED BIRDS. I sat on my porch and admired their colors—red, blue, yellow. During recent years, I became an actual bird enthusiast. I discovered the red bird was a cardinal, the blue one was a blue jay, and the yellow one was an American goldfinch. I bought a *Birds of Alabama* book and a pair of binoculars.

In April, I glanced up from the papers covering my desk and saw a multicolored beauty perched on a feeder. I reached slowly for the binoculars, hoping the movements wouldn't startle him. I turned the focus wheel…jet-black head, neck, and eyes…snow-white belly and rump…black-and-white-mingled back…and a stunning chest of rosy red. The rose-breasted grosbeak graced my yard for about a week before continuing his northern migration.

I don't know all the birds yet, but Jesus does. He gave each one a distinct design. He chose its size, tail length, bill shape, and wingspan, variations I've learned to notice for identification. Then Jesus splashed the bird with His creative color. He selected one, two, three, or many hues for decoration and a pattern to display them. Jesus also placed instincts within the bird to find food, locate or build shelter, care for its young, and in some cases, migrate from continent to continent like the rose-breasted grosbeak.

When I observe the creatures that fly, my soul flies too—higher and higher toward the heavens—in delight of the birds' Creator and mine. —BECKY ALEXANDER

FAITH STEP: *Find a picture of a rose-breasted grosbeak. Consider its intricate features and striking color combination. Praise Jesus for His work of art.*

FRIDAY, APRIL 25

. . . let us throw off everything that hinders and the sin that so easily entangles. And let us run with perseverance the race marked out for us. Hebrews 12:1 (NIV)

I'M WRITING THIS ON THE brink of spring when I start to get a mysterious, often totally random impulse to clean and organize. This time, it was my top two desk drawers. Both had compartmentalized trays that were once organized but had become chaotic: a jumble of paper clips, lipstick, rubber bands, odd keys, and way too many old business cards, among other things. I went to work.

It had evidently been a long time since I'd purged these drawers because I was able to toss so much, including 90 percent of the business cards. Some names looked familiar, some had cryptic handwritten notes, still others meant nothing to me, though they must have at the time. I know myself, and if I took and kept the card, there was a reason, but that reason had evidently come and gone.

In my Christian journey, I have sometimes held on to people, patterns, and practices long after Jesus had made it clear they were no longer useful for me. It has sometimes caused actual harm to me and others, created unhelpful spiritual clutter, or hindered my progress. Today, I know to tune in to that spring-cleaning feeling and ask Jesus if there is an area of my life I need to clean up. I pray for open hands and a willingness to purge whatever He commands. —ISABELLA CAMPOLATTARO

FAITH STEP: *Ask Jesus if there's something or someone He wants you to let go, then sit quietly with pen in hand to jot down what comes to your heart. Ask Him for the grace to let whatever—or whoever—go.*

SATURDAY, APRIL 26

When I am in distress, I call to you, because you answer me. Psalm 86:7 (NIV)

AS AN EXPERIENCED CYCLIST, I knew better than to bike after a rain, but I was determined to get my daily ride done before dark. The pavement was mostly dry and I could do my 7 miles in 30 minutes and still get home in time to fix supper. So off I raced.

I was two blocks from coasting into my driveway when my bike hit a mud slick, lost traction, and off I flew, landing with a splat on the pavement. Mortified, I scrambled to get up before anyone saw

me, but a searing pain in my left shoulder immo-
bilized me. What had I done to myself? *Oh, Jesus,
help me!*

Much to my dismay, a crowd gathered. There I
sprawled, dazed, in the middle of a circle of legs.
Someone asked if I was dead. Another said, "Ooh,
the blood!" Not helpful. A neighbor who knew
where I lived ran to get my husband, Jeff. I'd never
felt so alone and helpless. *Jesus?*

A man wearing a name tag that said Jim emerged
from the crowd and squatted down in front of me.
He asked me my name, and when I told him, he
said, "Pat, you are going to be fine. Your husband
is coming. You will get patched up and everything
will be OK. You'll be all right, Pat. I guarantee it."
In my loneliness and fragility, the words of that kind
man got through to me. Jesus's answer to my distress came in the form of a compassionate stranger
named Jim. —PAT BUTLER DYSON

FAITH STEP: *List two times you have called out to Jesus when
you were in distress. Write down how He responded.*

SUNDAY, APRIL 27

*So, if you think you are standing firm, be careful that
you don't fall! 1 Corinthians 10:12 (NIV)*

DEAR LORD, NOT SIRENS! My least favorite thing is drawing attention to myself, but someone had called 911 after I'd experienced a devastating fall off my bike. My husband, Jeff, ran over and crouched beside me, concern on his dear face. "We need to get you to the hospital," Jeff said. "Do you want to go in the ambulance or my truck?"

"Your truck!" I cried. Several people helped hoist me into Jeff's truck, and we drove to the hospital. Jeff found me a wheelchair, and I joined the ranks of suffering humanity in the emergency room. I yanked at my skimpy bike shorts, cringed at my torn, bloody shirt, tried to fluff up my helmet hair. The embarrassment of looking this awful in public coupled with the pain of my injuries was excruciating.

Finally, a nurse came to retrieve me and take me to imaging. There wasn't a part of my body that wasn't X-rayed. I pride myself on being tough, but I couldn't suppress a few moans. "Looks like you broke your collarbone, scapula, some ribs, and punctured a lung," the ER doctor pronounced. "We need to admit you."

I protested but no one listened. The last place I wanted to be was in this hospital. I wanted to crawl in a hole and never come out. Alone in the room, I knew I needed to talk to my Comforter. *Jesus, I did this to myself. My pride. My notion that I am indestructible. But I'm alive! Thank You for being there to catch me when I fall.* —PAT BUTLER DYSON

FAITH STEP: *Recall a time when you fell, literally or figuratively. How did Jesus help you?*

MONDAY, APRIL 28

He who was seated on the throne said, "I am making everything new!" Then he said, "Write this down, for these words are trustworthy and true." Revelation 21:5 (NIV)

EVERY YEAR I MAKE IT a point to try something new. This year I started doing CrossFit because I was recently diagnosed with osteoporosis and needed to do more weight-bearing exercise. CrossFit is a strength and conditioning workout at a high-intensity level with a group of others who cheer you on. It's also designed around movements used in day-to-day life, like pulling, pushing, lifting, and walking up and down stairs. After a few months, I felt significantly stronger and had a new group of friends.

I've found learning something new adds zest to life. New experiences invigorate me because I'm introduced to new people, my confidence is increased, and it's fun. I think God places this craving for newness into our DNA. When we decided to follow Jesus, we became a new creation. "If anyone is in Christ, he is a new creation. The old has passed away; behold, the new has come" (2 Corinthians 5:17, ESV). And as believers, we look forward to Jesus making "all things new."

I can get into a spiritual rut too. Seeking new ways of connecting with Jesus motivates me to delve deeper. When in a spiritual doldrum, I'll join a new Bible study, memorize scripture verses I haven't before, ask a trusted friend to be a prayer partner, or listen to new worship songs. Just as CrossFit has made me physically stronger, seeking new ways to connect with Jesus has resulted in giving my soul and spirit new strength. —JEANNIE BLACKMER

FAITH STEP: *What's one thing you can do to refresh your spiritual life with Jesus? Start it today.*

TUESDAY, APRIL 29

Charm is deceptive, and beauty is fleeting;
but a woman who fears the LORD is to be praised.
Proverbs 31:30 (NIV)

LAST WEEKEND I MET TWO close friends for dinner. In the months since we'd seen each other, I'd gained weight and added forty-seven wrinkles. In my heart, I wanted to focus on my friends instead of my pants size and how I now looked like my mom. But I'd fallen for the lie that skinny, wrinkle-free women are more valuable than, well, ones who look like me.

The tables in the restaurant were closely spaced. Inches away from me sat a girl of perhaps three or four. Her face was heart-shaped, her eyes bright. I sat down, smiled, and said, "Am I too close?"

Mother and daughter spoke at the same time. The mom reassured me I wasn't in their space. But not hearing what the girl said, I looked at the mother and shrugged.

"She said, 'You're beautiful.'"

My eyes felt suddenly prickly and wet. A sense of Jesus's affection washed over me. I said to the child, "Thank you. You're beautiful too." And I turned back to my dinner, thanking Jesus for His custom-made message, spoken through the lips of a small stranger.

Suddenly, I sat up straighter. I talked to my friends with renewed confidence. And I marveled that Jesus saw me in a more accurate light than I'd seen myself. Not from the outside. But from the heart, where I long to please and honor Him.

Finally, I could believe how Jesus sees me. I am beautiful. —JEANETTE LEVELLIE

FAITH STEP: *Write down everything you don't like about your appearance. Close your eyes and ask Jesus what He thinks of you. Now take a Sharpie and write across the list, "I'm beautiful!"*

WEDNESDAY, APRIL 30

Take delight in the LORD, and he will give you the desires of your heart. Psalm 37:4 (NIV)

SOME TRAITS WE INHERIT, like blond hair or brown eyes. Even daydreaming! I'm a dreamer, something I inherited from my father. We'd fantasize about woolly monsters and sailboats and faraway places during my growing-up years. My practical mother stood by shaking her head and smiling, proof that Mary-Martha households can work—or play, if Dad and I had our way. Daddy taught me to set goals, and Mom showed me how to reach them.

One of my lifelong desires has been to go up in a hot-air balloon. I'm hoping to experience that adventure this summer. I wonder, might hovering so high be like floating in the clouds, a sweet taste of heaven? If I stood on my tiptoes, could I touch just the edge of it? I plan to find out.

Just like my parents, Jesus guides me, helping me hatch and achieve my goals. Like my father, the dreamer, and my mother, the doer, Jesus makes things happen. From a happy marriage to world-wide travel to working as a writer, Jesus is a part of every blessing in my life. I want to know Jesus better and trust Him more deeply as He makes the dreams in my heart align with His plan for me.

There is one desire richer and grander than any other I possess. I long to see Jesus face-to-face. And as much as I love to daydream, Jesus promises that's a goal I'll achieve. —HEIDI GAUL

FAITH STEP: *Make a list of your dreams and unfulfilled desires. Pray that Jesus makes them come true.*

Thursday, May 1

Truly I tell you, anyone who will not receive the kingdom of God like a little child will never enter it. Luke 18:17 (NIV)

I WENT TO THE PUBLIC LIBRARY today earlier than usual. Story time was just letting out. Now that my kids are teenagers, I forgot what it was like to be in the company of preschoolers. Outside, one little boy was walking backward like it was the greatest adventure of all time. Inside, two siblings were quarreling over who got to sit on the step stool used to reach books on the upper shelves. Yet the minute their mom pressed the handicap button to open the front doors, they forgot all about their argument. Wide-eyed with wonder, they watched the doors magically open just for them. Following them out, I heard the brother exclaim, "Let's do the stairs!" as if taking the stairs, rather than the ramped walkway, was the biggest thrill of his life.

Driving away I wondered: *When was the last time I was overwhelmed by some small wonder in God's world? When was the last time I bothered to look through the eyes of a child and see the way Jesus wants to amaze me on a minute-by-minute basis?* There's a reason Jesus said to receive the Kingdom of God like a child. Children have an innocent faith and trust. They embrace the world as a magical place created by a loving God.

Back home, I opened my eyes with childlike vision and let Jesus mesmerize me by the amazing wonder of the earth. And I may have even walked backward a few steps. —CLAIRE MCGARRY

FAITH STEP: *The next time you leave your house, use your childlike vision. Be wide- eyed with wonder and let Jesus mesmerize you in everything you encounter.*

FRIDAY, MAY 2

Draw near to God and He will draw near to you.
James 4:8 (NKJV)

AS THE MOTHER OF SEVEN adopted kids, I find it easy to spot the weary gaze of another mom who needs a few words of encouragement. Recently, I was interviewing another adoptive mom named Shelly on my video podcast. When she greeted me on our video call, I noticed the look of defeat on her face.

"So, friend, how are you doing?"

Pain pierced her smile as she shrugged. "Oh, you know how things are."

After recording, I asked if she had a few minutes to chat. "I know you're struggling with your teens," I told her, "and you may question if there's any hope. I've discovered that giving them a little space and allowing them to approach me instead of trying to chase them down has helped our relationship. Building close bonds looks different when dealing with kids from trauma, and sometimes the best way to grow closer is to take a step back." Then I smiled. "At the same time, draw closer to Jesus. He alone can help transform our hearts."

Shelly's eyebrows lifted. Her eyes widened. A genuine smile broke through, and I knew she took this message to heart. More than anyone, Jesus knew what it was like to open His arms of love and watch others walk away. For mothers, it's only natural to want to nurture our children and build a bridge toward our kids' hearts. Sometimes the best encouragement is knowing Jesus waits to draw near to us while we are waiting for our children. —TRICIA GOYER

FAITH STEP: *Reach out today to a mother who has a child at home. Offer encouraging words or do something that could help her and you draw near to Jesus.*

SATURDAY, MAY 3

Let your eyes look directly forward, and your gaze be straight before you. Proverbs 4:25 (ESV)

ONE OF MY FAVORITE THINGS about where my family lives is our proximity to several cities. For instance, Louisville, Kentucky, is only a 2-hour drive. It's home to Churchill Downs, famous for the Kentucky Derby.

On a recent visit, my daughter and I watched the horse races. Those beautiful animals appear so smooth as they move so fast. It amazes me that the horses don't run into each other more often, and I know this is due in part to the blinders they wear to keep them from being distracted.

I learned something new about why horses wear blinders. Horses interpret surprises as threats to their safety. Blinders guard their field of vision, blocking out fears and thus helping them relax. Blinders guard horses against their own reactive vulnerability, which could cause danger to itself, other horses, and jockeys.

This idea of wearing blinders to block fear beyond other distractions made me think about my relationship with Jesus. In a similar way, Jesus invites me to focus on His face and block out fears by trusting Him so I don't react from fallible human instinct. At times I sense Him urging, "Look at Me." When I do, my entire being relaxes.

Jesus calms. He wants us to put on spiritual blinders that guard against our own vulnerability to real or perceived threats. In this way, we can live steady and secure.

We can't remove every source of distraction or danger. But by focusing on Jesus, we can relax as we live each day with His calming strength.
—ERIN KEELEY MARSHALL

FAITH STEP: *What fears distract you? Ask Jesus for spiritual blinders so you can focus on Him.*

SUNDAY, MAY 4

But the fruit of the Spirit is love, joy, peace, patience, kindness, goodness, faithfulness, gentleness, self-control; against such things there is no law. Galatians 5:22–23 (ESV)

AS A CHILDREN'S MINISTER, I tried several creative ways of teaching the fruit of the Spirit to kids. A volunteer in a banana costume greeted them on arrival. Nine fake fruits in a bowl became a memory verse game, a fruit toss competition, and the visual for the Bible lesson. Treats and prizes included Fruit Stripe gum, Froot Loops cereal, and cherry Popsicles. But the best idea of all came from an eight-year-old boy.

"Miss Becky, I can show you how to remember the fruit of the Spirit," Lucas said. "The first three words are one syllable." He stomped once for love, once for joy, and once for peace. "The second three are two syllables." He stomped twice on patience, kindness, and goodness. "And the third three are three syllables. Faith-ful-ness, gen-tle-ness, self-con-trol."

"That's brilliant, Lucas!" I stomped through the verses myself. In many years of ministry, I had never discovered that helpful trick.

Teaching children to follow Jesus kept me in the Word and on my knees. The eternal importance of the task energized me. I learned so much every week while preparing for Sundays. Truths I had heard during adulthood grew clearer when considered on a child's level. As I sought to lead the little ones closer to the Savior, I found I moved closer to Him too.

Love, joy, peace...patience, kindness, goodness... faithfulness, gentleness, self-control. To this day, I need my feet to say those verses. —BECKY ALEXANDER

FAITH STEP: *Try Lucas's method for stomping the syllables in the fruit of the Spirit list and memorize the nine attributes of a Spirit-filled life.*

MONDAY, MAY 5

Do not fret because of those who are evil or be envious of those who do wrong; for like the grass they will soon wither, like green plants they will soon die away. Psalm 37:1–2 (NIV)

OXEYE DAISIES HAVE ALWAYS BEEN one of my favorite gifts from God. Where I live, they grow in roadside ditches throughout the month of May. As a child, I gathered fistfuls of daisies and sat cross-legged on the grass, plucking the delicate white petals, one by one.

"He loves me, he loves me not," I'd whisper, hoping that when nothing remained except the stem and yellow center, I'd have proof of a boyfriend's affection.

I gave up that silly game when I became an adult, but I still adored daisies. In spring, I often stopped my car beside a patch of wild daisies and cut a bouquet for my table. Eventually, I realized it would be easier to grow my own. Late one autumn, I dug up a sunny patch of ground and scattered seeds. The daisies that appeared the next spring were just as lovely as those that grew wild. But when summer's heat became intense, they withered.

Like those daisies, I wither under the intensity of life. But Jesus offers me what I need to grow and thrive when I trust Him: "Trust in the LORD and do good; dwell in the land and enjoy safe pasture. Take delight in the LORD, and he will give you the desires of your heart" (Psalm 37:3–4, NIV).

Before I began cutting down those withered plants, I noticed a single perfect daisy smiling up at me. I picked it and sank down onto the grass, grateful that every May, God sends me daisies. And no matter how the petal-plucking comes out, I know He loves me. —JENNIE IVEY

FAITH STEP: *Write down one simple blessing God has given you.*

TUESDAY, MAY 6

Then, because so many people were coming and going that they did not even have a chance to eat, he said to them, "Come with me by yourselves to a quiet place and get some rest." Mark 6:31 (NIV)

I'D SPENT NEARLY 30 YEARS in neonatal intensive care with its alarms, interruptions, and life-and-death situations. As a transport nurse, then a nurse practitioner, I learned to pray under pressure, even if it was only to say, "Jesus, please help this baby!" under my breath while doing compressions. I took calls on my nights off to attend deliveries at two hospitals. My career was loud, busy, challenging, and rewarding. But I was ready to stop.

Then my husband, Mike, and I moved to a tiny cabin in the Hiawatha Forest.

The people I love were concerned when I lived alone for 2 years in our isolated cabin. Mike had found a temporary job a thousand miles away while I rested alone in a quiet place for a long time.

God knew this was exactly what I needed, though I wouldn't have chosen it for myself. That time was precious and served as a detox from the noise of the NICU, the wail of sirens, and the thump of helicopter blades. We had a landline put in for emergencies, but that phone never jarred me from sound sleep into adrenaline overload like when I was working.

Jesus lived quietly on earth for His first 30 years. During His ministry years, He drew crowds and mentored His disciples, but sometimes He withdrew. Jesus balanced His life with times of solitude, rest, and prayer. So can I. —SUZANNE DAVENPORT TIETJEN

FAITH STEP: *Just as Jesus did, carve out time for stillness and silence today.*

WEDNESDAY, MAY 7

You have rescued me! I will celebrate and shout, singing praises to you with all my heart. Psalm 71:23 (CEV)

I JUMPED A FOOT WHEN I saw the colorful snake basking in the sun by the window in my den. I live near woods, so I'm used to encountering lots of critters— possums, armadillos, squirrels, raccoons, mice, snakes. None of them bother me—*if* they remain outside.

The snake was very still. Dead or preparing to strike? And those colors. Was it "red on yellow, kill a fellow"? I couldn't remember. One thing I knew—I wanted this snake outside. I could get the broom and try to shoo it out of the house, but would it slink up the broom handle and slither up my arm? I stood still and watched. I didn't want to lose sight of it for fear it would sneak into my bedroom after dark and cozy up to me in bed.

Jesus made some daring rescues in His day. He saved His disciples from the waves, Noah from the flood, Lazarus from death. Praying He wouldn't think rescuing me from a snake was too trivial, I called out, *Jesus, help!*

Just then, my husband, Jeff, having forgotten his laptop, came through the back door. I pointed to my visitor, and Jeff quickly ascertained the reptile was deceased. I thanked Jeff and I thanked Jesus, who undoubtedly orchestrated my rescue. Being saved from a snake is a small thing when you think of the magnificent rescue Jesus made for all mankind, dying on the cross for our sins. But what a relief to be able to call out to Jesus when I am afraid.
—PAT BUTLER DYSON

FAITH STEP: *Recall a time when Jesus rescued you. Did you thank Him for it?*

THURSDAY, MAY 8

Don't be afraid, for I am with you. Don't be discouraged, for I am your God. I will strengthen you and help you. I will hold you up with my victorious right hand. Isaiah 41:10 (NLT)

I HAD JUST LANDED IN Toronto when a text message arrived from the airline. It said that my connecting flight to Baltimore that afternoon had been cancelled. The airline had booked me on a different flight leaving the next day at 6 a.m.

I was Baltimore-bound to speak at a women's retreat beginning the next day, so this was not welcome news. I'd deliberately planned to arrive a day early so the retreat director and I could address any potential last-minute hiccups. Now this.

The change left me stranded in Toronto's airport for 16 hours. I couldn't justify spending a fortune on a hotel room, so I stayed in the terminal knowing I wouldn't sleep. But wait—there's more. I'd suffered a foot fracture a couple of weeks earlier, and I was now hobbling in a knee-high air boot. My circumstances were far from comfortable or convenient.

I shot more than a few arrow prayers heavenward asking Jesus to get me to the retreat center on time and to give me strength to present my message coherently. He exceeded my expectations. When I took the podium the next evening, I'd been awake nearly 40 hours, yet everything went well. True to His promise, Jesus strengthened me, helped me, and literally held me up. —GRACE FOX

FAITH STEP: *Hold your right hand palm up and visualize your worries on it. Now give them to Jesus, and thank Him for holding you in His victorious right hand.*

FRIDAY, MAY 9

Don't pick on people, jump on their failures, criticize their faults—unless, of course, you want the same treatment. Matthew 7:1 (MSG)

I HAD A FRIEND I saw maybe once a year because of the miles between us, but I loved her. We kept in touch on social media, where we encouraged each other and shared funny photos and memes. We saw each other's general posts and knew we had different opinions about current events, but that didn't seem to matter.

Occasionally we discussed these differences in private emails and messages. It was good to hear another point of view. I prayed for wisdom, tact, and kindness before pushing "send," and based on her beautiful, gentle words, she might well have done that too. At least once, she changed my mind on an issue.

Time passed and I gradually realized I wasn't seeing her posts anymore.

I checked and discovered I'd been unfriended.

I was surprised by my sadness. I cried off and on for 2 weeks.

On social media, I often like or dislike posts that I wouldn't comment on face-to-face. This habit of judging people and what they have to say has carried over, if not into my actions, at least into my thought life. Has exercising so many judgments effortlessly online made me more judgmental offline?

Was that what happened here? I may never know, but this hard experience has made me more careful, less quick to judge, and, hopefully, kinder.

We've run into each other since in public. She smiled, helped me with a problem I had with my tablet, then hurried away. I hope it's a new beginning. —SUZANNE DAVENPORT TIETJEN

FAITH STEP: *When you feel like being critical, pause to pray for wisdom. Then let Jesus guide your words and actions.*

SATURDAY, MAY 10

Whatever you do, do it from the heart, as something done for the Lord and not for people. Colossians 3:23 (CSB)

I'M A PEOPLE PLEASER BY nature and I go out of my way to accommodate others. On the surface, doing things I am capable of and enjoy that also happen to please people is harmless. But people pleasing becomes a problem when I allow someone else's need to disregard my own—like the time I participated in a dramatic scene for our church's anniversary service.

I stood near the back of the church doors in my heavy wedding gown until I heard Tamela Mann's song "Take Me to the King" piped into the sanctuary speakers. Then I walked down the long, sloping aisle while acting out the lyrics. Once I reached the front, I stepped onto the stage and sat in a chair that was set up for me near the podium. The guest pastor started to preach his sermon on the bride of Christ. I followed the script and sat still in my hot bridal garb with my eyes closed under the scorching spotlights for more than an hour. I was so overheated that I needed help getting off stage. I was in so much pain from not moving a muscle that my body ached for hours afterward, and I had an excruciating headache.

There was nothing wrong with my desire to serve that day, but I disregarded my well-being in the process. Seeking to please others will sometimes leave us in pain and despair. Thankfully, seeking to please Jesus will lead us to healing and hope. —ERICKA LOYNES

FAITH STEP: *Write down all of the reasons it's most important to please Jesus.*

MOTHER'S DAY, SUNDAY, MAY 11

Listen, my child, to the instruction from your father, and do not forsake the teaching from your mother. Proverbs 1:8 (NET)

I DISCOVERED AT AN EARLY AGE that not all moms are alike. My own mother, Linda, died when I was ten, and my dad married my second mom, Sammie, when I was twelve. Though they were both amazing women who loved Jesus and served their families well, as moms, Linda and Sammie were as different as night and day.

Linda taught me to love literature, dream big dreams, and serve Jesus with imagination and creativity. Our home was always a mess, but we knew how much we were loved. Sammie taught me how to keep house, manage a large family, and serve Jesus with organization and structure. Our home was never a mess, but we knew how much we were loved. Later, I gained a third mom—my mother-in-law, Sherryl. Sherryl taught me how to live generously, worship through music, and serve Jesus with laughter and joy. We've never shared a home, but I know how much I'm loved.

When I became a mother myself, I thought about the lessons I'd learned from each of the moms in my life. Everyone says that a woman turns out to be just like her mother, and every mother has her own set of strengths and weaknesses. I determined to take the best traits of all my moms and become the greatest version of myself as a mother that I could be. Now, as I love Jesus and serve my family, I know my best moments are because of them. —EMILY E. RYAN

FAITH STEP: *Make a list of the best lessons you've learned from each of the mother figures in your life. How can you become more like Jesus through their examples?*

MONDAY, MAY 12

See, I am doing a new thing! Now it springs up; do you not perceive it? I am making a way in the wilderness and streams in the wasteland. Isaiah 43:19 (NIV)

WHEN I WAS AT MY orthopedist's office for my annual visit, the doctor looked at my worn sneakers. "You need something more supportive. It's time for an upgrade." Give up my favorite sneakers? I had been wearing the same style for more years than I could count, but I listened as she advised me what to buy for optimal joint cushioning.

Stepping into the shoe store days later, I half-heartedly tried on several of the recommended pairs. Amazingly, walking around the small shop, I immediately felt less knee pain. Though these sneakers were more of an investment than my usual kicks, I happily purchased them.

Marveling about the difference a new shoe made, I drove home. What else had I been hanging on to for more years than I could count? Lately, I felt like my time with Jesus was uninspired and stale, with the same prayers for the same people, over and over. Like my joints, my life was different when I was younger. Shouldn't my prayer habits be different too?

Pushing past the comfortable bookmarks in my Bible, I ordered a few new devotionals to add to my rotation. I even found myself unexpectedly talking to Jesus more throughout my day, instead of only reciting rote prayers and pleas in the morning. An upgrade indeed! —Gloria Joyce

---

Faith Step: *Examine your time with Jesus. Do you need an upgrade?*

Tuesday, May 13

So you are no longer a slave, but God's child; and since you are his child, God has made you also an heir.
Galatians 4:7 (NIV)

While shopping, I heard someone call me by my maiden name, which didn't quite fit anymore. Moments later, I was tangled in a hug with a friend I hadn't seen in decades. As we reminisced on the past and caught up on the present, I thought about the girl my friend remembered me as. I vaguely recall that child, but I'm not her anymore. A lot has changed between then and now.

Then and now. That reminds me of how Peter identifies himself in 2 Peter 1:1 (NIV): "Simon Peter, a servant and apostle of Jesus Christ." When Jesus called him to be a fisher of men, he was known as Simon (Mark 1:16–17). After sitting under Christ's teaching and witnessing miracles, Jesus asked the disciples, "Who do you say I am?" Simon answered,

"You are the Messiah" (Matthew 16:15–16). Then Jesus gave him a new name, Peter (Matthew 16:18).

Peter makes a tremendous statement by introducing himself by both names—Simon Peter. Why not claim the seemingly better of the two—Peter? I think it was because he never forgot who he once was—a frustrated fisherman in need of a Savior. Simon Peter signifies the change that happened between not knowing Jesus then and knowing Him.

In Christ, I have a new name too—child of God. In the space between my given birth name and my new title, much has changed. Like Simon Peter, I don't want to forget who I once was. —KAREN SARGENT

FAITH STEP: *Make two columns in your journal. In one column, list who you were before Jesus. In the other, list who you are now. Thank Jesus for filling the space between.*

WEDNESDAY, MAY 14

On that day a great persecution broke out against the church in Jerusalem, and all except the apostles were scattered throughout Judea and Samaria. Acts 8:1 (NIV)

A FEW MONTHS BEFORE OUR church's new student building was complete, our congregation gathered on a Wednesday evening for a special night of worship. We sang songs of praise in response to the powerful way Jesus was already moving among our students. We asked Him to provide the funds we needed to complete the building debt-free. Then we dedicated the next chapter of our student ministry to Jesus, aligning our collective hearts for His purpose and glory once again. The highlight of the night came at the end when the entire church body walked in procession to the new, unfinished building for our first look inside. Since it was still under construction, we were able to write prayers and Bible verses on the beams and walls as we dreamed about the lives that would be reached in the years ahead.

As I drove home, I thought about something our college minister had said that evening. He'd prayed, "Thank You, Jesus, for the opportunity to meet free from persecution." It was such a simple line, but it made me realize how much I take my religious freedom for granted. Not only can I attend church, but I can also own a Bible, openly pray in public, and speak the name of Jesus without fear of imprisonment. I thought of the early church and of oppressed believers in other countries who face persecution even now. I thanked Jesus for my freedom to worship Him openly and prayed for persecuted believers around the world. —EMILY E. RYAN

FAITH STEP: *Research the persecuted church to discover how you can help believers in oppressed countries. Begin by praying for them.*

THURSDAY, MAY 15

Jesus said, "Let the little children come to me, and do not hinder them, for the kingdom of heaven belongs to such as these." Matthew 19:14 (NIV)

MY FOUR-MONTH-OLD GRANDDAUGHTER, OLIVIA, DOES not take after me. I adore naps. She fights sleep with every ounce of her tired little body cradled in my arms. I sway back and forth. She blinks long and slow. Just as her eyes close, pop! She looks at me with a sleepy grin. When she begins to squirm and fuss, I pull out my Mimi magic. "Jesus loves me; this I know," I sing. Olivia watches my lips and listens to my voice. Eventually, she falls asleep.

As I repeat the words of the song over and over, I think of a man whose name I cannot recall. He took his family to church, then picked up my brother and me for Sunday school. Afterward, he drove us home and returned to church for service.

I remember sitting on a green wooden bench my first time in Sunday school, singing, "Jesus loves me; this I know." I didn't know who Jesus was, but somehow my four-year-old heart knew the words were true. Eventually, someone invited my mom to a Bible study, and she accepted Jesus. My brother and I raised our families in church, and now my grandchild spends Sunday mornings in the nursery.

I wish I could tell that man about the generational and eternal impact his sacrificial act of kindness had on two kids he didn't even know. Someday, in the Kingdom of Heaven, I will. —KAREN SARGENT

FAITH STEP: *How can you share Jesus with a child in your neighborhood? Give a child a picture-book Bible, take a child to vacation Bible school, or invite a family to church.*

FRIDAY, MAY 16

But he said to me, "My grace is sufficient for you, for my power is made perfect in weakness." Therefore I will boast all the more gladly about my weaknesses, so that Christ's power may rest on me. 2 Corinthians 12:9 (NIV)

AFTER A BONE-CRUSHING BICYCLE ACCIDENT, I'd spent the night in the hospital, icing my broken collarbone, scapula, and ribs and getting pain medication. *Jesus, get me home!*

My husband, Jeff, settled me on the couch in the den and brought me my cat. He wanted me to eat, but I wasn't hungry. I was broken and scared and I hurt everywhere. I was mad at myself for riding after a rain, at the bike that had betrayed me, at the world in general.

Over the next week, I shuttled from couch to recliner, seeking a position that didn't hurt. Jeff had to help me get up and down, take a shower, go to the bathroom. *Jesus, I hate this weakness!* And I heard Him whisper to my heart, *Embrace it.*

I had surgery to repair my collarbone involving an unsightly combo of plate and screws. Back home on the couch, I moaned to Jeff, "I'll never be the same."

Friends and family called, sent cards, brought food. It was hard for me to accept help, but I had no choice. *Embrace it.*

A friend told me, "You were lucky. Without your helmet, you'd have had a head injury. Jesus's grace, Pat. I know you're grateful." Yikes! Not so far. I'd been too busy feeling sorry for myself. Then and there, I thanked Jesus for my weakness, causing me to depend on Him and on people who loved me. —PAT BUTLER DYSON

FAITH STEP: *Remember a time when you felt weak. How did you feel Jesus's power?*

SATURDAY, MAY 17

Therefore encourage one another and build each other up, just as in fact you are doing. 1 Thessalonians 5:11 (NIV)

IT HAD BEEN A LONG TIME since my husband and I had hiked down a trail to see a waterfall—maybe too long. Sweat dripped down our faces, and our joints silently but persistently complained about the rocky, uneven terrain. We wondered how much farther we had to go. Then a smiling couple approached from the opposite end of the path. Seeing that we had paused, they offered encouraging words: "You're almost there! It's just a little bit farther. The rest of the way isn't too bad." I asked if the view would be worth the trouble; they assured us that it would be. We thanked them and continued our trek.

I'll admit I get weary sometimes and feel tempted to give up. Whether climbing a steep nature trail on a sweltering day or navigating through a difficult season of life, it helps to hear from someone who's been there. Part of being a Christ follower means speaking words that encourage and build up those around me, just as Jesus did. Jesus demonstrated this beautifully in His conversations with His disciples during His final days as He prepared and strengthened them for the trials and turbulence that lay ahead (John 14).

One of the best ways I can honor Jesus is to help others find the strength to keep going on their spiritual journey during rough patches and to assure them that the destination is most definitely worth the trip. —DIANNE NEAL MATTHEWS

FAITH STEP: *Keep watch today for someone who could use encouragement to continue their journey with Jesus. Ask Jesus to give you the words that person needs to hear.*

SUNDAY, MAY 18

The LORD appeared to us in the past, saying: "I have loved you with an everlasting love; I have drawn you with unfailing kindness." Jeremiah 31:3 (NIV)

MY MOM IS A LETTER WRITER. She has turned it into an art form. Every Sunday night, she sits down and writes to a group of friends and relatives whom she cares deeply about. She shares the comings and goings of the week, what she and my dad have been doing, and the beauty surrounding her. She talks about us—her family. And she talks about Jesus and what she is learning about Him. Her letter is laced with encouragement and hope. The friends who receive her letters cherish them. Who wouldn't?

Today when my husband, Scott, brought in the mail, there was a letter for me. I recognized Mom's handwriting. When I opened it, a ten-dollar bill fell out. The card said, "Dear Susanna, you are the best! Mom." (I have a hunch she sent a similar letter to my siblings.) The money and precious note reminded me that Mom is thinking of me and loves me. I put the card in my file of important letters. I cherish it.

Jesus has written me a love letter too—His Word. He tells me over and over again about His everlasting love. I am His child (1 John 3:1). He is thinking about me, and His thoughts of me outnumber the grains of sand (Psalm 139:17–18). His letter is laced with encouragement and hope. Jesus's Word is precious and endures forever. I cherish it. —SUSANNA FOTH AUGHTMON

FAITH STEP: *Cherish the love letter Jesus sent to you in the Bible. Read about His enduring love in Psalm 136 and then write a love letter back to Him in your journal.*

MONDAY, MAY 19

Then the two told what had happened on the way, and how Jesus was recognized by them when he broke the bread. Luke 24:35 (NIV)

BECAUSE OF AN AUTOIMMUNE ISSUE, I'm required to eat gluten-free. For the rest of my life. I jokingly tell people my first meal in heaven will include croissants.

A friend sent me a short inspirational thought today that imposed the words "recognize Him in the breaking of the bread" over an image of the most glorious-looking torn-open, hearty, airy yet rustic loaf of bread.

My attention was fixed on that image with what I'd have to describe as longing. The bread. Oh. The Bread.

After Jesus's Resurrection, two men on the road to Emmaus walked for hours with Jesus by their side, but they didn't recognize Him...until He tore apart a loaf of bread and offered it to them. With that act, their eyes were opened to finally realize who they'd been talking to, needing, longing for. They saw Jesus in the bread. Perhaps their aha moment was from the way His hands handled the bread as He would have during the Last Supper. Perhaps His sleeves slid back as He handed the bread to them, and they noticed the scars.

It's hard to find a loaf of gluten-free bread with satisfying flavor and texture and at a reasonable price. But today, I see how little that matters compared to the enormous price Jesus paid to give us Himself—the Bread of Life. Gluten-free or not, may I ever "see" Jesus in the Bread He offers. —CYNTHIA RUCHTI

FAITH STEP: *If bread is part of any of your meals today, pause a little longer than you normally would, not just to give thanks for it but also to "recognize Him" in it—the Bread of Life.*

TUESDAY, MAY 20

The generous will prosper; those who refresh others will themselves be refreshed. Proverbs 11:25 (NLT)

ON A RECENT TRIP TO FRANCE, my husband, Zane, and I had a 24-hour layover in Barcelona. We decided to explore the city. At the end of our self-guided tour, we entered the old Jewish quarter. During the time of the Nazis, Jews were confined to this impoverished area. We found the Ancient Synagogue of Barcelona, hoping to go inside, but it was closed. We read some of the signage on the building and learned that in 1931 the Jews of Barcelona were massacred. Then, as we were leaving, I noticed Proverbs 11:25 etched into the stone of the building.

Walking back to our hotel, I pondered how Jesus calls us to be generous and provide refreshment to those who are thirsty or hungry, like the Jewish people were during this dark time in history. They suffered at the hands of others, and yet on this synagogue was a scripture about generosity and refreshing others. At that very moment, I noticed a homeless person sleeping on a stone bench. Covered in a mint-green blanket with pink flowers, the top of his head and the tips of his sock-covered toes stuck out from underneath. Next to him sat a liter bottle of Coca-Cola, half full. Some kind person had given him refreshment. Just what I imagined Jesus would do.

I snapped a picture because I didn't want to forget this powerful image as a reminder for me to do what Jesus says—to refresh others, even during difficult times. —JEANNIE BLACKMER

FAITH STEP: *Ask Jesus to show you someone today who needs refreshing. Have some kind words and a bottle of water ready to give them.*

WEDNESDAY, MAY 21

*And we know that all that happens to us is working
for our good if we love God and are fitting into his plans.*
Romans 8:28 (TLB)

RECOVERING FROM SURGERY TO REPAIR my collarbone after a serious bicycle accident, I was eager to get back to doing the things I loved—riding my bike, practicing yoga, toting my chubby granddaughter. I yearned to resume my life, but my left arm wouldn't cooperate. I couldn't lift it much, and when I did, stabbing pain overwhelmed me. When my doctor recommended physical therapy, I was ready. Anything to get the old Pat back!

I swaggered into the rehab department and met Paola, my physical therapist. Paola's sweet smile belied a wicked taskmaster. The exercises for range of motion and strength were killers! How many times I pled with Jesus to help get me through those rigorous sessions, I can't say. But He was there. And He got me through. The day Paola released me 8 weeks later, she said, "Get back on that bike!"

That very day, I went home, put on my biking gear, and hopped on my old friend. A little wobbly at first, I found my balance, and although I wasn't zipping along as I had before, I was riding again.

Never would I have imagined that anything good could have come from my awful wreck. I'd been right about one thing: I would never be the same. Thankfully! I discovered I was not indestructible. I learned to allow others to help me. I began to practice gratitude. And in my weakness, I learned to lean on Jesus, and our relationship blossomed. —PAT BUTLER DYSON

FAITH STEP: *Write down something that happened to you that was devastating at the time but from which Jesus worked something good.*

THURSDAY, MAY 22

The steadfast love of the LORD never ceases; his mercies never come to an end; they are new every morning; great is your faithfulness. Lamentations 3:22–23 (ESV)

MY DAUGHTER EXCELS AT MAKING holidays and even ordinary days special for her children. Holly gets an early start, setting out seasonal décor and arranging a stack of holiday-themed books on the hearth. Last year she bought an English tea set and scheduled "Tea & Poetry Thursdays" with her two younger daughters. They're a military family, so she sometimes gives the kids "Goodbye" and "Welcome" gifts to acknowledge the state they're leaving and the one they're moving to.

Celebration is a theme found throughout the Bible. In Deuteronomy 16:16, God instructed the Israelites to observe three festivals, meeting at the temple to celebrate His faithfulness. Nehemiah 12:27–29 describes how people dedicated Jerusalem's rebuilt walls with massive choirs and joyful praise. Revelation 19:9 refers to a future wedding banquet as He welcomes His followers home.

Although every season and holiday can draw me closer to Jesus, they eventually end. I'm grateful that our Savior's love, mercy, and grace are everlasting. Each morning I wake up to a fresh day filled with opportunities to praise Jesus, to receive His blessings, to follow His will, and to share His love and forgiveness with others. That's more than enough reason to celebrate every day of the year. —DIANNE NEAL MATTHEWS

FAITH STEP: *Take out your calendar and schedule some activities you enjoy doing. Think of how you can use these times to celebrate what Jesus means to you.*

FRIDAY, MAY 23

I no longer call you servants, because a servant does not know his master's business. Instead, I have called you friends, for everything that I learned from my Father I have made known to you. John 15:15 (NIV)

My friends Amy, Rhys, and I chatted after worship one Sunday about our favorite snacks. "I'm addicted to hummus and celery," I chirped. Rhys and Amy looked at each other and grinned. "I was about to say chocolate mousse," Amy said. We all burst into laughter.

A few months later, my birthday fell on a Sunday. Amy made a dramatic production of giving me a brightly wrapped package of…yes, ma'am: hummus and celery. It remains one of my favorite birthday gifts ever.

Because I know Amy and Rhys like me, I don't mind their teasing. It means we're comfortable with each other. We've spent enough time together to develop trust.

Because Jesus is my friend, I long to feel comfortable talking with Him. Not only when I first get up in the morning or before I sleep but also throughout the day. To recognize His constant presence in my everyday life. To acknowledge Him.

When I see a gorgeous rose, to tell Him He did a great job. When I'm confused, to ask for His wisdom. When I've snapped at my husband, to ask for His forgiveness and an extra dose of patience. When I have a decision to make, to get quiet and listen for His input.

To discover if He prefers hummus and celery or chocolate mousse. Or both. —Jeanette Levellie

FAITH STEP: *Right now, stop and tell Jesus something you'd say to a best friend. Throughout the day, talk to Him and listen for His voice.*

SATURDAY, MAY 24

Now devote your heart and soul to seeking the LORD your God. 1 Chronicles 22:19 (NIV)

I HAD NOT SEEN MY younger son in 10 months. Our family finally managed to schedule a weekend gathering near a theme park. Unfortunately, Kevin joined us late and could only stay 24 hours. While everyone else explored lunch options, I stayed on the phone with Kevin, figuring out which entrance he'd used and how to direct him to my location. I stood by the gift shop, scanning the crowd passing by, barely blinking. Finally, I glimpsed someone who looked familiar, except the hair was too long. As the figure drew closer, I had no doubt about it: this was the face I had been searching for.

When I pray, I often have an agenda in mind. I might need wisdom for a tough decision or guidance to help me order my activities for the day. I may be focused on specific needs such as health problems or financial issues. Or I may be looking for comfort or strength. Instead of immediately bringing my needs and requests to Jesus, it might be a good idea to look first for His face.

I don't know what Jesus looks like in physical form, but reading the Bible gives me an accurate picture of His nature and His thoughts toward me. I can imagine Him looking at me with eyes of compassion and love, with His ears always listening to my prayers, and His mouth lovingly speaking words I need to hear. If I begin my day by "looking" on my Savior's face, I can be assured that I already have everything I'm searching for. —DIANNE NEAL MATTHEWS

FAITH STEP: *Take time right now to look for Jesus's face and imagine His expression as He looks on you with love.*

SUNDAY, MAY 25

Do not let any unwholesome talk come out of your mouths, but only what is helpful for building others up according to their needs, that it may benefit those who listen.
Ephesians 4:29 (NIV)

WHEN MY OLDER CHILDREN DECIDED to catch an early ride to church with my husband, my youngest son, Solomon, and I had a rare moment alone in the car. We shared stories and commentary about the previous week at school, and I was enjoying our back-and-forth banter and relaxed conversation. Then, after one of my more animated anecdotes, instead of laughing, he sighed and shook his head. "You're becoming way too PG-13, Mom."

I was taken aback. What did he mean by *that*? With respect and childlike candor, he mentioned some words I'd used that weren't exactly inappropriate but also weren't the best choice for ten-year-old ears to hear. Some pseudo cuss words people often use as stand-ins for really bad words. I thought I showed restraint to avoid using profanity, but Solomon thought my creatively colorful speech was borderline indecent.

I told him I appreciated his honesty, and we had a great conversation about how our words should honor Jesus and point others to Him. Solomon was right. Even if my speech hadn't been overtly vulgar, it hadn't been entirely wholesome either. I thanked him for holding me accountable and for reminding me to guard my tongue. Everything that comes out of my mouth should be G-rated—godly to honor Jesus. —EMILY E. RYAN

FAITH STEP: *What PG-13 words have crept into your vocabulary? Ask Jesus to help you silence any unwholesome talk that comes out of your mouth and choose words that bless and benefit others instead.*

MEMORIAL DAY, MONDAY, MAY 26

*Have I not commanded you? Be strong and courageous.
Do not be afraid; do not be discouraged, for the LORD your
God will be with you wherever you go. Joshua 1:9 (NIV)*

MY RED POPPIES ARE IN BLOOM. These resilient flowers grow in the toughest of settings and blanket areas with their silky red petals and lush greenery, almost daring a person to smile. How can this simple flower symbolize such hope? By showing up and growing where others won't. Our military heroes do that every day. Most come home, but many do not.

Red poppies are also a symbol of remembrance. During World War I, Lieutenant-Colonel John McCrae noticed red flowers popping up on battlefields all over Europe. Continual bombardment disturbed the soil and brought the seeds to the surface. They were fertilized by nitrogen in the explosives and lime from the shattered rubble of the buildings. It was as if the flowers reflected the bloodshed and rose from the ground as a promise of new life. Seeing these poppies touched McCrae so deeply he wrote the famous poem "In Flanders Fields." His poem inspired the red paper flowers many of us now pin onto our collars in honor of fallen warriors every Memorial Day.

Jesus watched over and walked into battle with those brave soldiers. For some, when their time had come, He carried them home. Just as Jesus was ever-present with our servicemen and women in the past, He guides them today and always will. I'm honored to pay homage to these brave individuals who, like Jesus, made the ultimate sacrifice. Their courage and willingness to serve provide us all with hope. —HEIDI GAUL

FAITH STEP: *Bring red poppies to a senior facility. Listen as veterans remember their fallen friends.*

TUESDAY, MAY 27

The heavens declare the glory of God; the skies proclaim the work of his hands. Psalm 19:1 (NIV)

MY YOUNGEST SON, ISAAC, HAS Down syndrome, but I daresay he enjoys life more than the average person. He's totally immersed in the activities at hand and is undistracted by the cares of this world. I absolutely believe Isaac has a special heavenly connection because he's less fettered by the limitations of this earthly dimension. Moreover, Isaac doesn't wrestle with some of my human failings like overanalyzing with intellectual skepticism, something I struggle with, for sure.

Isaac also has a great imagination and engages dolls, stuffed animals, and leaves in elaborate scenarios and dialogues. Yes, I said *leaves.*

Since he was a tiny tot, Isaac would say, "Mommy, I want to play leaves." This means he'd like to sit in front of the plants that line the sidewalk and play. He talks to them or pulls some branches or leaves (I keep meaning to train him to weed the flower bed!) and has the leaves talk to each other. Sometimes he names them and wants them to come in the house or run errands with us.

At first, this seemed a little odd, but God's Word plainly tells me nature declares His glory. In fact, science confirms talking to plants really helps them grow. They've done studies, people!

I honestly don't know if plants are truly audibly singing God's praises to the spiritually attuned, but Isaac's warm chatter with plants gives me pause. I see nature with fresh appreciation and wonder because of Isaac's example. —ISABELLA CAMPOLATTARO

FAITH STEP: *After you talk to Jesus, talk to your plants. Journal what you learn from both of them.*

WEDNESDAY, MAY 28

I instruct you in the way of wisdom and lead you along straight paths. When you walk, your steps will not be hampered; when you run, you will not stumble.
Proverbs 4:11–12 (NIV)

AS ANOTHER SCHOOL YEAR WINDS down, I remember how much I anticipated field day as an elementary student. My favorite event was the three-legged race. My friend Sherry and I practiced at recess, my left leg bound to her right leg. I loved the smooth stride when we ran in step. But if we were out of step, our bodies jarred side to side, knocking into each other. We had to stop and adjust or we'd fall flat on our faces.

Walking with Jesus is a bit like a three-legged race. When I cling close to Him, my steps feel fluid, making it easier to float over the bumps in my day. But recently, I was out of step. A new grandbaby, traveling, work deadlines, and coffee dates made it difficult to commit my mornings to Jesus. When I sat and opened my Bible, my eyes were in Ephesians, but my mind wandered to what I needed to accomplish. Sometimes I settled for a quick moment with a Bible app or promised Jesus I'd meet Him in prayer in the car...unless I forgot. "I'll do better tomorrow," I'd tell myself. But the tomorrows started adding up.

And so did the jarring and knocking of being out of step. It was time to make an adjustment. I thanked Jesus for remaining beside me, asked forgiveness for neglecting my Partner, and renewed my commitment to start each day in His presence, practicing for the daily race ahead. —KAREN SARGENT

FAITH STEP: *Are you out of step with Jesus? Is it time to adjust? Stop right now, turn to Him, and get back in step.*

THURSDAY, MAY 29

Call to Me, and I will answer you, and show you great and mighty things, which you do not know.
Jeremiah 33:3 (NKJV)

WHEN I WAS A KID growing up in our church's youth group, I memorized Jeremiah 33:3. The youth director told us it was God's phone number. Although that seems silly now, I am glad I memorized it because in my heart I learned to believe that when I call on Jesus, He answers me.

I have been going through a season of feeling hopeless. I am usually a happy person who sees the sunny side of things, but when things go wrong or the problems in the world seem so difficult to solve, it can be hard to keep a positive perspective. The only thing I know to do when I am feeling this low is to go back to the basics of my faith, many of which I learned in youth group. God's phone number—the idea that I can call on Jesus and expect an answer—is one of them.

I started calling Him, meditating and listening for His voice. It has not come in any loud or dramatic form. No wind, no rushing water, no lightning bolt.

But it has started to trickle in like light through a crack or, as stated in 1 Kings 19:12, in a still small voice.

Not all of my problems are solved immediately, but God promises me the hope and assurance that when I call on Jesus He will answer. —GWEN FORD FAULKENBERRY

FAITH STEP: *Light a candle as you call on Jesus today. Concentrate on the flicker of the flame as you wait for Him to answer.*

FRIDAY, MAY 30

Trust in the LORD with all your heart and lean not on your own understanding. Proverbs 3:5 (NIV)

I DIDN'T UNDERSTAND HOW CHALLENGING emotions can be until I had five teenage girls under the same roof. Over the course of a day, I felt joy, sadness, anger, fear, and love. While I enjoyed our conversations and banter, I also became frustrated at their snarky and, at times, disrespectful remarks.

Becoming more aware of my emotions allowed me to understand what needs one of my daughters was trying to fill. For example, a rude remark by one who was really seeking out connections to fill a void when she was lonely. Another felt left out, but instead of sharing that, she acted angry.

I can't always trust my feelings, but I can always trust Jesus. By journaling and praying about these emotional situations, I took it to the One who truly understands and can help.

Especially with the teen girls in the house.
—TRICIA GOYER

FAITH STEP: *Write down a troubling situation and the emotions you felt in a journal. Ask Jesus to guide you in relationship decisions and help you trust in Him completely.*

SATURDAY, MAY 31

Human anger does not produce the righteousness God desires. James 1:20 (NLT)

I NEEDED TO GET A booster shot, so I made an appointment at a nearby pharmacy. The plan was to dash over there and not miss too much time from work.

I had completed the paperwork in advance online and checked in on time for my appointment upon arrival. I took a seat and waited…and waited and waited. As the minutes ticked by, I found myself becoming irritated and angry. What was taking so long? After about 30 minutes, I asked the pharmacy attendant when I would be called in. He said it would be soon. I returned to my seat. *Help me, Jesus,* I thought. A family of four then came in, and a few minutes later, they were called for their appointments. That was the last straw.

"Excuse me. I've been waiting here 45 minutes and I still haven't been called," I said. The family stopped in their tracks and apologized. I was immediately summoned by the pharmacist and received the vaccination. Still fuming, I quickly left the exam room. On my way out, I walked by a gentleman who apparently had witnessed everything. "Thank you for being so patient," he said. It was as if Jesus was speaking to me. I was glad He had held my tongue and guarded my words earlier. Although I was angry, I didn't act on it. While I may have failed to stay as calm as I would have liked, that stranger's comment was like a booster shot of encouragement to my soul. —BARBRANDA LUMPKINS WALLS

FAITH STEP: *Think about the last time you were angry. Did you represent Jesus well? If not, what will you do differently the next time?*

SUNDAY, JUNE 1

*Consider how the wild flowers grow. They do not labor or
spin. Yet I tell you, not even Solomon in all his splendor
was dressed like one of these. Luke 12:27 (NIV)*

I HEADED DOWN THE DRIVEWAY to retrieve my
mail and noticed my neighbor going wild with
weed spray. I waved and said good morning. "No
matter how hard I try, I can't get rid of all this," he
said, sighing.

"Poison ivy?" I asked.

"Nope. These pesky wild violets. Seems like no
matter how much I spray, they come back every
spring stronger than ever."

I wished him luck. Then I went inside and took
from a cabinet a juice glass that had belonged to
my mother. In springtime, that glass became a
wildflower-filled vase that rested on the windowsill
above our kitchen sink. I ran water into it, headed
back outside, and picked some wild violets.

Then I looked up toward heaven. "I got it,
Mother," I said. "Our first bouquet."

I can hear her telling me the story of why violets were her favorite flower. "They're one of the first
signs of spring," she said. But that's not the main
reason she loved violets so. "God does all the work,"
she said. "All we have to do is enjoy them."

My neighbor was still at it with his weed spray while I raised the glass of violets to my nose and inhaled their sweet perfume. *Thank You, God, for the wild violets of spring. And for a mother who loved them and passed her appreciation along to me.* —JENNIE IVEY

FAITH STEP: *Write a note to a relative or friend, reminding them of something special between the two of you and thanking them for it.*

MONDAY, JUNE 2

If I go away and prepare a place for you, I will come again and take you to myself, so that where I am you may be also. John 14:3 (CSB)

A FEW YEARS AGO, MY HUSBAND, Richard, and I had to postpone our Easter visit with our daughter's family for 2 months. I knew our grandchildren looked forward to our visit, but five-year-old Lilah went above and beyond. She had chosen a bouquet from the grocery store to decorate the guest room nightstand. On our pillows, Richard and I found chocolates, handmade paper crowns, love notes, and unicorns she had drawn, cut out, and even personalized. I had never felt so welcomed at any time in my life.

During another visit last week, Lilah and I browsed through photos and saw the pictures I took of those welcome gifts 3 years earlier. At the time, she had just initiated a conversation about what heaven would be like—specifically, if there would be lots of candy and puppies. Lilah and I talked about how we'll be different when we get to heaven, after leaving behind our earthly needs and desires. But once we meet Jesus, we can be sure we'll have exactly what we need to be happy forever.

I wouldn't mind having more details about what heaven will be like, but I'm thankful the Bible tells us what *won't* be there: sadness, sickness, aging, death, and sin. And I have Jesus's promise that He is preparing a place especially for me. I have no doubt that He will go above and beyond anything I can imagine to make me feel welcomed.
—Dianne Neal Matthews

FAITH STEP: *What creative ways can you show Jesus that He is welcome in your home? Decorate a prayer closet or put flowers near the place you have your mornings with Jesus.*

TUESDAY, JUNE 3

I sought the LORD, and he answered me; he delivered me from all my fears. Psalm 34:4 (NIV)

PARENTING THREE YOUNG CHILDREN exhausted me. My senses were constantly on high alert because I didn't want them to go missing or get hurt. My eyes watched to ensure their safety, and my ears listened for their cries, which came both day and night.

My kids are in their late thirties and early forties now. Exhaustion from caring for their physical needs became a non-issue decades ago, but my senses remain on high alert because I still care about their well-being. Fear for them and their families exhaust me as I watch our society distance itself from godly principles. What will their lives look like as Christian values become less tolerable to the mainstream population? I wonder how they'll be able to sustain themselves as housing costs soar and groceries cost more. I see them suffer emotional bumps and bruises, and I want to kiss their boo-boos away, but I can't.

I've suffered a few sleepless nights in the recent past, but I don't want fear for my loved ones' well-being to dominate my life. When anxious thoughts rise in me, I hand them off to Jesus. When they return, I hand them off again. Repeat.

I seek Jesus's face and ask Him to help me keep my focus there, and those fears give way to peace. He's wise, strong, sovereign, loving, and always good. He holds the people most precious to me in His hands, and there's no better place to be. —GRACE FOX

FAITH STEP: *Write your fears about your loved ones' well-being on a piece of paper. Ask Jesus to address the issues or concerns, then throw away the paper.*

WEDNESDAY, JUNE 4

The LORD will keep you from all harm—he will watch over your life; the LORD will watch over your coming and going both now and forevermore. Psalm 121:7–8 (NIV)

I OFTEN RIDE THE METRO, the subway system that runs throughout Washington, DC, and surrounding areas. One morning as we stopped at Ronald Reagan National Airport on my way to work, I noticed the control tower where air-traffic controllers track plane arrivals and departures. I thought about the traffic controllers' great view of the nation's capital and how they direct hundreds of pilots flying over the Potomac River every day to safely land aircraft on the various runways.

Those air-traffic cops have an awesome vantage point from their tower, but it couldn't possibly compare to the view Jesus has of me from His seat in heaven at the right hand of God (Hebrews 1:3). Not only can He see me, but Jesus also has a full view of everybody and everything. He sees not just my comings and goings but also my troubles and pain.

He sees me as I zigzag through life. And He lovingly directs me, even when I fail to follow His way. It's especially those occasions when I know I'm off course that I seek His guidance. Sometimes the landings are a little bumpy, but I always get to where Jesus wants me to go. —BARBRANDA LUMPKINS WALLS

FAITH STEP: *Imagine Jesus keeping His sights set on you today. What would He have to say about where you go, what you do, and who you're with? Ask Him to continually correct your course as He keeps watch over you.*

THURSDAY, JUNE 5

Know therefore that the LORD your God is God; he is the faithful God, keeping his covenant of love to a thousand generations of those who love him and keep his commandments. Deuteronomy 7:9 (NIV)

MY TEEN SON, MASON, HAS been offered a job at a construction company for the summer. The owners are both in their seventies and desperately need a hardworking, dependable young person who can do all the heavy lifting for them. But Mason is hesitant to commit. He enjoys his free time and loves his friends. He's concerned that if he takes this job, he'll have to follow through. Showing up every day, Monday to Friday, means he'll have to miss out on whatever fun things his friends plan during the summer weekdays.

Fortunately, I have a God who doesn't hesitate to commit. He promises to follow through on His vow to love me and even turned His promise into a covenant—a pledge that cannot be broken. His covenant lasts forever through thousands of generations. Even when I break my side of the agreement and make choices that I shouldn't, He still abides by His. He continues to offer me forgiveness, mercy, and grace through His only begotten Son, Jesus, who took on my sins and nailed them to the cross with His very own body (1 Peter 2:24). It is Jesus's commitment and His heavy lifting that lighten my load, redeem my soul, and remain faithful to me no matter what. —CLAIRE McGARRY

FAITH STEP: *The next time you're reluctant to commit to something, reflect on all that Jesus has committed to do for you and say yes!*

FRIDAY, JUNE 6

Finally, brothers and sisters, whatever is true, whatever is noble, whatever is right, whatever is pure, whatever is lovely, whatever is admirable—if anything is excellent or praiseworthy—think about such things. Philippians 4:8 (NIV)

THESE PAST FEW YEARS, I have developed a reading habit that isn't so great. When my alarm goes off in the morning, I reach for my phone. I find myself scrolling through the headlines, checking what is going on in the world. The problem is that I am confronted with all kinds of sadness, pain, distress, conflict, and horror—even before my feet hit the floor.

This habit has been hard to break. By the time I put down my phone, I'm feeling anxious and fearful. This week, I've been trying something different. I've been starting my mornings by reading the Psalms instead of my news feed. The Psalmists turned their worries and heartaches into prayers. Checking the headlines leaves me feeling anxious and fearful about the world, but checking in with the One who made the world reassures me. Then I can turn those headlines into prayers.

Jesus designed my mind to dwell on lovely, pure, admirable thoughts. Thoughts about Him, His goodness, His power, and His great love. When I focus on Him, I can put my phone down and leave the problems of this world in His capable hands.
—SUSANNA FOTH AUGHTMON

FAITH STEP: *As you watch the news or read it online, turn those headlines into prayers.*

SATURDAY, JUNE 7

My dear brothers and sisters, take note of this: Everyone should be quick to listen, slow to speak and slow to become angry. James 1:19 (NIV)

I SELECTED TWO MOTHER-OF-THE-GROOM DRESSES, one sequined light purple and one satin green. Both worked with the wedding party colors, but both were too long. I took them to a local tailor to see if the hems could be raised. I explained what I needed and asked if the sequined one would be impossible to change. Instead of answering my question, he launched into how much he liked the sequined dress. He thought it was more elegant and loved the pattern. After several times of me asking if he could shorten the length, he finally answered, "Oh yes, no problem."

Because he was opinionated about which dress he preferred and wanted to voice his thoughts, he didn't hear my question. *How often do I do that to others?* I know I sometimes don't listen well when I'm eager to express my views. I know I am quick to speak and slow to listen, which is the opposite of Jesus. Jesus had the art of listening perfected. He was in constant communication with God the Father and listened to the needs of those He encountered. He frequently followed up with questions to their requests, another good practice in communication.

When I left the tailor, I hadn't decided which dress to wear, but I did decide to work on listening better to others and not giving unasked-for opinions. God gave me two ears and one mouth for a good reason. —JEANNIE BLACKMER

FAITH STEP: *Practice listening well to someone today. Like Jesus, follow up with a question or two to show you are listening.*

SUNDAY, JUNE 8

So he answered me, "This is the word of the LORD to Zerubbabel: 'Not by strength or by might, but by my Spirit,'" says the LORD of Armies. Zechariah 4:6 (CSB)

I'M A PERFORMER AT HEART. I tend to memorize most of the material when I have to give a presentation or train a class. I don't like being caught off guard. I prefer to prepare and know my content well enough to adjust it or change course if needed without anyone else being the wiser. I can't help it. Since participating in church programs as a kid, I have memorized speeches and scripts with the intent of presenting a flawless performance.

One Sunday morning, a friend's pastor encouraged me not to concern myself with perfection—to just let my words naturally flow and resonate with people. Little did I know that the agenda for an event my friend and I were hosting that afternoon would change to become a more formal presentation at the start. We quickly chose something to read, prayed for Jesus's spirit, and shared a few impromptu words. I would have preferred to practice beforehand, but a perfect performance didn't matter to our guests. At the end of the day, they shared how blessed they were by what they'd heard from us.

I may want to prepare in order to perform everything perfectly, but Jesus doesn't ask me to. He simply asks that I do everything from the heart and for His glory (Colossians 3:23). There's no need for me to avoid mistakes or cover up inadequacies. Jesus's definition of perfect is complete, and I am made perfect in Him (Hebrews 10:14). —ERICKA LOYNES

FAITH STEP: *This week, refrain from trying to get your words exactly right. Trust Jesus for the right words at the right time.*

MONDAY, JUNE 9

That person is like a tree planted by streams of water, which yields its fruit in season and whose leaf does not wither—whatever they do prospers. Psalm 1:3 (NIV)

EARLIER THIS SPRING, I FINALLY decided to put on my gardening gloves and boots. I needed to tackle the "tree situation" in our backyard. The line of trees and bushes that formed a U around the yard had been allowed to grow freely and wildly with just a trim here and there, but recently I noticed some of our pretty flowering trees were less than spectacular when they bloomed. I traipsed around and discovered some taller half-dead trees had overtaken the smaller flowering ones and weren't allowing sunlight to get through. I began trimming.

I also noticed that fallen leaves were piled around the base of the tree trunks, preventing rainwater from reaching their roots. As I raked the leaves and pulled the hose around to give those trees a much-deserved drink, Jesus showed me that I had the same problem: I wasn't letting enough of His light or His Word help me grow on a regular basis.

I had been inconsistent in meeting Jesus. It had been months since I'd waded deeply in His Word. Instead, I coasted on the revelation and knowledge I gleaned years ago—and my withered leaves were starting to show. My seemingly urgent daily activities had overtaken the time I used to set aside to soak up Jesus. I needed some pruning and a daily drink from the Source of Living Water.

In the days to come, I sought the Son more consistently. I felt myself starting to bloom again just like the vibrant pink and purple buds that emerged from those well-watered trees that could now see the sun. —PAMELA TOUSSAINT HOWARD

FAITH STEP: *Make a habit of spending time with Jesus each day. Promise Him and yourself to never let the busyness of life overtake this precious discipline.*

TUESDAY, JUNE 10

The LORD their God will save his people on that day as a shepherd saves his flock. They will sparkle in his land like jewels in a crown. Zechariah 9:16 (NIV)

THIS YEAR I FOUND A treasure I'd hunted for several decades.

In my twenties, I started collecting goblets from the Madonna Inn, a spectacular hotel in San Luis Obispo, California. These unique goblets remind me of precious jewels. The rich red of a ruby. A sparkling indigo sapphire. The deep green of an emerald. Gems fit to adorn a king's crown.

Because the goblets seem like an extravagance, I asked for one each Christmas and birthday, building up a collection of nearly forty. But one color was missing.

I'd seen the chocolate brown beauty in the Madonna Inn gift shop back in the 1980s and almost bought it. Shortly afterward, the manufacturer discontinued that color. It took me 40 years to find one of those cocoa-hued goblets, and I paid double the price I usually pay for a new goblet. But that long sought-after chalice was worth every penny to me.

My yearslong quest for this treasure reminds me of Jesus's search for me. Although I decided to follow Jesus when I was eight, I deserted Him during my teen years. I broke every rule, dated unsuitable boys, and made regrettable choices. In spite of all that, Jesus showed me I was still treasured through people who prayed for and counseled me and scripture verses that assured me of His forgiveness.

When I was lost in my sins and had turned my back on God, Jesus willingly paid the most expensive price, His precious blood, to purchase my freedom (Ephesians 1:7). Like my unrelenting search for that precious brown goblet, Jesus never gave up on His quest for my heart. —JEANETTE LEVELLIE

FAITH STEP: *Thank Jesus for the huge price He paid to buy you.*

WEDNESDAY, JUNE 11

Oh, the joys of those who . . . delight in the law of the LORD, meditating on it day and night. They are like trees planted along the riverbank. . . . Their leaves never wither, and they prosper in all they do. Psalm 1:1–3 (NLT)

AFTER SEVERAL RAINY WEEKS, OUR front flower bed was overdue for weeding. So I set to work, and one by one the roots released their grip from the damp earth. Even through a layer of fresh bark mulch, the weeds pulled up easily.

This hasn't always been the case. I've weeded more dry flower beds than damp ones, when those undesirable plants snapped and tore, leaving the worst part—the roots—behind in the soil.

"Weeding this season hasn't been overwhelming," I told my husband after taking a break from the chore.

As soon as the words were out, I realized nature was serving up another spiritual truth: sometimes I need to weed myself of stubborn roots that prevent me from growing.

A move, job change, relationship shift, health scare, or financial glitch can cause my spiritual soil to dry up, taking with it peace and tranquility. When I am resistant to change or to see the blessing in something new, roots of doubt, worry, and anxiety take hold.

Thankfully, God's Word keeps my spiritual soil moist, making weeding out harmful and stubborn behaviors easier. Tending my spiritual roots in Jesus's presence helps me release my concerns into His capable hands.

I went back outside to finish the job with a fresh perspective. As I tossed away each weed, roots and all, I asked Jesus to help me abide in the rich soil of His Spirit. —ERIN KEELEY MARSHALL

FAITH STEP: *Check your yard or garden for weeds. As you pull them out, ask Jesus to tend to the health of your spiritual garden as well.*

THURSDAY, JUNE 12

But whoever drinks the water I give them will never thirst. Indeed, the water I give them will become in them a spring of water welling up to eternal life. John 4:14 (NIV)

IT HAS BEEN 10 YEARS since our first visit to Hawaii's enchanting Big Island. Excited, my husband and I rented a car and explored every corner of the gorgeous place. When we stumbled upon an orchid nursery, it was as if a long-forgotten wish had come true. Brightly colored exotic blooms filled that incredible space, and we placed an order for several orchids and one plumeria to be mailed to our home in the Pacific Northwest.

Years passed, and the orchids repeatedly brightened our kitchen nook—and our spirits. The plumeria grew from a 6-inch stick to more than 8 feet tall. Though leaves sprouted, grew, and dropped, the plant never put forth a single blossom. Still, I continued watering and feeding it. I told myself it was an exercise in patience.

Last month, the plumeria finally budded. Not just one or two flowers but four of the most exquisite, fragrant pink blooms I've ever seen. After waiting so long, I almost cried.

When I consider the many detours and side trips I've taken along the path leading me to Jesus—and all the years it took—I'm grateful He chose to wait on me. Throughout my faith journey, He's nurtured and guided me in the right direction. Then, when my hopes ran dry and my soul grew parched, He offered me the water of eternal life. Today, like a prized blossom, I can open and bloom in His light forever. —HEIDI GAUL

FAITH STEP: *Purchase an indoor plant and nurture it to bloom. Reflect on the endless patience Jesus shows you as you grow in Him.*

FRIDAY, JUNE 13

Our eyes look to the LORD our God, till he shows us his mercy. Psalm 123:2 (NIV)

A VIDEO ON MY TABLET caught my attention. A silhouette of a computer- generated ballerina twirled, one arm raised, one leg gracefully bent at the knee. The video narrator, an optical illusion expert, asked, "Which way is she spinning, clockwise or counterclockwise?"

Obviously, the girl was twirling clockwise. No question. Final answer: clockwise.

The narrator explained, "It depends." He said that if my brain's right hemisphere was in the driver's seat, I would see the girl spinning clockwise. If the left side was dominant, I'd see her spinning counterclockwise.

How intricately God created the human brain to function!

Viewers like me—convinced we were right—were encouraged to keep looking. Then I saw it. The ballerina began to twirl in the opposite direction of the one I assumed. The left side of my brain viewed the same scene differently.

Just like that ballerina, I need to keep watching what Jesus is doing. *Does it appear He's turned His back?* No, keep looking. He said He wouldn't abandon me (John 14:18). *What else could it—* Aha! He's standing in front of me, facing my giants, protecting me (2 Thessalonians 3:3). *Why am I getting the opposite of what I prayed for?* If I keep seeking, I may discover the wrong part of my brain was in the driver's seat. That's not what He's doing at all. He's working out His plan. I need to look harder, longer, and allow for the possibility that what I am sure of may be my mind playing tricks on me.

One glance won't always show me the scene accurately, but this I see clearly: Jesus is no illusion—He's real. —CYNTHIA RUCHTI

FAITH STEP: *Look up the spinning ballerina illusion on YouTube, then journal about a time you trusted what you saw rather than what Jesus or His truth told you.*

SATURDAY, JUNE 14

Put on your new nature, and be renewed as you learn to know your Creator and become like him. Colossians 3:10 (NLT)

"THE SHAGGY BARK HICKORY IS finally dropping its leaves," my husband said as he sipped his morning coffee, surveying other signs of spring's arrival: yellow daffodils, purple phlox, red tulips.

Unlike the barren trees surrounding it, the hickory does not shed its leaves in the fall. Instead, the tree holds on stubbornly through the blustery winter. In the spring, new buds form on its branches, forcing the shaggy bark to release its brown, crusty foliage. The dead leaves and the new leaves cannot occupy the same space.

Looking at the tree, I couldn't help but think about my own life. *What dead leaves am I holding on to far past the season?* An unrealized dream, an emotional wound, a loved one who passed too soon. I sometimes wonder, *When will my winter end?* In reality, it may be time for a new season to arrive, but here I am, still clinging to old leaves. New life tries to sprout, but there's no room on my heavy branches.

Like me, Jesus endured emotional wounds on earth. His closest companions betrayed and abandoned Him. He lost loved ones too. In His sorrow, Jesus modeled how we can become like Him. He prayed, "Father, forgive them" (Luke 23:34) and "Not my will, but yours" (Luke 22:42).

I joined my husband at the kitchen window. A spattering of dead leaves circled the hickory's trunk. Little nubs poked out along its branches. I, too, am ready to let go and welcome renewal.
—KAREN SARGENT

FAITH STEP: *Have you been clinging to a past hurt for too long? Ask a trusted friend to pray with you and walk into a new season with Jesus.*

FATHER'S DAY, SUNDAY, JUNE 15

We all, like sheep, have gone astray, each of us has turned to our own way; and the LORD has laid on him the iniquity of us all. Isaiah 53:6 (NIV)

WHEN MY HUSBAND AND I decided to replace our kitchen countertops, my father offered to save us hundreds of dollars by cutting down our current split-level countertop and moving the electrical out-lets himself. A few days later, after the countertop was removed, I explored the progress. The cabinets were in a curved island, so the dead space between the individual sections was exposed. I looked inside, and that's when I saw it—Isaiah 53:6 written in pencil on the back side of the drywall. Right away, I recognized the verse and knew who had written it. It was my father's favorite verse. The entire Gospel, squished into one sentence, pointing the reader to Jesus.

I've watched my dad manage construction proj-ects my whole life. He's built swing sets, churches, patios, birdhouses, buildings, and a cross so tall that airplane pilots navigate around it. I've also watched my dad grow in his walk with Jesus. He's never taken for granted the grace that he, an admitted sinner, has received through Christ. He knows it's unlikely someone will find his hidden messages, but he still leaves Isaiah 53:6 behind when he builds. It's hope for the future. An answer to a question not yet asked. Salvation for sinners not yet born. If just one person sees the reference, looks up the verse, and follows their curiosity to find Jesus, it'll be worth it.

Dad, I saw your hidden message. But more so, I see your love for Jesus. —EMILY E. RYAN

FAITH STEP: *Write the reference to your favorite Bible verse and leave it as a breadcrumb for someone to find.*

MONDAY, JUNE 16

At that day you will know that I am in My Father,
and you in Me, and I in you. John 14:20 (NKJV)

THE GROUND BEEF AND SAUSAGE waited in the pan, browned and drained. I spooned the meaty mixture into the slow cooker and added a few additional items. By dinnertime, the tomato sauce and herbs, mushrooms, onions, and red pepper I'd placed in the slow cooker would meld into an irresistible pasta topping. My mouth watered as I imagined the deep, rich flavor.

Without even one of the many ingredients, my sauce would be lacking. Each is necessary to make the best sauce. I'm that way with Jesus too. I can't be my best without Him. He is in the Father and I'm in Him, and vice versa. My brain short-circuits as I struggle to grasp even the tip of this wisdom. I trust I will understand fully when I see Him face-to-face. Until then, I simmer and wait.

I don't need to complicate this promise. The security, strength, and freedom Jesus lays out in these words are enough. How can such a love so deep exist?

Sometimes this knowledge overwhelms me. And it changes my perspective on life. I know I'll make mistakes. That's part of being human. But my goal is to please Jesus, to meld beautifully and completely into His image, just like the spices in my sauce.

I'm only one ingredient in this melting-pot world, but I'm confident that I'm a necessary part of His divine purpose. I plan to add zest, depth, and love. —HEIDI GAUL

FAITH STEP: *Make any recipe requiring a number of ingredients. Think about how each of those items comes together as one. Then share the bounty!*

TUESDAY, JUNE 17

But he said to me, "My grace is sufficient for you, for my power is made perfect in weakness." 2 Corinthians 12:9 (NIV)

MANY PEOPLE REMARK ON THE kind and cooperative co-parenting relationship I have with my ex-husband. We are always polite to one another. We make a sincere effort to accommodate each other's schedules and needs, pinch-hitting rides and childcare, even when it's not our week. How do we do it? Not to be overly simplistic, but the answer is Jesus and His amazing grace.

Jesus gave me grace to see my part in the marriage, both my contributions and my failings. There is no ego in His grace, and this diffuses the potential bitterness and blaming that can make co-parenting terribly tense, if not downright impossible.

I also cannot deny the fact that Jesus loves my ex-husband as much as He loves me. I want to treat Him like a Christian brother, understanding he (just like me) is a sinner in need of grace. The Golden Rule (Matthew 7:12) helps me make a sincere effort to treat him as I want him to treat me.

It is Jesus's love that enables both me and my ex to keep our children's well-being at the forefront, promoting the most loving, safe, positive environment for them *and* for us. The goal is more love and peace, not more strife and destruction. When there's a potential conflict, Jesus's grace comes to my rescue, reminding me that I can rely on Him to help me through any challenge because He is all I need. —ISABELLA CAMPOLATTARO

FAITH STEP: *Pray for the grace and clarity to see your part in a difficult relationship and consider ways in which Jesus can help you bridge the gap.*

WEDNESDAY, JUNE 18

Then he said to them all: "Whoever wants to be my disciple must deny themselves and take up their cross daily and follow me." Luke 9:23 (NIV)

I PUT THE DIRECTIONS INTO my maps app on my phone and started driving to meet some friends at a restaurant about an hour away. I love Google Maps because it's a calm voice telling what direction to go, when to turn, and my estimated arrival time. But sometimes I still think I know best.

On my recent trip to meet my friends, I decided to ignore the voice coming through my car stereo telling me to take a specific exit. I thought if I went a little farther down the highway, there would be a better route. Of course, I was wrong. The next exit was 3 miles down the road. The voice directed me to "return to the route." Eventually, I did and made it to my destination late.

How often do I think I know better in my journey of following Jesus? He simply says, "Follow Me." I haven't heard an audible voice with specific directions telling me what path to take when making decisions, but I have God's Word that is pretty specific with directions for life. I also have Jesus's example in Scripture on how to live. And I have the Holy Spirit, who lives in me guiding me into all truth (John 16:13). When I think I know better and take a wrong turn, I feel an uneasiness in my spirit and a nudge in my heart telling me to "return to the route." Eventually, I figure that out and get back on track. —JEANNIE BLACKMER

FAITH STEP: *Map out a specific course to follow Jesus as you plan your day.*

JUNETEENTH, THURSDAY, JUNE 19

I am the LORD your God, who brought you out of
Egypt to be your God. I am the LORD your God.
Numbers 15:41 (NIV)

AS I LISTENED ONE MORNING to a reading of Psalm
46, I noticed that "the God of Jacob" was repeated
a couple of times. Although I had heard that psalm
countless times, those words resonated with me
throughout the day.

I kept thinking that the Lord, who is often referred
to as the God of Abraham, Isaac, and Jacob, the
revered patriarchs of the Israelites, is also my God.
The One who promised to give land to Abraham
and his descendants and make them as numerous as
the stars in the sky is the same One who freed my
ancestors from slavery, which we celebrate today, and
blessed them with many descendants. The Almighty
God who kept His promise to Isaac and Jacob is the
same One who has kept me and my family throughout our trials and tribulations. "I am your God,"
He constantly told the Israelites throughout their
history. His Word tells me that as well.

My mind can hardly wrap around the fact that
the God who made those declarations to Abraham,
Isaac, and Jacob thousands of years ago is the same
who sent Jesus to save me and all humankind from

our sins. Jesus is my personal Savior. He is the God of Barbranda. And the God of those who came before me. Jesus is known by many names—Immanuel, King of kings, Messiah, Teacher, Master, Holy One of Israel, and more—but He is ultimately the One who saves and gives freedom. Jesus, my God. —BARBRANDA LUMPKINS WALLS

FAITH STEP: *Insert your name in the blank: Jesus, the God of _____. What does it mean to you to have Jesus as your God?*

FRIDAY, JUNE 20

Sing and make music from your heart to the Lord.
Ephesians 5:19 (NIV)

THE "UNKNOWN NUMBER" APPEARED ON my phone screen, and I let the call go to voicemail. Later that day, I listened to the message: "Hello, Becky. This is Suzanne from WayFM. You've won two concert tickets for the My People Tour, featuring Anne Wilson, We the Kingdom, and Crowder. Give us a shout back for more details." I squealed like a teenager and dialed her immediately to claim my prize.

Jesus created a beautiful June evening for the outdoor event. First, my daughter and I ate hot dogs with popular radio personalities at a tailgate party. Then we made our way to great seats in the amphitheater. When the music started, we sang along to familiar tunes we'd heard on the radio and at church.

I snapped a few pictures throughout the concert, but one captured the experience best. The sky was dark by the time David Crowder and his band performed. Thousands of believers stood with hands raised, singing praises to Jesus. And projected on a screen above the stage, the song lyrics proclaimed: "Jesus when the sun goes down." I'm still not sure how I managed to catch such an inspiring shot.

Music helps us step into the presence of Jesus. In the Bible, Miriam played a tambourine and sang after Pharaoh's horses, chariots, and horsemen were swallowed up by the Red Sea and the Israelites were delivered out of Egypt (Exodus 15:20–21). Deborah sang about God's power following a victory in battle (Judges 5). Paul and Silas prayed and shared hymns, even while chained in prison (Acts 16:25). These accounts from Scripture and winning free concert tickets are certainly something to sing about. —BECKY ALEXANDER

FAITH STEP: *Step into the presence of Jesus today by listening to the melody and message of a favorite hymn or song.*

SATURDAY, JUNE 21

You, LORD, keep my lamp burning; my God turns my darkness into light. Psalm 18:28 (NIV)

WHEN MY ELECTRIC WALKWAY LIGHTS gave out this year, I bought solar lights to replace them. They were sold in sets of six. After lining the path to my front door, I had three left over. I decided to put them in my flower garden.

All day long, sun shone on the top panels, charging the small battery tucked inside. When the sun went down and darkness fell, the lanterns clicked on like magic, illuminating the space. I was able to enjoy my beautiful garden well into the night.

I can be like those solar lights if I choose to be. When I spend time in God's Word, soaking up His grace and storing it in my heart, I'm charged up and prepared for any difficulty that comes. Whether it's my own struggle or that of a friend, I'm able to shine God's light into the darkness and illuminate hope.

God's plan is always as elegant and beautiful as any flower we plant. That doesn't change just because the sun goes down or turmoil blocks out the light. If my heart is constantly recharged through time spent with Him, my faith and trust become steadfast, illuminating His grace and hope into the darkness. —CLAIRE MCGARRY

FAITH STEP: *Raise your face to the sun—and Son—today, soaking in the warm rays as you store up Jesus's grace in your soul.*

SUNDAY, JUNE 22

But she said, "I swear by the LORD your God that I don't have a single piece of bread in the house. And I have only a handful of flour left in the jar and a little cooking oil in the bottom of the jug. I was just gathering a few sticks to cook this last meal, and then my son and I will die."
1 Kings 17:12 (NLT)

EVER FEEL LIKE YOU'RE DOWN to your last bit of flour and oil and there's nothing more in your jugs? I know I've felt this way at times, especially about finances. Some years ago, my husband and I were looking for an inexpensive investment property to buy, fix up, and rent as a way to supplement our income. Housing was in huge demand in our state, and most sellers required all cash. How were we going to purchase anything without securing a loan since we didn't have enough discretionary income to pay cash?

A recent sermon about the widow of Zarephath (the subject of the scripture verse above) began to simmer in my mind. *What we had could be enough for Jesus to help us achieve our goal.* We pressed forward through the adversities with this in mind, and a unique door for financing opened to us where we could use zero-interest credit cards to purchase a low-cost fixer-upper. We closed on the home a few months later.

If we'd looked only at what we had financially, or even emotionally and physically, we could have fallen into anxiety and quit. Instead, we gave Jesus our handful of flour and trusted Him to show us how to make it into a feast. —PAMELA TOUSSAINT HOWARD

FAITH STEP: *Ask Jesus to show you an area where you feel you're lacking and let Him guide you to the hidden riches.*

MONDAY, JUNE 23

There are different kinds of working, but in all of them and in everyone it is the same God at work.
1 Corinthians 12:6 (NIV)

IN MY BEDROOM, ISOLATED FROM my family due to illness and praying I would get well soon, I was lonely and out of lozenges. My husband brought me one of the kids' unwanted lollipops instead. It wasn't a throat drop, but I was consoled by the fact that it was grape. My favorite flavor always soothed my soul, bringing me back to simpler days when my time with Jesus was not rushed and there was more time for fun.

My mind wandered away from my undone to-do list to my childhood, visiting the bank with my mom, being rewarded for good behavior after church, going door-to-door with my friends on Halloween. I recalled my toddlers, now teenagers, giggling over their stained tongues in the mirror. Closing my eyes, I thanked Jesus for the people in my life, savoring the memories as they washed over me lick by sweet lick. I took the downtime I didn't always have and spent it with my friend Jesus. That unexpected lollipop not only provided physically what my throat needed that day, but it wound up being just the blessing my lonely spirit needed as well. —GLORIA JOYCE

FAITH STEP: *Treat yourself to your favorite candy today and savor it as you sit with Jesus. Use the uninterrupted time to thank Him for the memories evoked within you, patiently praying for those who come to mind.*

TUESDAY, JUNE 24

He asked me, "Son of man, can these bones live?"
I said, "Sovereign LORD, you alone know."
Ezekiel 37:3 (NIV)

TELEVISION SHOWS FEATURING CRIME SCENE investigators are popular, but I'm too squeamish to watch much since some scenes and dialog are graphic. When I was younger, I felt disturbed by images conjured up by Ezekiel's vision: dried-out, scattered bones noisily attaching to each other; tendons, flesh, and then skin covering the skeletons; breath entering the bodies and allowing them to stand up. My attitude changed when I understood the relevance of this Old Testament passage.

In Ezekiel's day, Israel was a nation divided, scattered, and seemingly dead. But God shared His plan to one day restore and bring new life to His people. What seemed to be a hopeless case was not. Personally, I need this reminder that there is never a reason to give up. Not when I'm grieving for a broken relationship or feeling burdened for a loved one who seems spiritually dead. Not when I'm struggling with a self-destructive habit that has long held me in its grip. Not when I'm longing for a cherished dream that now seems impossible.

On-screen crime scene investigators solve the crime by the end of the episode, identifying the perpetrator and revealing the motive. But there is never a happy ending because there's been a loss of life. Thankfully, my life is different when Jesus comes on the scene. For many years, He has been working on me, bringing new life where there was death. And when my episode on earth is finished, I'll

have the happiest ending of all with Him in heaven.
—DIANNE NEAL MATTHEWS

FAITH STEP: *Have you given up on a relationship, a problem situation, or a goal? Ask Jesus to give you a "dry bones" vision of how He may want to change your circumstances.*

WEDNESDAY, JUNE 25

Two are better than one, because they have a good return for their labor: If either of them falls down, one can help the other up. But pity anyone who falls and has no one to help them up. Ecclesiastes 4:9–10 (NIV)

A COUPLE YEARS AGO, MY son Nathan and I embarked on an exciting journey to write a historical fantasy novel that would entertain, inspire, and educate. As we wrote our story amid Nazi-occupied Prague, the novel's theme resonated: "Even in the darkest of times, hope can still be found." By weaving together historical events and imaginative elements, we intended to offer readers a glimpse into the past and inspire them to consider how they can make a difference in today's world.

Working on this project together, Nathan and I realized we were able to bounce ideas off of each other, as well as encourage and support one another throughout the writing process. When I felt over-whelmed by my busy schedule, Nathan lightened my load. Then I pointed out Nathan's talents and skills when he felt insufficient for the task.

Not only did our collaboration draw us together, but it also caused us to lean on Jesus. When we needed ideas, inspiration, or wisdom, Jesus was a prayer away. What an exceptional opportunity to turn to Jesus in prayer with my son as we crafted a fiction story. Two really are better than one, and that's a fact! —TRICIA GOYER

FAITH STEP: *What project would be made easier if you collaborated? Pray that Jesus inspires you to find a partner and reach out.*

THURSDAY, JUNE 26

Every time you cross my mind . . . is a trigger to prayer.
I find myself praying for you with a glad heart.
Philippians 1:3–4 (MSG)

IT STARTED YEARS AGO WITH a simple pair of ear-rings. Whenever I'd reach for them, I'd find myself praying for my pastor's wife. I'd come to associate those particular earrings with her because I remember serendipitously running into her that day at the craft fair where I bought them. I've long since transferred my church membership to a congregation closer to home—in the town where I now live. Nevertheless, I still pray for my former pastor's wife whenever I wear that particular pair of earrings.

From that tiny prayer habit has grown an ongoing opportunity for similar prayers of blessing. For it occurred to me that whenever I see, touch, or use certain items that someone gave to me, I can say a quick prayer of blessing for that person. Whether it's the gift of a cherished, perfectly smooth stone, a beautiful handmade pottery mug, or a luxuriously snuggly blanket that I'm enjoying, I can ask Jesus to bless the giver of that gift.

Meanwhile, I recognize that all gifts come from God (James 1:7). So, whenever something in my home causes someone to cross my mind and triggers me to pray for them, I ask Jesus to bless them, knowing He's the One who gave them the desire to bless me. With a glad heart, I'm continually grateful for how He blesses me through the people in my life. —CASSANDRA TIERSMA

FAITH STEP: *Look around the space where you're sitting. Notice something that reminds you of someone. Ask Jesus to bless that person. Thank Him for showing His love to you through the people in your life.*

FRIDAY, JUNE 27

Seek the LORD and his strength; seek his presence
continually! Psalm 105:4 (ESV)

"Pat, will you come take a look at my head?
And bring towels," my husband, Jeff, called from
the garage. *Oh, Jesus, don't let this be as bad as it
sounds.* I rushed to the garage where Jeff had been
tinkering with an old generator when the door had
swung open and gashed his head. I cringed when I
looked at the bloody wound. Jeff asked if I thought
he needed stitches. I couldn't tell because of the
blood. Jeff had planned to go to our grandson
Winston's baseball game, but should he get medical
care immediately? I needed advice.

So I took several pictures of Jeff's gash and sent
them to Erin, our daughter-in-law, to see what she
thought. Erin, an optometrist, was our medical
go-to for weekend family boo-boos. Erin couldn't
determine from the picture whether Jeff needed
stitches but said she'd get other opinions. In the
meantime, Jeff left for Winston's game, pressing a
washcloth to the hole in his head.

For the next hour, I fretted until I heard from
Erin. Two of her friends in the medical profession
agreed Jeff needed stitches. After I relayed the message to Jeff, it hit me. What was I thinking? I'd

called out to Jesus early in the crisis, but did I ask for His direction after that? No, instead I'd taken pictures and consulted others. Jesus would have led me in the expedient course to take. How foolish of me to neglect to ask for guidance from the One who knows best. *He* should always be my go-to! —PAT BUTLER DYSON

FAITH STEP: *List three instances in which you called out to Jesus in a crisis. How did He help you?*

SATURDAY, JUNE 28

Be completely humble and gentle; be patient, bearing with one another in love. Ephesians 4:2 (NIV)

I'M A RETIRED SHEPHERD, so when a neighbor had an issue with new triplet lambs, she called me for help. Two of the three lambs were nursing, but the mother was rejecting and pushing the third away. The lamb was up and trying to nurse, but Mama wasn't having it. The group of us finally figured out that the lamb's baby teeth were sharp and hurting the ewe's teats. We dulled his teeth with a nail file and I headed home. Problem solved.

Except it wasn't. The ewe wouldn't give the lamb another chance. She made the situation worse by rejecting one of the other two lambs she'd previously accepted. I guess she'd been hurt, and in trying to protect herself, she overcorrected.

How often do I do the same?

Recently, when a doctor's office staff inadvertently left me for hours in the waiting room, I fumed rather than approaching the desk to check. By the time I did, the receptionist said the doctor was gone. He thought he'd seen all his patients and had left early to beat a snowstorm. I overreacted and cried, taking it personally.

When I'm hurt in other areas of my life, I tend to overact or withdraw, acting like that mama ewe. But there's a better way of working through the pain— relying on Jesus in order to move forward.

If the ewe doesn't allow her lambs to nurse, even though it hurts, her udder would swell and become more painful, risking infection and its consequences. In the same way, I must trust my Good Shepherd to know what's best for me, even when I've been hurt.

—SUZANNE DAVENPORT TIETJEN

FAITH STEP: *Recall a way you've overreacted recently. Talk your hurt over with Jesus, your Good Shepherd.*

SUNDAY, JUNE 29

Therefore, if anyone is in Christ, the new creation has come: The old has gone, the new is here!
2 Corinthians 5:17 (NIV)

I GLANCED AT MY FRENCH country teapot resting on the bistro table in our front yard. It's one of the oldest I own and the largest by far. But this year, I noticed crazing on its interior surface. Harmful bacteria could grow in the tiny cracks in the glaze and cause illness. The time had come to retire this gorgeous piece. Still, it was too beautiful to toss in the trash. I considered displaying it in the sitting room, but that would only provide me with one more item to dust. And dusting is not my favorite pastime.

I had an idea. Looking around the garden, my focus settled on a grouping of carnations. After my husband drilled a drainage hole in the pot, we filled it with soil and added a flower. Now this lovely teapot turned flowerpot cheers my spirit when I take a break on the patio.

As I get older, Jesus is making changes in me too. Like my teapot, I'm beginning to show signs of my age, but I still have worth. And like that pot, the things that fill me—my time and my thoughts—have evolved. My life serves a different purpose now, one He's chosen for me.

Running my fingertips along my teapot's smoothness, I sniffed the flower's light scent and smiled. I'm pleased with my creation. I trust Jesus has found delight in His, as well. —HEIDI GAUL

Faith Step: *Scavenge your home, a thrift shop, or a garage sale for an item you can repurpose. When you use it, consider the new creation you've become through Jesus.*

MONDAY, JUNE 30

Now to him who is able to do immeasurably more than all we ask or imagine, according to his power that is at work within us, to him be glory in the church and in Christ Jesus throughout all generations, for ever and ever! Amen. Ephesians 3:20–21 (NIV)

I AM CURRENTLY EXPERIENCING AN amazing season of God's blessings. Prayers I've whispered for years are now being answered favorably. Dreams I've kept close to my heart are finally coming to fruition. The joy I imagined for my future is what I am feeling today. Some days I have literal "pinch me" moments as I think about all Jesus is doing in my life.

But as blessed as I am, nothing has unfolded exactly as I asked or envisioned. In my imagined future, I was thinner, richer, funnier, and way more successful. I worked for fun, not to pay the bills. My children cleaned their rooms without being asked. My car never broke down. My husband and I never disagreed over what to eat for supper or how we would pay for the kids' college.

Quite simply, I thought the perfect future was a life without trouble so I could praise Jesus and glorify Him in every blessing. Instead, the life I'm living is immeasurably more than the one I imagined. It's one in which I can praise Jesus in good times *and* bad. That's the real reason I am experiencing an amazing season of God's blessings. It's not that a few things are finally turning out well. It's that I've found joy in Jesus that gives me the "pinch me" life. —EMILY E. RYAN

FAITH STEP: *Think about how the future you imagined when you were younger is different from the life you're living now. How has Jesus made it better?*

TUESDAY, JULY 1

I will place on his shoulder the key to the house of David; what he opens no one can shut, and what he shuts no one can open. Isaiah 22:22 (NIV)

I STAND, DOOR AJAR, LETTING the air-conditioning rush out while my cat, Winnie, stands at the threshold. She sniffs the outdoors, tail twitching. Her eyes track birds flying past. Losing patience, I ask, "In or out?" Apparently, she's asking herself the same question. On such a gorgeous summer day, why would she not take advantage of the open door? I give her a gentle nudge, which she resists.

I wonder how often Jesus has held a door open, waiting on me to stop sniffing around and just go through it already. How many times have I walked away, declaring the place beyond the threshold too risky, uncomfortable, or simply not what I had planned? What opportunities have I missed?

Sometimes I've known when Jesus has opened doors: a job change requiring a move, a coffee date with an acquaintance who became my mentor. I've known when Jesus has closed certain doors too. But sometimes I'm not sure if He's holding one door open or another door shut.

I'm trying to set aside my own plans, read Scripture to illuminate my steps, and seek wise counsel from my mentor. I pray, trying my best to be still and discern a

252 | MORNINGS WITH JESUS 2025

divine nudge. I don't want to miss another open door or try to force one that has been closed by Him. I'd rather trust Jesus as my Doorman. —KAREN SARGENT

FAITH STEP: *Are you uncertain about a door Jesus may be opening or closing? Seek counsel from a wise friend who will speak truth to you.*

WEDNESDAY, JULY 2

Some of his disciples began talking about the majestic stonework of the Temple and the memorial decorations on the walls. But Jesus said, "The time is coming when all these things will be completely demolished. Not one stone will be left on top of another!" Luke 21:5–6 (NLT)

I'VE HAD THE OPPORTUNITY TO visit historical cathedrals in countries including Poland, Ukraine, Russia, and Cyprus. As I gaze at the lofty vaulted ceilings, intricate designs, and paintings, I contemplate how early craftsmen invested time, energy, and resources into building these monuments for God's glory.

Some structures are more than a thousand years old. Made of stone and adorned with marble, gold, and stained glass, they stand like fortresses and appear indestructible, but they are not. Someday, Jesus says, they will collapse into heaps of rubble.

A quote by C. T. Studd, a British missionary who lived a hundred years ago, challenges me to consider the difference between temporal and eternal. He wrote, "Only one life, 'twill soon be past. Only what's done for Christ will last."

The older I get, the more I want my life to count for Jesus and His kingdom. And so I prayerfully consider opportunities that come my way. Before I invest time, energy, and resources, I ask this question: Will this impressive-looking project or pursuit stand the test of time and reap eternal results, or will it be reduced to nothingness when Jesus returns? I ask Jesus for wisdom and clarity, and He shows me what to do. —GRACE FOX

FAITH STEP: *Write C. T. Studd's quote on a note card or your screen saver. Ask Jesus to help you determine how to best invest your time, energy, and resources into what is eternal.*

THURSDAY, JULY 3

Jesus Christ is the same yesterday and today and forever.
Hebrews 13:8 (NIV)

WHEN WE MOVED INTO OUR little town 16 years ago, I loved everything about it: the small beach, the new park, the full-service gas station. I couldn't understand why my neighbor was always

254 | MORNINGS WITH JESUS 2025

complaining about it. Turns out, there were only 600 residents when he moved here as a kid. A lot has changed to accommodate the current population of 15,592. Something recently happened to help me understand where he's coming from.

When I went to the full-service gas station the other day, I was shocked to find it's now self-serve! I don't mind pumping my own gas. It's more the fact that it's a major cultural shift that's not for the better. Everyone in town went to that station and chatted with the attendants. It felt like "the good old days" and a little bit like the town of Mayberry from *The Andy Griffith Show.* The change feels like the end of an era, and it's unsettling.

It brings me an immense amount of comfort to know that Jesus never changes. He's the same yesterday, today, and tomorrow, no matter what happens in my small town or the big world. As the landscape continues to change and I don't recognize where I live anymore, I need not complain because Jesus is always the same. He's the full-service Attendant who'll fill my heart with whatever I need to cruise through life with security and peace.
—CLAIRE MCGARRY

FAITH STEP: *The next time you're filling your tank with gas, imagine it's Jesus filling your soul with everything you need.*

INDEPENDENCE DAY, FRIDAY, JULY 4

It is for freedom that Christ has set us free. Stand firm, then, and do not let yourselves be burdened again by a yoke of slavery. Galatians 5:1 (NIV)

THE FOURTH OF JULY HAS always been one of my favorite holidays. I love the parades, the patriotic songs, the beautiful fireworks, and the delicious food. But nothing prepared me for the Fourth of July in our new neighborhood. The first thing that surprised me was that people shot off full-sized fireworks from the comfort of their driveways. The displays were phenomenal and deafening. One of our neighbors, who had served in the military, had someone play the national anthem on the trumpet and we joined in.

Then my family took a walk behind our subdivision. There is an irrigation canal with a path running alongside it that gives a great view of the entire Treasure Valley here in Idaho. We stood up on the path and watched as hundreds of fireworks displays illuminated the skies around the valleys, each city's beautiful show. It was awe-inspiring. Freedom is like that. We all want to be free.

Jesus is the one who truly set me free. Because He gave His life for me, I don't have to be trapped anymore—trapped in sin, temptation, and separation from Him. His gift of righteousness flung open the door to a different way of living. He offers me a new life of purpose and hope. I have a new life in Him. Now that is something awe-inspiring and really worth celebrating! —SUSANNA FOTH AUGHTMON

FAITH STEP: *As you celebrate our nation's freedom today, take time to thank Jesus for forgiving your sins and setting you free.*

SATURDAY, JULY 5

The eye cannot say to the hand, "I don't need you!" And the head cannot say to the feet, "I don't need you!" On the contrary, those parts of the body that seem to be weaker are indispensable. 1 Corinthians 12:21–22 (NIV)

NEW FRIENDS OFTEN ASK ME what kind of work our two grown children do. When I tell them that our son is a supervisor in a university library, I hear a wee note of pride in my voice. But I've noticed that my voice isn't as chipper when I tell people our daughter is a supermarket clerk. As if overseeing a group of student workers is more important than helping people feed their families.

Jesus, forgive me. Because You, of all people, understand what our daughter experiences as she serves the public. You made wine for whiners at a wedding

(John 2:7–10), multiplied a meal for a mob (Mark 6:41–42), and healed a horde of heathens (Luke 4:40).

Who am I to make distinctions based on someone's choice of a career? That's not Your way, Jesus. You value each individual based on the fact that they're fashioned in God's image, therefore worthy of respect. Regardless of the job they do (Acts 10:34–35).

From now on, Lord, when someone asks what type of work my kids do, I'll say, "One works in a big building helping people find information; the other works in a big building and helps people find lightbulbs and ice cream. I'm very proud of them both." —Jeanette Levellie

Faith Step: *Think of two very different careers and how each of them is essential. Then thank Jesus for the unique talents He's given you.*

SUNDAY, JULY 6

And let us run with endurance the race God has set before us. We do this by keeping our eyes on Jesus, the champion who initiates and perfects our faith.
Hebrews 12:1–2 (NLT)

I NORMALLY JOG 2 TO 4 MILES a day. I seldom do any other exercise, but last week, I decided to go for a bike ride instead. I hopped on my bike, intending to ride with vigor to burn some calories. Honestly, I expected it to be easier than running. Boy, was I wrong!

I set off, pedals pumping furiously, chugging along. About halfway through the ride, my legs were burning and the sweat was pouring off me, but I still had to make it home. I mustered my mental energy, along with a little bit of ego, to keep myself going. I prayed aloud for Jesus to strengthen me.

Glancing ahead, even the slightest rise looked like Mount Everest. I redoubled my focus, praying, visualizing the route, redirecting my thoughts, looking at the scenery, and remembering where I was headed. Eventually I made it home, relieved and pleased with myself.

Life can be like that. We embark on journeys not knowing what it will cost us or how hard it will be. Sometimes, the routine challenges of living can wear me out and make me wonder if I'll be able to make it. Overwhelmed or weak, I cry out to Jesus for help and strength. Just like my difficult bike ride, the solution is the same. I need to keep my eyes on Jesus and the goal, praying and enjoying the scenery along the way. —ISABELLA CAMPOLATTARO

FAITH STEP: *Are you dealing with an especially arduous challenge right now? Visualize your goal, turning your thoughts to Jesus and praying.*

MONDAY, JULY 7

And call on me in the day of trouble; I will deliver you,
and you will honor me. Psalm 50:15 (NIV)

AT A PARK IN ALBANY, Oregon, a travel writer
erected something called a Telephone in the Wind.
Attached to a post is an old-fashioned rotary-dial
phone, the kind with the long corkscrew cord from
days gone by. Beside it, a sign explains the phone's
purpose. "This phone is for everyone who has lost
a loved one. The phone is an outlet for those who
have messages they wish to share with their lost
friends and family. It is a phone for memories and
saying the goodbyes you never got to say."

Many of us have lost someone dear when they've
moved away, moved on to heaven, or when the relationship cooled over a disagreement or misunder-
standing. To have that chance to stand at a phone
and speak the words "I love you" or "I'm sorry" one
last time could help heal a deep pain.

This park phone reminds me of the loved ones
Jesus has blessed me with and the importance of
maintaining those relationships. Jesus taught the true
meaning of the words *love* and *forgiveness* so I can be
there for loved ones, willing to listen no matter what
they say, whether they're silly or angry or sad.

And I remember my best friend, Jesus. The most
satisfying communication I can experience is in prayer

with Him. I don't need to drive to a park and reach for a special phone to talk to Him. His line—and His heart—is always waiting for my calls. —HEIDI GAUL

FAITH STEP: *Reconnect with friends you've lost contact with. Rejoice in your relationship.*

TUESDAY, JULY 8

Let the redeemed of the LORD say so . . . Psalm 107:2 (KJV)

A WOMAN AT CHURCH HAS been in a wheelchair for years. When her husband pulls close to the building so she can power-wheel herself into church, it's only moments before this gracious, quirky woman with a deep and charming Southern accent is surrounded by children. She's at their eye level. They gather around her because she has extended them her love and care, her interest in their stories, her humor, and her devotion to Jesus.

Most days, pain is as constant a companion as her Savior. But she ministers from where she is to those she can reach. I only know some of the details of her life before her wheelchair. This Sunday, I learned a little more. She said, "Someday, I'll have to tell my whole story. It's a hard one."

I noted the ache in her eyes, but I saw light there too—the light of Jesus that cannot be dimmed despite what she's been through. "The hard stories," I said, "are the ones that last. Fluffy stories are easy for a listener to forget. The hard stories, those with redemption in the telling, are the ones that endure."

She looked toward heaven before answering, as if seeking Jesus's confirmation that her story was worth telling. When she lowered her gaze again, His peace was written all over her face.

"Hard stories are the ones that endure." The words had come out of my mouth, but I think they were as much for me as they were for her. Lord Jesus, help me seek Your perspective on every one of them. —CYNTHIA RUCHTI

FAITH STEP: *Share your redemption story with someone today. Seek Jesus's perspective before speaking the words.*

WEDNESDAY, JULY 9

And you will seek Me and find Me, when you search for Me with all your heart. Jeremiah 29:13 (NKJV)

"I HAVE TO LEARN THIS Bible verse, Grammy," Sadie said, shoving a yellow paper into my hand after vacation Bible school. "If I can say it tomorrow, I'll get a giant Hershey bar!"

My five-year-old granddaughter loved attending VBS at the old country church in our small community. The fun theme, "Destination Dig," taught kids about real-life archaeological finds in Israel that proved biblical events really happened. The candy contest helped them hide Jeremiah 29:13 in their hearts. And the simple motto pointed them to the Savior: "Seek truth! Find Jesus!"

On Sadie's yellow paper, I circled three action words—seek, find, search. With a little practice, she mastered the order of the actions and memorized the verse. She quoted it to her teacher the next day, easily winning the prize. Then, she shared her chocolaty reward with me.

The familiar words of Jeremiah 29:13 took on new energy for me as the week of VBS progressed. I contemplated the three action words. Seek... I committed my life to Jesus as a child and followed Him for decades, but did I seek Him daily as I should? Find... I felt secure in my relationship with Jesus, but did I fully appreciate the assurance and joy of that great find? Search... I sought Jesus by praying, reading the Bible, attending church, and serving, but did I engage my whole heart in the search?

You see, even grammies can learn a lot at vacation Bible school. —BECKY ALEXANDER

FAITH STEP: *Write the words of Jeremiah 29:13 on bright paper. Circle the action words, and pray about their role in your life.*

THURSDAY, JULY 10

Your ears shall hear a word behind you, saying, "This is the way, walk in it," whenever you turn to the right hand or whenever you turn to the left. Isaiah 30:21 (NKJV)

TWO OF MY BEST FRIENDS are a mother-daughter pair named Cheryl and Emily. We have been friends for decades and have shared many good times and bad: graduations, marriages, births of children and grandchildren, divorce, sickness, loss of loved ones— the normal heartaches and joys that make up a life. A few weeks ago, Cheryl had COVID-19 and Emily got some disturbing news at a routine checkup. Two spots showed up in her lungs that concerned the doctor so much that she was immediately ordered to have further testing and a follow-up appointment with an oncologist.

I have been walking with Jesus a long time now, and I'm in such constant contact that I can't say I did any kind of formal praying. I was beside myself with worry since Cheryl couldn't be with Emily when a question for Jesus arose in my spirit. *What do I need to do?* And before the question was even fully formed the answer came: Go. So I drove almost 2 hours to meet Emily at the oncologist's office. And I went home with her after and stayed for dinner and a visit. This is something I might have done anyway even without Jesus's urging, but that day I realized I always need to ask for His guidance and wait for Him to tell me, "This is the way, walk in it." —GWEN FORD FAULKENBERRY

FAITH STEP: *Set a timer for 5 minutes and ask Jesus, "What do I need to do today?" When you know the answer, step out in faith and obedience.*

FRIDAY, JULY 11

Be hospitable to one another without grumbling.
1 Peter 4:9 (NKJV)

I HUSTLED ACROSS THE MEDICAL office waiting room, anxious to get on with my errands. "Joyce, is that you?"

The voice came from a man in the corner. Since we were the only two people there, I assumed he was talking to me.

"No, I'm not Joyce," I said.

The man asked me if I was *sure* I wasn't Joyce because I looked just like her! *Jesus, I don't have time for this.* I replied I was sure and headed for the door.

Before I could escape, he asked if I'd grown up in Katy.

I responded, not very cordially, that I'd grown up in Orange.

He told me I looked enough like Joyce to be her twin, and he beckoned me over to see a picture of her he had on his phone.

This was getting ridiculous. *Jesus, do I really need to look at this stranger's pictures?*

As I drew nearer, I noticed the man's pallor, his frailty. I'd been here for a checkup, but he looked very ill. I sat beside him while he scrolled through his phone. He couldn't find Joyce's picture, but he hoped he'd see her at their upcoming fiftieth high school reunion, if he lived that long.

Softening, I asked him if Joyce was cute.

He assured me Joyce was adorable! A cheerleader. Had I been one?

He laughed when I said I was a klutz.

Just then, the nurse called the man, and as he rose painfully and shuffled toward her, he said, "See ya, Joyce." I gave him a thumbs-up.

Thank You, Jesus, for making me take the time.
—Pat Butler Dyson

FAITH STEP: *Ask Jesus to place a lonely person in your path. Engage them, cheerfully!*

SATURDAY, JULY 12

Even there Your hand shall lead me, and Your right hand shall hold me. Psalm 139:10 (NKJV)

MY TWELVE-YEAR-OLD DAUGHTER POINTED TO the brightly colored wheel standing 100 feet into the sky on Gillian's Wonderland Pier in Ocean City, New Jersey. She pleaded with me to ride, but I declined as always. Ana's smile faded. The ride was one of her favorites, but I was afraid of heights. I'd tried to ride years earlier, but when I was that high in the sky, I gripped the rickety cage with both hands and prayed that Jesus would get me through. I disliked disappointing my daughter, but what could I do?

"Let's go to the bumper cars," I suggested. We hustled to their location, as those were *my* favorite. Bumping around the enclosure, Ana and I howled with delight, chasing and crashing into each other around the track. Disembarking, we walked down the ramp. "Remember how scared I was the first time?" Ana said with a laugh. I nodded. "We sat together and I had one hand on the wheel and you squeezed my other hand. I loved sharing my ride with you!"

Just then, a knowing bumped through my heart. I pulled my girl into a side hug. "Promise to hold my hand if we go on *your* favorite ride?" With one hand in Ana's and my other hand in Jesus's, I was able to share my daughter's favorite ride. My fear didn't leave, but with Ana and Jesus holding my hands, I made it through. —GLORIA JOYCE

FAITH STEP: *What fear is keeping you from connecting with someone you love? Envision Jesus holding out His hand to give you courage, then write down steps to move past your fear.*

SUNDAY, JULY 13

Commit your way to the Lord [roll and repose each care of your load on Him]; trust (lean on, rely on, and be confident) also in Him and He will bring it to pass. Psalm 37:5 (AMPC)

MY GUINEA FOWL ARE THE size of pheasants and are supposed to taste as good. We wouldn't know because we keep them to work. They kill rattlesnakes and eat all the ticks without destroying the garden. Keeping our guineas fed in winter is the hard part. Their high-protein feed comes in 40-pound bags. At the farm store, I can tip the bag off the shelf and into the cart, letting gravity do the work. An employee cheerfully loads it into my car. But once I'm home, it's beyond my strength to carry the feed 50 yards to their pen.

In all kinds of weather, my old ice-fishing sled makes the job easy enough that I don't need help. I position the sled behind my old station wagon and roll the feed bag into it. Once it is in the sled, a child could pull it.

The Hebrew word for *roll* is *galal*, meaning to commit or trust. When I roll that feed bag, there's a "teetering" moment when the outcome is certain, but it just hasn't happened yet. Every time I roll a feed bag, I think of my commitment to Jesus. With Him, my outcome is certain, no matter how much teetering there is in my spiritual life.

Just as my guineas trust me to provide food in summer and winter, so must I trust Jesus in all seasons. —SUZANNE DAVENPORT TIETJEN

FAITH STEP: *Do you have a burden today? Imagine yourself rolling it into the arms of Jesus as you pray. Release the weight of it to Him.*

MONDAY, JULY 14

Be still, and know that I am God; I will be exalted among the nations, I will be exalted in the earth!
Psalm 46:10 (NKJV)

THE DAY AFTER MY FAMILY and I visited the Grand Canyon on a summer road trip, we drove to Yuma, Arizona, to spend an afternoon with my husband's relatives. I was so enamored with the distant mountains and thorny vegetation that I almost missed the large wooden sign that hugged the side of the road on a sparse stretch of US 95. Its bold message—"Pause, Rest, Worship"—was like an oasis in the middle of the desert, and I craned my neck to see more as we flew by in our rented minivan. "We need to turn around!" I shouted and convinced my husband to go exploring. To my delight, the sign led us to a beautiful, one-room tiny church that stood strong and sure in the middle of a desolate field.

Hot pink blooms exploded from the shrubs in front, the only color in a sea of browns and grays. Inside, light poured in from small windows, illuminating a simple pulpit and six miniature pews. The entire church was barely 100 square feet, but it was the perfect size for our family of six to pause, rest, and worship Jesus, just as the road sign invited us to do.

After we left, I realized that the invitation followed me. I repeatedly felt the familiar longing to slow down and acknowledge Jesus, even in the least likely of places—the airport, the grocery store, the laundry room. That tiny church in the middle of the desert reminded me that Jesus can be worshipped anywhere. —EMILY E. RYAN

FAITH STEP: *Find an unlikely place to pause, rest, and worship Jesus today.*

TUESDAY, JULY 15

*A fierce storm came up. . . . When Jesus woke up, he rebuked
the wind and said to the waves, "Silence! Be still!"
Suddenly the wind stopped, and there was a great calm.*
Mark 4:37, 39 *(NLT)*

WHAT FIELD OF LEARNING WOULD you study if
you had time and resources to pursue it? Meteorol-
ogy would be at the top of my list. I'm fascinated by
tornadoes, waterspouts, tsunamis, comets, and all
aspects of the atmosphere and weather.

I've never lived on a coast, where tsunamis or hurricanes are threats. But I've lived in the Midwest and the
Ozarks, regions known for tornadoes.

For many years, I've heard the blare of a tornado siren. When I was younger, those warnings
were scary. Truth be told, there are times now when
a tornado warning doesn't faze me as it probably
should. I've usually had the blessing of being able
to find safety in a basement or storm shelter. One
time, however, my husband, kids, and I survived
in a closet while an EF2 tornado passed right over
our house. That experience reminded me that natural forces can cause destruction in immeasurable
ways—a sobering reality.

Nature's forces also remind me of the power of Jesus.
They put me in awe of Him, who is even mightier
than the strongest tornado or hurricane. I wouldn't

wish a natural disaster on anyone, but they awaken me to the One who can create life from destruction.

I'm sure we would all love for Jesus to prevent storms in our lives, both big and little. But even when He doesn't, Jesus remains sovereign over each tumult and whirlwind.

The best study I can undertake centers on Jesus and His loving power. It is Jesus who, regardless of the weather or atmosphere, is greater and higher above all. —ERIN KEELEY MARSHALL

FAITH STEP: *Next time a storm hits your area, thank Jesus for being the most powerful force in your life. (And find safety!)*

WEDNESDAY, JULY 16

The LORD your God is with you, the Mighty Warrior who saves. He will take great delight in you; in his love he will no longer rebuke you, but will rejoice over you with singing. Zephaniah 3:17 (NIV)

MY FRIENDS AND I WERE shopping on their yearly visit to my hometown, a tourist destination in Amish country. I bought a floral journal to support a local merchant, knowing I would need a new one the following year. I tucked it away when our weekend ended and didn't think much about it.

Months later, another friend and I were sharing our faith journeys. I confided struggling with some heartaches

I was carrying for my family. Bonnie responded by praying that God would show me His delight in me.

The word *delight* intrigued me. I sure didn't feel delighted in the situation. It felt heavy and hard. What did delight even mean? I imagined playing with my grandsons, who are toddlers. They brought me delight! I pictured Jesus having similar joy as He interacted with me, but my current burdens made it a fleeting vision.

The idea of delight prompted me to start a gratitude journal to focus on the Lord's goodness rather than my sadness. I found and unwrapped the journal I'd bought months earlier. On the cover was, "The Lord delights in you."

I giggled to myself. *Was Jesus engaging with me as I do with my grandsons?* I felt Him smile as I opened the journal and started a daily discipline of making gratitude lists. —BRENDA L. YODER

FAITH STEP: *Intentionally create experiences that foster gratitude and delight. Notice how it changes your relationship with Jesus.*

THURSDAY, JULY 17

Will You not revive us and bring us to life again, that Your people may rejoice in You? Psalm 85:6 (AMP)

THOUGH I LIVE IN AN area favored by anglers and fly fishermen, I know virtually nothing about fishing. My idea of a fresh fish dinner is fish and chips from the neighborhood burger joint. Nevertheless, I identify with fish. And not just because a well-meaning friend once awkwardly described a much younger, slimmer version of me as "sleek as a trout." No, my new revelation came to me when I discovered a map of local fishing holes posted outside our town's parks-and-rec building.

There I saw, for the first time, instructions on "How to Revive a Fish." Never having heard of such a thing before, I was intrigued. The first-aid protocol for reviving a fish is to hold the fish upright in water facing upstream so water runs through its gills. This newfound knowledge that a fish could be revived by the cleansing stream of river water illustrates how Jesus revives me when I place myself in the cleansing stream of His Word.

When I'm feeling spiritually lifeless, if I read the Bible, I'm breathing in the spiritual oxygen I need to keep swimming in the river of life. I may not have gills, but, like a trout worn out from fighting for its life, I, too, experience revival in the Lord's cleansing stream. God's Word—the Living Water of Jesus—runs through my heart, mind, and spirit to revive me and bring me to life again. —CASSANDRA TIERSMA

FAITH STEP: *While showering today, breathe deeply as you focus on the water running over your body. Feel yourself being revived. Rejoice in the Lord's restorative, life-giving power in you and your life.*

FRIDAY, JULY 18

For you were once darkness, but now you are light in the Lord. Live as children of light. Ephesians 5:8 (NIV)

"I'M GOING UP THE COUNTRY to help Randy install his water heater," my husband, Jeff, told me early that morning.

"What can go wrong?" I asked, and Jeff cackled. He and his friend Randy undertook multiple projects and often they hit snags—needing more parts, taking more time than they had anticipated, sometimes having to totally abandon the venture.

I wasn't trying to be humorous. Jeff and Randy's history with projects made me pessimistic about the success of this one.

If there is a pessimism gene, I'd inherited it. My dad was a good husband and father, honest and kind, but if ever there was a glass-half-empty person, it was Dad. His thinking, which my brothers and I adopted, was that if you expect the worst, the outcome is likely to be better than you had anticipated.

Then I married Jeff. If there ever was a glass-half-full person, it's Jeff. For over 41 years, Jeff's been working on me, remolding me and reshaping my negative thinking. He cheers me up when I'm down in the dumps. He turns my nos into yeses. He points out the hopeful when I am feeling hopeless. Jeff models Jesus to me.

Despite the way I was raised, I must rein in my pessimism. I've found that the more I immerse myself in the Word and spend quiet time with Jesus, the less likely I am to feel downhearted. Above all things, Jesus offers hope, even to a (former) pessimist like me. —PAT BUTLER DYSON

FAITH STEP: *When you are feeling down, make a list of five hopeful things that have happened in your life recently. Thank Jesus for these blessings.*

SATURDAY, JULY 19

You have searched me, LORD, and you know me. You know when I sit and when I rise; you perceive my thoughts from afar. Psalm 139:1–2 (NIV)

MY HUSBAND, HAL, AND I traveled to Kansas City to attend the wedding of our niece Amani. It was a lovely outdoor ceremony on the grounds of an art museum followed by dinner in a beautiful indoor courtyard. As we gathered to pick up our table seating cards before the meal, there was lots of chatter. When I got my card, I realized what all the buzz was about. On the seating card for each of the more than one hundred guests, the bridal couple had taken the time to write something about them.

Under my name were the words, "Wise wordsmith, generous and faithful, an elegant class act." Wow. I was touched and flattered. Those few words on each guest's card certainly made them feel special.

Amani knows me from her observations and the interactions we've had over the years. But nobody knows me better than Jesus. He knew me before I was born and still inside my mother's womb. He knows all my likes and dislikes, my deepest and darkest secrets, and the desires of my heart. He is aware of my strengths and weaknesses and the things I've done wrong that I have yet to confess. Because He is the God who sees me, He knows me very well. Because I believe in Him, He accepts me as a part of His royal family.

If there are table cards in heaven, I wonder what Jesus will say about me? I can't wait to see.
—BARBRANDA LUMPKINS WALLS

FAITH STEP: *How well do you know Jesus? Consider making Him a table card with words that describe Him. Put it somewhere you will see it often.*

SUNDAY, JULY 20

Then the LORD answered me and said: "Write the vision and make it plain on tablets, that he may run who reads it." Habakkuk 2:2 (NKJV)

A MAGNETIC DRY-ERASE CALENDAR IS stuck to the front of my refrigerator. On Sunday evenings, I transfer appointments from my phone to the fridge, filling the week with activity: babysitting, professional meetings, doctor visits, deadlines. I like to see my week at a glance.

Most weeks are filled with multiple commitments scribbled in each day's block. As I take in my weekly schedule, I realize many voices have input into my calendar. My husband and daughters, my colleagues, sometimes doctors or a repairman, and me.

I wonder how different my days would look if I allowed Jesus's voice to shape my agenda. What if I started each morning asking, "What can I do for You today? Do You have something You'd like me to do for someone?" What would He add to my calendar? What would Jesus delete?

Maybe I would visit a friend recovering from surgery instead of sending a text to say I'm thinking of her. Perhaps I would reschedule my hair appointment so I could attend a women's Bible study since I missed last week too. I think Jesus might like it if I'd mention Him when I meet with my quilting companions for a sit and sew.

One thing is certain about whatever is written on my calendar. As Habakkuk says, I'll be running through my week. Why not take Jesus along with me? —KAREN SARGENT

FAITH STEP: *Look at your calendar for the week. Ask Jesus what you can do for Him and pencil it in.*

MONDAY, JULY 21

Give thanks to the LORD, for he is good; his love endures forever. Psalm 107:1 (NIV)

I FREQUENTLY SCROLL THROUGH INSTAGRAM admiring the funniest animal photos of the year, award-winning landscape shots, amazing underwater images, and other pictures that fill my feed. I marvel at the beautiful images. In college I took photography classes and I wish I had kept up with it because it's a creative way of capturing God's glory in the world.

Recently, a friend mentioned he takes a photo every day and saves it in a gratitude album on his phone. This novel idea grabbed my attention. Research shows gratitude helps people feel happier, relish good moments, improve health, handle adversity better, and build stronger relationships. For many years, I've kept a gratitude journal as a practice for remembering and expressing my thankfulness to Jesus, who gave His life for me, provides new mercies every day, and loves me unconditionally. A photo album capturing and recording daily pictures I took would be a meaningful way for me to further express my thankfulness to Him. I started making it a part of my gratitude practice too.

So, every day I pray my eyes will be opened to see Jesus's goodness, and I record that moment with a visual memory. As I scroll through my gratitude photos, I have a picture-perfect reminder of all I am grateful for. —JEANNIE BLACKMER

FAITH STEP: *Today, snap a photo of someone or something for which you are grateful. Before going to sleep, look at that picture again and thank Jesus.*

TUESDAY, JULY 22

Peace I leave with you; my peace I give you. I do not give to you as the world gives. Do not let your hearts be troubled and do not be afraid. John 14:27 (NIV)

RECENTLY, MY HUSBAND AND I followed a trail through meadows and forested land. Our goal was to reach the top of Marys Peak, the highest mountain in Oregon's Coast Range. The trail we hiked proved easy and wide enough for us to walk side by side. We stopped several times to enjoy the scenery. Fog rolled in almost as quickly as we climbed, and our concern grew. What could we possibly see from the top?

The answer came to us as we reached the summit. A panorama as soft and elegant as down, as stunning and magnificent as the soaring of an eagle. We were on top of the world. Our view from above the clouds continued as far as our eyes could see. Mile after mile of undulating whiteness hid the busyness and the stark reality of our workaday world. Sounds were muffled in the fog we'd risen above. It was as if Jesus had wrapped all of our cares in cotton batting.

Jesus doesn't need mountaintops and cloud cover to connect with us. His peace is available every day, no matter what circumstances we encounter. His touch can be as sublime as the panorama atop a peak or as simple as a sigh when I read a familiar Bible verse. He speaks to me in ways I can hear Him, often without words. —HEIDI GAUL

FAITH STEP: *Take a nature hike or stroll around a park. Listen for the different ways Jesus speaks to you through nature, and let His peace wash over you.*

WEDNESDAY, JULY 23

Because he himself suffered when he was tempted, he is able to help those who are being tempted. Hebrews 2:18 (NIV)

THE CHURCH SERVICE HAD BARELY begun when I felt my phone vibrate in my back pocket. Annoyed that a notification alert was interrupting the moment of worship, I checked it quickly to make sure no one in my family needed me. They didn't. Instead, the notification read: "*Totally not spam* would like to share a photo." I rolled my eyes and ignored it. There was no way I was accepting photos from a strange account. Who knows what I would find if I did?

But a few minutes later, a second alert came through. "*Totally not spam* would like to share a photo." Someone in the church service was sending this request. I scanned the auditorium, looking for anyone who was on his phone instead of singing along with the praise band, but no one looked suspicious. I ignored the alert again but struggled to keep my mind on Jesus after that. I was so curious. Who was sending this request? What photo did they want me to see? And why was the urge to accept the request so strong even though I knew that *Totally not spam* was most certainly a spam account?

This is what temptation feels like, I realized. I knew what was right, but I still felt the desire to satisfy my curiosity. I thought about Jesus and His promise to help those who are being tempted by providing a way of escape (1 Corinthians 10:13). With a prayer of thanks, I turned off my phone, buried it in my purse, and began worshipping Jesus again. —EMILY E. RYAN

FAITH STEP: *Next time you feel temptation growing stronger, begin worshipping Jesus.*

THURSDAY, JULY 24

God is not a man, so he does not lie. He is not human, so he does not change his mind. Has he ever spoken and failed to act? Has he ever promised and not carried it through?
Numbers 23:19 (NLT)

ONE OF THE GUIDING BUSINESS principles I have lived by is to underpromise and overdeliver. I learned it early on from executives at a firm I worked for when I was a young professional. Colleagues, family members, and friends have always told me how reliable I am. But lately, I've felt as if I have been overpromising and underdelivering.

It's frustrating saying one thing and doing another, especially since I am usually known for following through on my word. In an attempt to understand what's different, I've discovered I've stopped certain practices such as creating a realistic schedule, clearly laying out plans, limiting interruptions while working, and making helpful checklists. These essential elements are what made me reliable in the first place.

Sometimes when I face adversity, I step away from my basic practices and routines. When Jesus faced adversity, he consistently followed after what was most essential: seeking God the Father in prayer. Because Jesus spent time doing what was most important to His work, the disciples and all of those who needed Him could always count on Him to be true to His Word. Jesus is always reliable. When He promises, He delivers! —ERICKA LOYNES

FAITH STEP: *What promises do you still need to fulfill? Choose one and ask Jesus to help you make good on it today.*

FRIDAY, JULY 25

How, then, can they call on the one they have not believed in? And how can they believe in the one of whom they have not heard? And how can they hear without someone preaching to them? Romans 10:14 (NIV)

RECENTLY, MY HUSBAND, JOHN, GOT hearing aids. After turning them on, John's eyes widened as he realized all he'd been missing out on. John lost much of his hearing in the military and didn't know how muted his world was until a hearing test pointed it out.

Sometimes it's easy to take hearing for granted. The same is true when it comes to hearing the Gospel. The Gospel is good news about all Jesus accomplished to give us eternal life. To have any response, we must first hear about it. We must understand our sins and acknowledge Jesus's death on our behalf. Only then can we become Jesus's redeemed and beloved children. While hearing is not enough, it is the first step toward belief and repentance.

Just as John realized how much he was missing only after his hearing was restored, I didn't understand what I'd been missing out on until the truth met my ears and I genuinely heard Jesus's message about His love for me and the eternal life He offered. It's essential I not take my hearing for granted physically and spiritually.

I guess John wasn't the only one needing to hear more clearly. I realized that I sometimes need to tune my spiritual ears to hear Jesus more clearly. —TRICIA GOYER

FAITH STEP: *How is your spiritual hearing? Sit quietly for 10 minutes. Listen closely to what Jesus wants you to hear, then write it down.*

SATURDAY, JULY 26

And behold, the glory of the God of Israel came from the way of the east. His voice was like the sound of many waters; and the earth shone with His glory. Ezekiel 43:2 (NKJV)

ALTHOUGH THE RIVER BEHIND OUR rented cabin was called Stillwater Creek, the water was anything but tranquil. A tributary of the Yellowstone River in Montana, it is famous for being a great fishery, with plentiful rainbow and brown trout. Stillwater is truly *wild* in places, with white water and huge boulders and drops. Again, it's hardly "still."

We could hear the roar of the river from the moment we turned off the car in front of the cabin. A few minutes later, while unpacking groceries in the kitchen, I wondered whether the sound of the thundering current would keep us from getting to sleep. It reminded me of the verse in Ezekiel that says God's voice was like the sound of "many waters." This river, like God's voice, was resoundingly loud but somehow calming. Constant, bold, powerful.

At the end of every day, after riding horses or hiking or trying our hands at fly-fishing, my family and I slept soundly in that house. But I knew our good rest was not only due to physical exhaustion. The sound of that flowing water was like God's voice promising comfort and rest whenever we needed it.
—Jennifer Grant

Faith Step: *Today, play a short video and listen to the sounds of the ocean or a rushing river. Close your eyes as you listen to it, imagining you are hearing God's voice as He promises you comfort and rest.*

SUNDAY, JULY 27

For where two or three are gathered together in My name, I am there in the midst of them. Matthew 18:20 (NKJV)

A SPECIAL STORY FROM MY family tree occurred at a summer picnic in 1916. Friends and family rode in horse-drawn carriages to a favorite spot in the woods. While the adults spread blankets on the grass and unloaded food baskets, the children skipped happily and played ball.

My great-aunt Treva, only five at the time, ran to visit one of the horses. Just as she raised her arm to pet him, he squealed and opened his massive mouth. Before she could back away, the horse clamped his giant teeth on her little face.

A doctor in the crowd rushed to help her. He did his best to close Treva's gaping skin and clean the wound. Her parents held her still for the many stitches, though she screamed in pain. Her young brothers, traumatized by the scene, wept nearby. All the people formed a circle around Treva, grasped hands, and cried out to Jesus for a miracle.

Jesus answered their prayers, and Treva survived to bless others for 91 years. Occasionally, she brushed her fingers over her face and told me again how Jesus saved her life. I hardly noticed the scars. She was beautiful to me, inside and out.

Divine power flows when believers come together in prayer or worship or proclamation of the Word. Jesus graces us with His presence, listening to our pleas, our songs, and our sermons. I feel blessed that the stories of His faithfulness have been handed down in my family through generations. —BECKY ALEXANDER

FAITH STEP: *Think of a faith story when two or more gathered together to pray. Share it with someone in a younger generation.*

MONDAY, JULY 28

Do nothing from selfish ambition or conceit, but in humility count others more significant than yourselves.
Philippians 2:3 (ESV)

"GO, BRAVES!" I HOLLERED, AS I hung on the fence at the Little League baseball park. In the last inning of the playoff game, my grandson Winston's team, the Braves, were beating the Astros 8–7. And Winston was pitching!

As I nervously gripped my husband Jeff's arm, a mom wearing an Astros T-shirt came up behind me, invading my space, and shrieked, inches from my ear, "Kill it, Josh!" I turned and gave her a withering look, but she continued to yell while she shot a cell phone video over my shoulder. When Josh struck out, I jumped up and down, applauding loudly.

Jeff stared at me in disbelief. "Pat, you *clapped* when that kid struck out!"

"I wasn't clapping *because* he struck out," I retorted. "I was clapping *against* his rude mom and *for* the Braves." Jeff gave me a disgusted look. If he was that disappointed in me, I knew Jesus was crushed.

Little League baseball had made me a monster! When my sons were in Little League, I'd preached good sportsmanship to them, encouraging them to be humble, in victory or in defeat, thinking of other players' feelings. What a hypocrite I turned out to be!

The Braves won the game, but for me, the victory was tainted by guilt over my behavior. Little League baseball had not made me a monster; I'd made *myself* a monster! I tried to find Josh and his mom to apologize, but they were long gone. So I asked Jesus to forgive me and promised Him that in the future, I'd practice what I preached. —PAT BUTLER DYSON

FAITH STEP: *Read Philippians 2:3. It's good advice, in sports or in life.*

TUESDAY, JULY 29

We are hard pressed on every side, but not crushed; perplexed, but not in despair; persecuted, but not abandoned; struck down, but not destroyed. We always carry around in our body the death of Jesus, so that the life of Jesus may also be revealed in our body. 2 Corinthians 4:8–10 (NIV)

A SOON-TO-BE YOUNG ADULT GRANDSON and I were having a conversation about serious issues—grave disappointments he'd experienced and a habit or two he wanted to kick. "Yeah, about that, Grandma. I'm gonna wait to deal with it until I'm not broken."

Behind his words lay so much more—distress far more serious than the fractured wrist he was nursing.

It was a privilege to gently assure him that we don't ever have to wait until we're not broken to invite Jesus to help us with whatever the need. It's a truth I cling to with deep gratitude. Jesus never asks us to heal first before we dare ask for His healing, to scrub our souls before we ask for His cleansing, to hose off our feet before coming to Him for a soul-changing foot washing.

And He never says, "Figure it out the best you can first before you seek My wisdom." For Jesus, it's never an inopportune time for His intervention. After all, He gave me a brain. But He also gives me an invitation to seek Him. Why would I spend a minute trying to solve any problem if I haven't consulted Jesus as the first order of business?

If I "wait to deal with it until I'm not broken," I've simply prolonged the pain, exacerbated the distress, and let the bad habit dig deeper. From my experience, the best time to deal with brokenness is now. —CYNTHIA RUCHTI

FAITH STEP: *Find the above passage in your Bible. Insert a sticky note and write on it the concern you think you need to figure out before bothering Jesus with it.*

WEDNESDAY, JULY 30

Cast all your anxiety on him because he cares for you.
1 Peter 5:7 (NIV)

ONE SUNDAY AFTER SERVICE, I mentioned to Eva June, a friend from church, that my favorite bumper sticker read "Jesus Cares." Several Sundays later, she brought me a sign she'd made. In pink needlepoint on a white background, she'd stitched "Jesus Cares." Neither Eva June nor I had any idea of how that thoughtful little gift would change my world.

Every morning as I pace and pray in my bedroom, I look over at Eva June's needlepoint sign dozens of times. I whine to the Lord that the healing I'd asked for hasn't arrived yet and I'm still in pain. *Jesus cares.* I remind Him that I've prayed for a certain relative for decades and they don't seem any closer to making a decision to follow Him. *Jesus cares.* I tell Jesus that we need to buy a house this year because we're not getting any younger and if we wait much longer the bank won't loan us money. Can you please make Kevin agree to buy a house since we can't live in a parsonage all our lives? *Jesus cares.*

No matter what challenge I bring to the Lord, no matter how impossible the situation appears to me, no matter how knotty the relationship, the answer remains the same: *Jesus cares.*

And it finally started to sink in. Jesus is a real person. He's not sitting on a golden throne in heaven watching me walk around my bedroom and worry. Because He cares, He will help. At last, I rest in Jesus's love. —JEANETTE LEVELLIE

FAITH STEP: *Say to Jesus, "Because You care for me, I give all my worries to You," and then rest in His love.*

THURSDAY, JULY 31

For I am convinced that neither death nor life, neither angels nor demons, neither the present nor the future, nor any powers, neither height nor depth, nor anything else in all creation, will be able to separate us from the love of God that is in Christ Jesus our Lord. Romans 8:38–39 (NIV)

KEEP CALM AND CARRY ON. How many times have we seen this popular phrase on memes, clothing, mugs, and home décor? The slogan originates from morale-building posters the British government printed during World War II but never circulated. Today, we have untold variations to replace the original ending, including *Knit On, Drink Tea, Hug a Tree, Call Batman.*

Choosing to keep calm is easier said than done. We all occasionally find ourselves sidetracked by sudden troubles. Staying calm is especially difficult for people who are emotional, prone to worry, and tend to overreact (I'm looking in the mirror here). I've always admired the Apostle Paul for his ability to seem cool and collected even when suffering unjust accusations, beatings, a shipwreck, and a lengthy imprisonment. Regardless of his circumstances, Paul revealed a deep assurance that absolutely nothing could ever separate him from Christ's unconditional, sacrificial, life-giving love.

One day I saw that familiar slogan and realized something: the Word was in the word. Now, whenever I see or read *calm*, I welcome the reminder that Christ Always Loves Me. The next time my emotions or my circumstances push my panic button, I'll choose the C.A.L.M. mode instead and carry on with Jesus. —DIANNE NEAL MATTHEWS

FAITH STEP: *Memorize today's verse and recite it once a day or as needed to make sure you're convinced that Jesus's ever-present love will never waver, no matter what happens.*

FRIDAY, AUGUST 1

And he directed the people to sit down on the grass. Taking the five loaves and the two fish and looking up to heaven, he gave thanks and broke the loaves. Then he gave them to the disciples, and the disciples gave them to the people.
Matthew 14:19 (NIV)

MY BACK'S BEEN GIVING ME TROUBLE. I'm doing all the right exercises and stretches to help. And I'm heeding the suggestions to work on my posture. In first grade, I had the honor of being named Posture Queen. That's the last time it was perfect. But I'm working on it.

Biblical postures for prayer and praise have fascinated me for some of the same reasons as spinal posture—pain relief (confessing what's hurting), greater flexibility and agility (pivoting when Jesus says to move), and putting the focus where it belongs (on the Healer). Bowed down. Hands raised. Eyes lifted toward heaven.

I've wondered, since heaven isn't a visible entity right now, if lifting my eyes to heaven was more symbolic than an important practice. Considering Jesus and His habits resolved that curiosity. No one knew more about being present with God the Father than Jesus did. The Son, perhaps as an example for us, visibly turned His focus and gaze to seek the face of the Father in prayer. Jesus prayed with His arms spread wide on the Cross (Luke 23:34), on His knees in the Garden of Gethsemane (Luke 22:41), and with His hands and face lifted to heaven before miraculously feeding 5,000-plus people. What an inspiring posture lesson. —CYNTHIA RUCHTI

FAITH STEP: *What's your preferred prayer posture? Consider choosing one of Jesus's prayer postures as you seek His face today.*

SATURDAY, AUGUST 2

I will be glad and rejoice in Your mercy and steadfast love, because You have seen my affliction, You have taken note of my life's distresses. Psalm 31:7 (AMPC)

I RECENTLY BOOKED A LAST-MINUTE, round-trip flight with horrible connections. Two were so tight that I missed one of them. During the other three seemingly endless layovers, I people-watched. Nearly everyone's eyes were on their screens. No one made eye contact with me or chatted with passengers who weren't in their party. The seats at the gate were full, yet I felt alone and invisible.

Then I heard a distressed traveler at the service desk exclaim, "I feel seen!" Someone must have listened to whatever her problem happened to be and fixed it. The traveler thanked the airline employee profusely.

The worker softly smiled. "Is there anything else I can do to help?" she asked.

"No. Thank you so much!"

Being seen, noticed, or understood is affirming, a welcome exception to being alone or feeling like a face in the crowd.

Jesus really saw people—the children His disciples were preventing from running to Him (Luke 18:16); the woman crippled by a spirit of infirmity (Luke 13:11–16); the man at the pool of Bethesda who couldn't get in the water (John 5:5–9); and the widow dropping her two tiny coins into the offering (Luke 21:2–3). Jesus didn't just physically see these people; He *noticed* them (Proverbs 15:3). No one is invisible, even today, when everyone is looking at their phone screens. —SUZANNE DAVENPORT TIETJEN

FAITH STEP: *Put down your phone and pay attention to the people Jesus puts in your path. See them. Notice them. Ask them how they're doing.*

SUNDAY, AUGUST 3

Before they call I will answer; while they are still speaking I will hear. Isaiah 65:24 (NIV)

As I sit rocking on the porch this morning, my mind is in turmoil. The neighborhood appears just as it always has. Neighbor boys play in the lane with their cardboard swords and foil-covered crowns, careful not to upset the invisible steeds only small children can see and mount. Clouds billow softly in the sky, as our resident squirrel, Dirty Harry, offers his warning bark to an imaginary enemy.

Like the others on my street, I'm fighting a private battle. Turbulent thoughts are stealing away my peace, stripping my awareness of blessings from the day. No one else knows about the disagreement I just had with a family member or the prayer request I'm repeating as often as the woman in the parable of the widow and the judge (Luke 18:1–5). I feel I'm alone in this struggle.

But I'm wrong. I'm never alone. Jesus knows. He sees the unseen, and He grieves with me, just as He grieves alongside my loved one. He knows the pain I'm experiencing despite my silence. He will help me work toward peace within and between the two of us, meshing and melding our differences until harmony once again reigns in our relationship. I can't see, hear, or touch it, but I sense He's at work inside me, leading my attitude away from being right toward being at peace.

I watch as a leaf skitters by along the asphalt just past our garden gate, on a breeze I can't even feel. And I understand. —HEIDI GAUL

FAITH STEP: *Write a list of challenges that are troubling you. For each entry, pray Jesus reveals the unseen ways He's working toward solutions.*

MONDAY, AUGUST 4

A heart at peace gives life to the body, but envy rots the bones. Proverbs 14:30 (NIV)

A PICTURE POSTED BY MY friend Mary Ann popped up in my Facebook feed. Her son, Noah, and daughter, Emma, were holding hands and skipping through a grocery store parking lot. The caption was true, judging from the huge smiles on their faces: "Pure joy." Had the photo been taken when her kids were in elementary school, I wouldn't have thought twice about it. But Noah and Emma were sixteen and eleven at the time. The same ages as my son and daughter, who, most certainly, had never held hands and skipped through a parking lot.

The second my heart started to warm at Noah and Emma's sweet display of sibling love, comparison attempted to snuff it out with doubts about my own children and their affection for each other. *Why haven't they held hands and skipped through parking lots? Do they love each other at all? Is our family not healthy? Am I failing as a mother?*

That's when Jesus interrupted my downward spiral. He reminded me that I was comparing a tiny moment in someone else's family to the entire story of my family. It wasn't an accurate comparison and, if left unchecked, could lead to jealousy and rob me of the joy I have in my own blessings. I looked at the picture of Noah and Emma again, this time with a clear heart. I thanked Jesus for the friendship they shared with each other and the friendships they had with my own kids. —EMILY E. RYAN

FAITH STEP: *Think of a time when comparison or jealousy popped up for you. Bring it to Jesus so envy won't rob you of the joy of your own blessings.*

TUESDAY, AUGUST 5

"For I know the plans I have for you," declares the LORD, "plans to prosper you and not to harm you, plans to give you hope and a future." Jeremiah 29:11 (NIV)

MY DAD LOVES TO TRAVEL. Some of his earliest childhood memories take place on board ships heading to and from India in the late 1940s and early 1950s. His parents were missionaries there. He has passed on his love for travel to his family. This summer, Dad will be taking my son Addison and my husband, Scott, on a trip to Italy.

I am the trip coordinator. I have been researching hotels, reading up on the beaches in Positano, and locating Neapolitan pizzerias. I've looked up tours of Pompeii and the Vatican. I am already a little jealous of all the gelato they will be eating. I chatted with Dad on the phone last night about the pros and cons of rental cars, trains, and ferry rides. I could sense his excitement in getting to share his love of the journey with Scott and Addie.

Jesus has invited me on an amazing journey of following Him. He knows exactly where He wants to take me, the experiences that He has prepared for me, and the friends He has for me along the way. I don't always understand where Jesus is taking me on the journey, but I know He has planned every step with love and care. He promises me a hope and future. And I will follow Him each step of the way.
—SUSANNA FOTH AUGHTMON

FAITH STEP: *Where are you in your journey of following Jesus today? Think of some of the places you have gone with Him and how His plan is for your good.*

WEDNESDAY, AUGUST 6

You shall not covet . . . anything that belongs to your neighbor. Deuteronomy 5:21 (NIV)

When my son Jake was in a 2-year physician assistant program, he bought a baby chameleon and named him Ollie. He also bought a terrarium, filled it with live plants, and installed a complicated misting system. Apparently, chameleons prefer drinking water dripping from leaves rather than from a bowl. Ollie's shades were vibrant and beautiful. He would change colors with circumstances. When threatened, he was the brightest. When calm, he blended more into his environment.

During this time, most of my friends' children were having babies, not raising exotic pets. When they shared their grandbaby pictures, I shared my "grand-chameleon" photos. When they talked about the difficulty of giving a new baby a bottle, I shared the difficulty of the chameleon's drinking preferences. Although I enjoyed their stories, inwardly I wished for grandchildren. I was coveting something my friends had. The Tenth Commandment is clear: "You shall not covet...anything that belongs to your neighbor." Although covet sounds extreme, synonyms for it are wish for, long for, or desire.

I needed to talk with Jesus. I honestly admitted my jealousy of my friends who had grandchildren. I felt sorrow for my lack of sharing in their joy and prayed Jesus would help me with a change of attitude. I wrote my prayer of confession in my journal. The next time my friends shared their joys of grandparenting and photos of grandchildren, I chose to listen and enjoy their stories. Like Ollie, I could change—not my colors, but my attitudes and actions, with the help of Jesus. —JEANNIE BLACKMER

FAITH STEP: *Write a prayer of confession to Jesus in your journal about something you wish you had. Pray for repentance and change.*

THURSDAY, AUGUST 7

No discipline seems pleasant at the time, but painful. Later on, however, it produces a harvest of righteousness and peace for those who have been trained by it. Hebrews 12:11 (NIV)

I NEGLECTED MY FLOWER BEDS, and now I regretted it. If I'd started pulling those little green sprouts when they broke through the soil last month, it wouldn't be so overwhelming. For at least 6 weeks, I'd been watching the weeds grow like, well, weeds. I berated myself for having put it off. I made excuses for myself. I'd been too busy. I was too tired. It was too hot. But was I really just lazy?

I haven't always been a procrastinator. Through the years, I've found clarity or heard from God when my fingers were in the dirt. So why did I *put off until tomorrow what I could do today* when it came to pulling weeds? I resolved to turn my *maybe later* slogan into *just do it*. I made a date with my spade for the next day.

Early the next morning, I pulled on my gardening gloves and carried my caddy to the far end of the flower bed. Praise music played over the outdoor speakers. Breathing in the fresh summer air renewed my mind and encouraged my soul. I actually felt *happy* doing the job I'd avoided and even dreaded for more than a month.

After a few hours, I marveled at the progress I'd made. I realized that I'd spent much more time procrastinating doing what I knew I should do than it actually took to accomplish it. Thank You, Jesus, for giving me discipline that overcomes procrastination in all areas of my life. —STEPHANIE THOMPSON

FAITH STEP: *Today, identify one task you've been avoiding and take one small step toward accomplishing it.*

FRIDAY, AUGUST 8

But you would be fed with the finest of wheat; with honey from the rock I would satisfy you. Psalm 81:16 (NIV)

ONE OF MY FAVORITE ASPECTS of beekeeping is harvesting the honey. Honey truly is a miraculous substance. It takes twelve bees their entire lifetime to make a teaspoon of honey. They visit fifty to one hundred flowers on their flights to gather nectar each day. Honey is not only a delicacy, but it also has all sorts of health benefits. It's used as an antidepressant, anticonvulsant, and antianxiety supplement. It's also been shown to help prevent memory disorders, heal wounds, and lessen allergy symptoms.

Did you know honey is mentioned sixty-one times in the Bible and is often associated with provision? Such as when God called Moses to lead the Israelites out of slavery into a land flowing with milk and honey (Exodus 3:8). And in Psalm 81:16, the Psalmist writes God feeds us with "the finest of wheat; with honey from the rock." I've never heard of honey being found in a rock, making this honey a miraculous provision. Perhaps this verse is a foreshadow of Jesus, our Rock, and connecting His sacrifice to God's unending provision in our lives.

Only God, in His creativity, proves His provision through a tiny, winged insect. And honey is not only healthy but also meant to delight the one who eats it—just as Jesus's sacrifice not only gives us eternal life but also pleasure in the here and now. Every time I enjoy a teaspoon of honey, I remember what a miraculous substance it is. Jesus provides my basic needs, but often His provision is meant to nourish and delight me. —JEANNIE BLACKMER

FAITH STEP: *While enjoying a cup of coffee or tea sweetened with honey, make a list of ways Jesus has abundantly provided for you.*

SATURDAY, AUGUST 9

All Scripture is God-breathed [given by divine inspiration] and is profitable for instruction, for conviction [of sin], for correction [of error and restoration to obedience], for training in righteousness [learning to live in conformity to God's will, both publicly and privately—behaving honorably with personal integrity and moral courage].
2 Timothy 3:16 (AMP)

I DON'T TALK A LOT when I'm in the theater watching movies, but when I'm at home watching television it's a different story. I'm extremely vocal, sometimes turning what would be an hour of pure entertainment into 2 hours of disruptive dialogue.

Images constantly rewind, freeze, or unfreeze on screen depending on the barrage of questions I ask my family and the advice I hurl at the characters who frustrate me: the detective who doesn't admit wrongdoing, the captain with selective memory, the wife who manipulates situations, the roommate who plays the victim card, or the government agent who is self-absorbed. If I could just get my hands on those scripts, I would rewrite scenes to fix their flaws, force them to make better decisions, or even replace the characters altogether to experience more palatable behaviors.

I'm glad Jesus doesn't respond to my behavior the same way I respond to the television characters'. Instead of rewriting scenes in my life to fix flaws, Jesus asks me to read His life-changing Word. Instead of forcing me to make better decisions, He invites me to choose His way. Instead of replacing me with someone, Jesus reminds me that I have a specific part to play in His kingdom and, when I follow His script, my behaviors will accurately reflect Jesus's character. —ERICKA LOYNES

FAITH STEP: *Meditate on 2 Timothy 3:16. Ask Jesus to shed light on any behaviors that don't line up with His Word.*

SUNDAY, AUGUST 10

For now we see only a reflection as in a mirror; then we shall see face to face. Now I know in part; then I shall know fully, even as I am fully known.
1 Corinthians 13:12 (NIV)

I STARED AT THE IMAGE in my bedroom's full-length mirror. Turning side to side, I checked my appearance from every view. This dress's waistband pinched. That top's fabric had pilled. Just how many different outfits had I tried on?

Most of the clothes in my closet had been there for years. Though nice, they'd begun to show their age and hung a tad soft on the hangers. I might as well have described myself. Then I wondered, *Where did that come from?* My negative attitude wasn't about having nothing to wear.

Once again, the mirror had deceived me. I'm more than a two-dimensional figure striving to look attractive. My true beauty, the part of me that Jesus cherishes, lies hidden within. Victor Hugo said, "There is one spectacle grander than the sea, that is the sky; there is one spectacle grander than the sky, that is the interior of the soul."

To consider the complexities of the human spirit, the nuances and mystery hidden beneath our skin, is fascinating. Yet when I think of what lies unknown and unseen in the heavens, in the universe, in the simple term *eternity,* I'm overwhelmed. To know Jesus fully, to be able to comprehend His endless goodness, for now, I can only imagine. But someday I'll know. And my joy will be as limitless as His love. —HEIDI GAUL

FAITH STEP: *Consider the flat, two-dimensional image reflected in a mirror. Compare it to the incomprehensible depth and breadth of what lies ahead when we meet Jesus. Give thanks.*

MONDAY, AUGUST 11

... for not the hearers of the law are just in the sight of God, but the doers of the law will be justified. Romans 2:13 (NKJV)

DO YOU REMEMBER WHEN YOU were assigned your first school locker? This rite of passage occurred in seventh grade for me. I secured a combination lock on the handle to prevent my peers from stealing my homework or stacking my books so they would tumble out when I opened the door. The lock, however, posed its own problems, specifically the combination to open it. I had to align three numbers just right to make the lock work. If I misaligned the numbers even a hair, the lock would not budge.

Proper alignment is vital in combination locks and in my walk with Jesus. Instead of three numbers, I must align my beliefs, my actions, and my heart.

I believe in helping those in need, so I cover the cost of church camp for a child. But if I find ways to drop my act of generosity into conversations, my heart is probably misaligned.

I believe in forgiveness. In my heart, I tell myself I forgave the person who emotionally devastated our family. But if I refuse to tell him face-to-face, my actions don't align.

Until recently, I haven't given the alignment of my beliefs, my actions, and my heart much thought. Intuitively, I get it right much of the time. But I also get misaligned, more than a hair sometimes. Whatever the deed, I need to think it, do it, and feel it the way Jesus modeled. He healed the leper in secret (Matthew 8:2–4). He forgave Peter's betrayal and gave him a new mission (John 21:15–17). Whenever I align with Jesus, I always hit the right combination. —KAREN SARGENT

FAITH STEP: *Journal about a time when your beliefs, actions, and heart didn't align with Jesus. List ways you can make them work together.*

TUESDAY, AUGUST 12

...Be careful to guard against all forms of greed, because even if someone is rich, his life does not consist in what he owns. Luke 12:15 (CJB)

I SORTED THROUGH MY CRAFT room yesterday and verified that I have more tatting shuttles than anyone could possibly need. I've collected them for years. If I find one in a secondhand store, I buy it. I tell myself I'm rescuing them. That I'll appreciate them in a world that doesn't remember what they are. Yes, I tat and use them sometimes, but that doesn't excuse me from always wanting more shuttles. And thread! I find myself looking online for spools of antique silk and linen thread to add to my more than sufficient stash. I enjoy the suspense of possibly being outbid on the auction site and I feel pleasure when I win. We aren't talking about a lot of money here, but I don't need everything I buy.

When I went out to check the mail, what did I find but a catalog from a tatting supply company. Slick pages with color photos of shuttles and thread tempted me. And books—another thing I have too much of—with rediscovered tatting patterns. I started to circle everything I wanted.

Wait. I don't need any more tatting supplies. I haven't finished the projects I've started. I've let myself want and buy more than I could ever use. I've been training my heart to be greedy.

My craft room has too much stuff, but I can never have enough of what I really want—Jesus.
—Suzanne Davenport Tietjen

FAITH STEP: *Open a physical or online concordance and do your own word study on greed. Examine yourself and repent as necessary. Consider giving something away.*

WEDNESDAY, AUGUST 13

David said to Abigail, "Praise be to the Lord, the God of Israel, who has sent you today to meet me. May you be blessed for your good judgment and for keeping me from bloodshed this day and from avenging myself with my own hands." 1 Samuel 25:32–33 (NIV)

MY HUSBAND, JOHN, AND I have been married for more than 30 years. One thing that has kept our marriage strong and our family healthy is a willingness to communicate when one of us overacts in our parenting. Raising ten kids isn't easy, and sometimes we get it wrong. If one of us feels we didn't fully understand a situation, and a child's consequence didn't fit with a child's action, we pull the other aside. Then, with a humble attitude, we lovingly explain our thoughts to each other. Because of this, there have been times when we've lessened or dropped a child's consequences. And while it isn't fun being "wrong," a gentle reproof given out of love is sometimes needed.

The same is true in my relationship with Jesus. Sometimes my actions step out of line, and that's when Jesus's Spirit stirs within my soul. It's then I get away, pray, and open His Word. I don't like to be wrong, but I often am, and I'm thankful that Jesus humbly leads and directs me when I overact. Intimacy with Jesus means trusting His good judgment and knowing that any rebuke He offers is given out of love. —TRICIA GOYER

FAITH STEP: *Ask Jesus to point out areas where you need a gentle reproof. Ask Him to bring to mind anything you need to confess.*

THURSDAY, AUGUST 14

For with God nothing will be impossible. Luke 1:37 (NKJV)

I LOOK AT MY DAY PLANNER and see "Clean bathrooms." Ugh and double ugh. I'd rather train for a marathon or memorize Psalm 119 (the longest chapter in the Bible with 176 verses) than scrub a toilet. The Love to Clean Queen I am not.

Oh, yes, I've hired numerous people who enjoy housework to rescue me. One was allergic to cats and had my couch cushions strewn across the lawn, vacuuming them for an hour. Another wanted more money than my college graduate husband earns. The last one got testy when I asked her to pick up items and dust under, not around, them.

So I prayed a desperate prayer. "Lord, please cause me to enjoy housework."

I realized this might be one of those requests that takes Jesus a lifetime to fulfill. I wouldn't be dancing with my mop and singing as I scrub by the following Saturday. But I figured if Jesus could heal a leper, forgive a prostitute, and resurrect a dead girl, He'd be up to changing my cleaning-hating DNA.

Several weeks later, I was on a trip and popped into a cute boutique. When I felt compelled to buy a can of furniture spray instead of a garden flag, I realized Jesus was at work. And when I got home and actually used the spray, my heart burst with hope for all those other situations and people I've considered "impossible." The broken relationships. The stubborn habits. The stony hearts and closed minds.

As I breathed in the fresh lemony aroma and viewed the bright gloss on my coffee table, I smiled. Jesus is still in the miracle business. —JEANETTE LEVELLIE

FAITH STEP: *Get brave and ask Jesus to change something that yesterday you thought was impossible.*

FRIDAY, AUGUST 15

The LORD makes firm the steps of the one who delights in him; though he may stumble, he will not fall, for the LORD upholds him with his hand. Psalm 37:23–24 (NIV)

EARLIER THIS SUMMER, MY SISTER, Jenny; sister-in-law, Traci; and I took care of our great-nieces Emma (age four) and Avery (age three) and great-nephew Owen (age one) so their parents could attend a grandkids' birthday party for my mom's eightieth birthday. Traci strapped Owen in his baby carrier. Jenny played with Avery. I was Emma's aunt-on-call. We made chocolate chip scones. Emma and Avery helped measure and stir. Owen's expressive eyebrows were lifted high in surprise. The scones were eaten by all with delight.

Then we headed to a nearby park. Emma and I climbed every ladder on the structure. We went down both slides. We lay in the sand. We rode the metal animals on coils that almost whipped my back out of alignment. We waded into the little lake nearby to throw pebbles. Our goal for the afternoon? To keep the children happy and alive. Little ones tend to embrace fun with little or no thought toward safety. We delivered them back to their parents full, happy, and with no major injuries—a win all around!

As I move through life, I encounter all kinds of adventures and struggles. But when I trust Jesus, He oversees my care. He guides my steps. He guards my heart and mind. He heals my body. He encourages my spirit. It is a win all around! —SUSANNA FOTH AUGHTMON

FAITH STEP: *Go for a walk today and ask Jesus to come with you. Imagine Him upholding your life with His hand and making your steps firm.*

SATURDAY, AUGUST 16

Now faith is confidence in what we hope for and assurance about what we do not see. Hebrews 11:1 (NIV)

"LORD, I FEEL ALONE," I wrote in my journal during my morning with Jesus. Tears fell. I finally put words to what I had been feeling for a while. I felt foolish saying I was alone. People were all around me, both personally and professionally. Yet something was missing.

Journaling allowed me to be honest with Jesus and myself. I searched for love and companionship in people and experiences rather than seeking the face of Jesus. I didn't trust He was with me because I often didn't *feel* Him—no wonder I felt alone.

Jesus gently assured me He was with me amidst my loneliness, but I often dismissed His presence if my needs were not satisfied by others. He invited me to believe He cares, even if I didn't see or feel Him in the ways I expected. He told me I would experience more of His presence if I sought *Him* for my needs rather than putting that expectation on others.

Hebrews 11:1 assures me faith is not a feeling. It's a conscious practice of being sure of what you can't yet see. Jesus asked me to expect His presence with such belief.

I confessed I didn't have much faith on my own. Like the man in Mark 9:24, I began praying, *Jesus, help my unbelief.* Anticipating Jesus's presence, rather than the unmet expectations of others, built my faith and diminished my reliance on my feelings. Slowly, I felt less alone and more complete. —BRENDA L. YODER

FAITH STEP: *When you feel alone, find a scripture to pray that helps you rely on your faith instead of your feelings.*

SUNDAY, AUGUST 17

"For my thoughts are not your thoughts, neither are your ways my ways," declares the LORD. Isaiah 55:8 (NIV)

I GLANCED ACROSS THE AISLE before church service. There she sat—pretty, kind, and well-off. Men and women flocked around her, talking and laughing. *Shouldn't she let everyone take their seats?* Church was about to begin. In my lap, my fingers worked a tissue into knots, as envy pooled in my heart. Lowering my gaze, I opened my Bible to some characters I know well.

A jealous woman. A murderous, deceptive king. An adulteress. At times, when I read the stories of Martha, David, and Mary Magdalene, it's as if I'm looking in a mirror. I see my vulnerabilities exposed in these people. If I allow it, I can fall back into the shame and hopelessness I experienced before I met Jesus. But I won't. I know there is more to their stories, and to mine.

As I read, the Lord reveals His mercy. He focuses not on weaknesses but on the goodness within. Martha worked for Jesus's love and acceptance, not understanding she—like her sister—already had it. David's devotion to God was so deep He wrote poetry and music in praise. Mary Magdalene searched for love in the wrong places, until she found it in the one right place. Jesus. And she loved Jesus with all her being.

Jesus sees me and my sins, every single one of them. Even my envy over a kind woman's popularity. Like all stories in the Book of Life, mine has a happy ending. I am redeemed. —HEIDI GAUL

FAITH STEP: *Spend a few minutes journaling this week. If you find yourself focusing on negative self-talk, flip the wording to reflect the way Jesus sees you.*

MONDAY, AUGUST 18

My Father's house has many rooms; if that were not so, would I have told you that I am going there to prepare a place for you? And if I go and prepare a place for you, I will come back and take you to be with me that you also may be where I am. John 14:2–3 (NIV)

MY FAMILY IS IN THE process of moving. In 3 weeks, we'll leave our home of 16 years and settle into a new life on an unfamiliar street in the next neighborhood over. Yesterday we got the keys to the new house, and we spent the evening walking through the empty rooms and dreaming about how it will feel as our new home. We can't wait to move in.

But for now, we're living in both worlds. While I spent the day at our current house doing laundry, packing boxes, and getting ready for another week of work and school, my husband, Jason, spent the day at the new house. He cleaned and painted, moved bookshelves and furniture, and patched holes in the walls to prep them for a fresh coat of paint.

When the day ended, we were worn out but happy. I thought about how Jason had worked all day getting our new home ready for us, and it made me think of Jesus. I forget sometimes that while I am going through the everyday routines of living life, paying bills, or making dinner, Jesus is actively preparing an eternal home for me in heaven. I know I'll be with Him forever, and that makes me giddy with anticipation. —EMILY E. RYAN

FAITH STEP: *Imagine Jesus preparing a home for you in heaven. Ask Him to reveal His will for you as you await moving day.*

TUESDAY, AUGUST 19

Do not be interested only in your own life, but be interested in the lives of others. Philippians 2:4 (NCV)

TODAY MY HUSBAND INSTALLED curtain rods for our elderly next-door neighbor. We weren't always such good neighbors. Initially, I'd avoided the new neighbor man out of embarrassment.

Summer mornings, I check whether the air is warmer inside or outside by lightly moving my palm from side to side in an open, south-facing window. When the outside temperature is warm, I close all the windows. Once, while checking the outside temperature with my hand, I saw a man inside the previously vacant house next door, facing my direction. I was mortified, afraid he'd thought I was waving at him from my window! Worse, I worried that through the open windows he might've heard my screams at the peak "scarifying" moments in the British murder mysteries I watched. Doubly embarrassed about appearing to have flirted with a complete stranger by waving at him from my window and my nightly blood-curdling screams, I avoided welcoming the new guy to the neighborhood.

Later, while reading my Bible, it was as if Jesus were waving to me through His Word: "Love your neighbor as you love yourself.... Show respect to old people.... Remember all my laws and rules, and obey them" (Leviticus 19:18, 32, 37, NCV). So I forced myself to walk next door and confess the reason for my avoidance. The man and I shared a good laugh about it. Turns out, he hadn't seen me waving or heard my screams. Self-consciousness made me unneighborly. Now I'm more concerned about my neighbor's well-being than my own image, thanks to Jesus's reminder. —CASSANDRA TIERSMA

FAITH STEP: *Journal about an embarrassing incident. Ask Jesus to help you overcome self-consciousness so you can be more like Him.*

WEDNESDAY, AUGUST 20

When You said, "Seek My face," my heart said to You, "I shall seek Your face, LORD." Psalm 27:8 (NASB)

I LOVE, LOVE, LOVE THE early-morning quiet with Jesus. I rise before my husband wakes, the dawn peeps, and the birds chirp. Nestled on our vessel's settee with coffee and journal nearby, I read my Bible and savor sweet moments with my Savior.

I'll be honest—I haven't always considered those early-morning times delightful. I used to think that doing daily devotions was written on every good Christian's to-do list. Do it or die trying. My perspective changed when my husband, Gene, and I were involved in an all-consuming ministry while parenting three active teenagers. That's when I realized my desperate need for divine wisdom and supernatural strength, and I dived into my devotional time with fresh hunger.

I recall asking Jesus to wake me at the time He wanted to meet, and He did—5 a.m. At first, I thought He was joking, but an inner alarm prompted me to awaken at the same time every morning. Imagining Jesus waiting in my living room provided motivation to get up and get moving. If He wanted to spend time with me, then I didn't want to disappoint Him by not showing up.

My current life season allows me the flexibility to rise even earlier than 5 a.m. Time in Jesus's presence and soaking in His Word gives me strength, joy, and peace. It encourages me, answers tough questions, and anchors me amidst the storms of life. I can't imagine facing my day without first seeking His face. —GRACE FOX

FAITH STEP: *Ask yourself if you consider time with Jesus a duty or a delight. If not the latter, what needs to change?*

THURSDAY, AUGUST 21

Let us not become weary in doing good, for at the proper time we will reap a harvest if we do not give up.
Galatians 6:9 (NIV)

I HAD PLENTY OF REASONS for not attending my high school classmate's funeral. Torrential rains made driving conditions dangerous for the trip to my hometown. I had a sore throat and didn't want to spread my germs. I wasn't familiar with the location of the church where the funeral was being held and my GPS was unreliable. My black dress was at the cleaners. *But I'll go, Jesus,* I promised. *I'll go.*

Years ago, I read an essay by Deidre Sullivan that has been my guidepost ever since. Her admonition: always go to the funeral. As a child, Sullivan's father required her and her siblings to attend visitations and funerals to pay their respects to the grieving families. It was the right thing to do, her father told her. No matter if it wasn't convenient or easy to do, it was the right thing. I know Jesus expects me to do what's right and I don't want to disappoint Him.

Some time back, as I struggled to keep from breaking down while delivering my mother's eulogy, I spotted a couple in the congregation I hadn't seen for years. Buddy and Judy lived at the lake, over an hour away. They didn't really know Mom, but they'd come to the funeral to pay their respects and to support me. Their kind gesture touched my heart and reinforced my resolve to always go to the funeral. Having been on the receiving end of that kindness, I know how much it means.

—Pat Butler Dyson

Faith Step: *Always attend the funeral or the visitation. You will comfort the family. And you'll please Jesus.*

FRIDAY, AUGUST 22

In the multitude of my anxieties within me, Your comforts delight my soul. Psalm 94:19 (NKJV)

HOW CAN A MINIVAN GET so disgusting? I surveyed the crushed Cheerios on the floorboard and the mystery liquid hardening in the cup holders and whispered an anxious prayer: *Help me, Jesus.* I had been feeling out of control recently. The car was just one of many things I'd neglected over the past several weeks of grief and mourning for my late brother-in-law, Jared, who took meticulous care of his vehicles. He'd be so disappointed in me.

I was in the back row, hunched over a booster seat, digging candy wrappers out from the cracks, when I saw it. Large, scratchy writing, in pen, on the back of my tan leather seats. I almost came unglued.

Clearly, it was my daughter's writing, but I couldn't make out what it said. I called her outside and asked, in my most contrived calm voice, if she knew anything about the pen marks. Her face crumpled into a mess of tears. "I couldn't help it," she sobbed. "I'm sorry."

"But what does it say?" I asked, softening at her sorrow. These were more than the crocodile tears of a child caught in mischief.

"It says, 'I miss you,'" she said with a hiccup. "I tried to clean it, but it won't come off." I pulled her close and stroked her hair. "I wrote it when we left the cemetery after Uncle Jared's funeral. Are you mad?"

Instantly, I felt the Lord's peace. "No, baby. I understand," I assured her, knowing in my heart that even Jared would understand as well. Sometimes I think I can fix my messy sadness by cleaning things around me. But only Jesus can wipe away my tears. —Emily E. Ryan

Faith Step: *Next time you're feeling sad or out of control, reach out to Jesus for comfort and strength.*

SATURDAY, AUGUST 23

When the perishable has been clothed with the imperishable, and the mortal with immortality, then the saying that is written will come true: "Death has been swallowed up in victory." 1 Corinthians 15:54 (NIV)

MY HUSBAND AND I USED to throw *big* parties, but those shindigs have gone by the wayside in the busyness of raising three kids. Reminiscing about our backyard bashes, we got nostalgic. It motivated us to throw another one even though we didn't have a special occasion to celebrate. Instead, we chose a date that worked best for us and our friends and then researched what happened on that day in history.

We discovered that the day of this party was the day the Republic of Dubrovnik was conquered by the French Empire in 1808. I painted their flag on an enormous bedsheet that we hung from our basketball net. Everyone came dressed in the flag's colors of red, white, and blue. We had silly games called "Transfer of Power" relay, "Escape the Oppression" obstacle course, and "Sword Dueling for Freedom" with pool noodles. We even played their national anthem while crowning the victors of the games at the end. Clearly, we had a ton of fun. But we had to go looking for a reason to celebrate, and then we had to create party games around that theme.

Thankfully, there's no need to go looking for a reason to celebrate my faith. Jesus liberated me from my sins and conquered death so I can spend eternity with Him. No matter what day it is when I get to heaven, I anticipate the *biggest* party of all. —CLAIRE MCGARRY

FAITH STEP: *Think of a way you can celebrate Jesus's victory over sin and death. Get together with friends or maybe enjoy a slice of cake.*

SUNDAY, AUGUST 24

His master commended him: "Good work! You did your job well. From now on be my partner." Matthew 25:23 (MSG)

OUR GRANDSON DANIEL PLAYS DRUMS in his high school band. Quite expertly, if I may brag a little.

When he performed his first solo at a concert, my husband, Kevin, and I hooted and hollered and applauded. He told us afterward in the lobby that we'd embarrassed him. Of course. He's seventeen.

Kevin and I were quick to apologize, even though we weren't a bit sorry. I explained that since we didn't get to attend concerts and ball games when our three grands were small because they lived 10 hours away, we had to make up for it now that they lived in the same town. We were just proud of him.

He didn't buy it.

When our two children were small and displayed a godly character quality, I applauded them and said, "Jesus is so proud of you. He stands up from His throne, turns to His Heavenly Father and says, 'Will you look at that terrific kid? He's sharing toys with his little brother (or using polite manners, or showing kindness).' And Jesus and the Father jump up and down for you!"

I was definitely taking some theological license, but is it so far-fetched to think that when we act like Jesus, He's proud of us? And that Jesus might nudge the Father to share His joy?

Kevin and I embarrassed our grandson with our over-the-top praise, but I think Daniel would agree that making Jesus proud is nothing to be embarrassed about. —JEANETTE LEVELLIE

FAITH STEP: *Next time someone you love exhibits a Christ-like quality, applaud and compliment them. If they get embarrassed, tell them you're just acting like Jesus.*

MONDAY, AUGUST 25

Out of his fullness we have all received grace in place of grace already given. John 1:16 (NIV)

I WAS A LITTLE APPREHENSIVE about a work trip to Chicago because of the numerous flight delays and cancellations that were occurring regularly. As usual before I left, I prayed for smooth and safe travel. Unlike several of my colleagues, I had no problem reaching my destination.

But on the return trip to Washington, DC, I faced flight delays. The gate agent warned us that the plane was totally booked. I prepared myself to be scrunched up in my window seat for the 2-hour flight. A young man came to sit next to me. We greeted each other and watched as the other passengers boarded. The flow of people started to slow down. The guy next to me and I looked at each other—could it be on a packed flight that we would have an empty seat on our row and be able to stretch out? The flight attendant closed the door. The young man and I grinned and fist-bumped each other as he moved to the aisle seat. God's favor strikes again!

I've learned to recognize those little, ordinary blessings as "God nods," unexpected assurances of Jesus's grace and presence with me. It's when I'm running late and the traffic opens up so I can arrive to an appointment on time. Or when I'm feeling burdened and a stranger on the street tells me to smile because Jesus loves me. Jesus gives signals that He sees me, knows what I need, and provides it in some way. Sometimes it's even an empty middle seat on a packed flight. —BARBRANDA LUMPKINS WALLS

FAITH STEP: *Be on the lookout for "God nods" today and thank Jesus for them when they happen.*

TUESDAY, AUGUST 26

Jesus Christ is the same yesterday and today and forever. Hebrews 13:8 (NIV)

THE WEATHER ON THE GULF Coast of Florida, where I live, is less predictable than I thought it would be. I guess I imagined constant sunshine and year-round warm temperatures, but that just isn't so.

While my city has dodged the worst of the hurricanes in recent years, crazy summertime storms come up fast in the afternoon and don't always blow right on through, messing up a perfectly good beach day. Sometimes my weather app will call for overcast skies or rain, and it turns out to be glorious. Winter-time can be downright cold with lows of forties, can have highs of eighties, or can have days that linger at either end of the thermometer with no apparent pattern. It seems to be getting more erratic each year.

At times, my life has been like unpredictable weather patterns too. I've had certain expectations or a game plan, or have simply been chugging along, when out of nowhere the heat turns way up or warmth vanishes altogether. Here's what I've learned—coats and sundresses aside. If I keep my eyes on Jesus with unwavering faith, the "weather" is always fine because Jesus never changes. —ISABELLA CAMPOLATTARO

FAITH STEP: *Has the "weather" of your life been unpredictable? Sketch a thermometer that fills the page and note your current uncertainties at intervals. Then, in big letters, write "Jesus" right down the middle with Hebrews 13:8 across the bottom.*

WEDNESDAY, AUGUST 27

*Jesus said to them, "Come and have breakfast."
None of the disciples dared ask him, "Who are you?"
They knew it was the Lord. John 21:12 (NIV)*

JACK, OUR OLDEST, HAS LIVED in Southern California since he started college. He is a senior this year majoring in business management and humanities.

But business isn't all he knows how to manage. He is wise in the ways of apartment living. He knows his way around a food budget and is a great cook. He has mastered the art of making scones. And his homemade jam is unparalleled.

Jack and Will, our second oldest, decided to share an apartment at their school this year. When I helped Will move into their apartment, Jack invited me to come back later for dinner.

When I arrived at their apartment, there were flowers on the table. A delightful aroma filled the room. Jack had made lettuce wraps with delicious seared beef and a spicy sauce. The experience was nourishing in so many ways. I could see Jack's care in the way he made the food and his thoughtfulness in serving us. In that moment, I felt loved and cared for.

Jesus often used food to connect with people, from meals on the beach to miraculous wedding celebrations. Jesus wants to connect with me in the same way. He wants me to know, on the most basic level, that He cares for my body, mind, and spirit. Jesus is with me, nourishing me, and providing for me daily. I am loved and cared for.
—SUSANNA FOTH AUGHTMON

FAITH STEP: *Jesus wants to nourish you in body, mind, and spirit. As you sit down to eat your meals today, recognize and thank Him for His provision and His care for you.*

THURSDAY, AUGUST 28

---

*The LORD replied, "My Presence will go with you,
and I will give you rest." Exodus 33:14 (NIV)*

EVERY YEAR AS THE DATE of my breast cancer surgery passes, I celebrate. Nothing elaborate; no parties or expensive meals in fancy restaurants are necessary. In fact, the greater the length of time that goes by, the more introspective my observances of this blessing have become. For the last decade, I've shared my gratefulness and awe with Jesus alone.

One of the lessons He's taught me post-surgery was the importance of slowing down. For many years, I based my self-value on how much I could accomplish daily. Every waking minute that didn't produce tangible outcomes, I considered a waste. As a result, I adopted lifestyle choices that might have affected my emotional and physical health.

This week, as my special anniversary approaches, I once again find time crunched and busyness snowballing, threatening to avalanche my well-being. I call this condition "rest cancer," and it requires immediate action. Left untreated, it can lead to exhaustion, anger, and tears. The worst symptom is distancing myself from Jesus.

Thankfully, the ailment is treatable. Quiet time spent with Jesus proves the most effective cure. Communing with Him in prayer, reading the Bible, and seeking His peace in nature lead to the deep, restoring soul rest only He can provide.

For now, I sit on my porch rocker, breathing in the scent of sweet alyssum. Songbirds circle their feeder, and a warm breeze caresses my face. I meditate on His Presence and cast my endless to-do lists aside. Free of rest cancer, I rest in Him. —HEIDI GAUL

FAITH STEP: *No matter how full your day, set aside a few minutes to simply breathe, pray, and listen. Rest in Jesus.*

FRIDAY, AUGUST 29

Then she said, "Sit still, my daughter, until you know how the matter will turn out; for the man will not rest until he has concluded the matter this day." Ruth 3:18 (NKJV)

AFTER WEEKS OF INTERVIEWS, it was down to me and another candidate for a coveted media spokesperson position at a large nonprofit. I felt confident this job was right for me, the stepping stone I needed to broaden my career in journalism. The final interview went very well and I fully expected a job offer soon after. Two weeks passed. No offer. I called the senior executive who interviewed me. Voicemail. Days went by without a response. I was discouraged. Finally, the organization let me know the bad news: they'd hired the other candidate.

I cried out to Jesus. *Why, Lord? I really wanted that job!* My soul was crushed. How could I have been so sure of something that didn't happen for me? Inside my spirit, Jesus answered with a verse I'd meditated on from the book of Ruth. "Wait my daughter, and see how the matter turns out." I was confused but trusted God's Word. I chose to believe things would work for my good.

Two more slow weeks passed and the phone rang again. The same executive asked if I would still consider their offer. The person who they'd hired decided the job wasn't for him. The position was mine!

Not only did I receive the job of my dreams, but they also increased the salary. All this came as I stopped fretting and sat still, letting Jesus work on my behalf. —PAMELA TOUSSAINT HOWARD

FAITH STEP: *In difficult situations where things seem to be against you, practice stillness and allow Jesus to work it out.*

SATURDAY, AUGUST 30

Then Jesus said, "Whoever has ears to hear, let them hear."
Mark 4:9 (NIV)

WE STOOD IN THE APPLIANCE aisle at the big-box store the other day contemplating a major investment.

The time had come for a new dishwasher. The search had begun.

Not large enough capacity. Don't like this handle. Do you think we need a third rack? Look how flimsy this sprayer arm is. Price-wise, these five are automatic nos. We were down to a couple with similar options and little price difference when my eyes fell on a label with what might have seemed a small detail. The how-loud-is-this-while-running factor. We opted for the quieter of the two, not realizing the decision was no small thing after all.

Yesterday, I had to put my ear to the door of the dishwasher to make sure I'd remembered to start it.

Just like my new dishwasher, Jesus speaks quietly—in a still, small voice. It isn't that He doesn't want to be heard. Jesus wants me to listen and often started or ended teaching His life lessons in the Bible with words to that effect: "He who has ears, let him hear." Jesus used the admonition seven times in the Gospels.

Why then does He speak to me in a whisper? Why the still, small voice?

I think I found part of the answer in my new dishwasher. I had to get close, listen deeply, and lean in to hear. —CYNTHIA RUCHTI

FAITH STEP: *As part of your time with Jesus, make a list of those "He who has ears, let him hear" phrases. What truths do you hear?*

SUNDAY, AUGUST 31

Since, then, you have been raised with Christ, set your hearts on things above, where Christ is, seated at the right hand of God. Set your minds on things above, not on earthly things. For you died, and your life is now hidden with Christ in God. Colossians 3:1–3 (NIV)

I READ THE TEXT AGAIN while dread churned in my stomach. The other person's response sounded displeased by how I handled a situation. I thought I had done well, but worry over what this person thought of me felt as familiar as my own skin.

Breathing deeply, I willed my rising defenses to relax. Maybe I had made a mistake. Or maybe the other person simply would have done things differently.

In recent years, I've been coming to terms with how much energy I often sacrifice to gain and maintain the approval of other human beings. I've been learning how unhealthy people-pleasing can debilitate spiritual, emotional, and relational health.

Maybe you, too, struggle with fears of disappointing others or being misunderstood.

Today's verses provide hope for overcoming unhealthy people-pleasing. Sheltering my thoughts and emotions with Jesus has become a practical strategy to steer clear of placing too much weight on what others think. I imagine myself placing those worries in His hands. Then instead of berating or shaming me with accusations, these words soothe my spirit when I've made an innocent error, or am being misunderstood, or even when I *have* done wrong.

Focusing on Jesus and His heart frees me to live confidently in Him, relate with others well, make corrections when needed, and move forward in peace. —Erin Keeley Marshall

---

Faith Step: *Take inventory of any people-pleasing tendencies in yourself. Ask Jesus to meet you in those moments and guide your thoughts and emotions to Him.*

LABOR DAY, MONDAY, SEPTEMBER 1

Now may the . . . Lord Jesus, that great Shepherd of the sheep, equip you with everything good for doing his will, and may he work in us what is pleasing to him, through Jesus Christ, to whom be glory for ever and ever. Amen.
Hebrews 13:20–21 (NIV)

I HAVE SPENT MANY YEARS volunteering in a variety of settings—business organizations, my local community, my kids' schools, and, of course, church. On some occasions, I was asked and promptly agreed; on others, I actively sought out opportunities that interested me.

Sometimes I'd say yes to too much or to something I wasn't gifted to do and would find myself exhausted, ineffective, and, worst of all, a resentful martyr. This inevitably also depleted my bandwidth for my family. I admit I didn't always consult Jesus about what *He* wanted me to do. I also confess that sometimes I was working for perks—mainly, heavenly or human accolades.

I have a lot of skills, energy, and interests, but I'm not called to do everything, nor does Jesus equip me to do everything. It took me a while to understand that everything I do should be for His glory. Now I know that if what I do is not for Jesus, then it's no good for me. These days, I seek Jesus's direction before saying yes or jumping up to volunteer. —ISABELLA CAMPOLATTARO

FAITH STEP: *Does this devotional strike a chord? Take time to make a complete list of all you do. Consider praying and fasting for a week or more to seek Jesus's direction for what He wants for you.*

TUESDAY, SEPTEMBER 2

But seek the welfare of the city where I have sent you into exile, and pray to the LORD on its behalf, for in its welfare you will find your welfare. Jeremiah 29:7 (ESV)

AFTER LOSING OUR HOME TO a wildfire, we moved into a rental house while we rebuilt. I felt like an exile having to flee danger and resettle in a new community. Our situation is less dire than the Israelites', but I've gained a new understanding of God's desire for times of displacement. God told the exiled Israelites in Jeremiah 29:4–7 to build houses, plant gardens, multiply their families, and pray for the welfare of the place where He had sent them. God knew they were going to be there for a long time.

Jesus's permanent home was not here on earth. He moved from place to place. He prayed constantly and ministered wherever He went. He also talked about

His forever home in heaven. Knowing my husband and I were going to be living in our temporary place for a minimum of 2 years, Jesus's example inspired me to do more than see it as transitional housing. We decided to build a life where we were placed.

So, we planted a garden. We had family dinners every Sunday night. I walked with our neighbors and traveled back and forth between houses to give and borrow things. And I prayed for the welfare of Boulder, Colorado. This city has had some rough times, including a recent shooting at a grocery store and the wildfire that took our home along with more than one thousand others.

I look forward to having our home again. In the meantime, I'll bloom where I'm planted, pray for the welfare of this place, and look forward to our eternal home with Jesus. —JEANNIE BLACKMER

FAITH STEP: *Take time today to pray for the city where you live. Write down ways you can be more invested in that community.*

WEDNESDAY, SEPTEMBER 3

There is no fear in love. But perfect love drives out fear, because fear has to do with punishment. The one who fears is not made perfect in love. 1 John 4:18 (NIV)

THE FOUR TEENAGE FOSTER GIRLS my husband, John, and I adopted were excited and frightened by the idea of moving into our home. Their original home was unsafe, and being separated and sent to various foster homes was scary. When we welcomed them into our home, first for weekend visits and later permanently, I expected their hearts would settle and they would quickly trust our love for them. They didn't. Months passed, and they still resisted our affection.

John and I loved our girls, but from what they'd experienced, love was conditional. Opening their hearts to us was a risk, so they pushed our love away. Seven years later, we've watched their trust develop slowly, but even after all this time, our now-adult daughters don't understand or completely trust our unconditional love.

Just as our adopted daughters struggled to trust us, I, too, have struggled to fully trust Jesus's unconditional love. Why would He sacrifice His life for me? What if I did something and He rejected me? His plan of salvation seemed too good to be true. By taking a step of faith and opening my heart to Him, I made the conscious decision to not be afraid and completely trust Jesus's unconditional love as His adopted daughter. I pray our daughters will one day trust Jesus's unconditional love and ours too.
—TRICIA GOYER

FAITH STEP: *Write down any fears you have. Pray about them with Jesus and trust His unconditional love.*

THURSDAY, SEPTEMBER 4

The LORD is near to all who call on him, to all who call on him in truth. Psalm 145:18 (NIV)

WHILE I WAS WAITING AT the train station for my husband to pick me up, a young woman got out of a sports car and greeted me. "Hello, ma'am," she said. I smiled and asked, "How are you?" Expecting to hear the routine "I'm fine," I was a little surprised when she responded, "I'm exhausted!" before continuing on her way. I quickly uttered a few words of encouragement and bid her a good evening.

A few days later, I got on an elevator and said hello to a young man I didn't know. He immediately shared with me that it was his first day back to work after paternity leave and he was concerned about leaving his wife at home alone with their three-month-old twins.

What struck me about those two encounters is that both people had told me, a total stranger, just how they felt or what was going on with them. Jesus is certainly no stranger to me, but do I always tell Him exactly how I feel? Truth be told, not always.

Maybe it's because I know He already knows what's happening, so why repeat the obvious? Perhaps it's because I think I shouldn't complain. But just as I was willing to listen and encourage two complete strangers, wouldn't Jesus do the same for me? I want to take every opportunity to honestly seek His guidance, help, or strength. Or just bare my soul. Whatever it is, Jesus is near and ready to listen.
—BARBRANDA LUMPKINS WALLS

FAITH STEP: *Take a moment to tell Jesus what's on your mind. Nothing is too trivial or too big. He's listening.*

FRIDAY, SEPTEMBER 5

Do not harden your hearts as you did in the rebellion, during the time of testing in the wilderness.
Hebrews 3:8 (NIV)

ONE OF MY GOALS THIS YEAR was to teach our granddaughter, Grace, to drive. She's a great kid and very smart. Which is what worried me.

The first time out, I instructed Grace on the basics, showing her the location of each item on her steering column, which were the gas and brake pedals, and how to adjust her rearview mirrors.

In a fifteen-year-old's version of politeness, Grace explained that she'd already learned all this in driver's education. I refrained from a snippy comment and continued my lesson with the actual driving instruction.

Although we'd planned on a 30-minute session, Grace was done in fifteen. "It's harder than it looks, huh?" I said, failing to keep the smugness out of my voice. But then I remembered Jesus.

Sometimes He has to remind me of the basics. *Be nice. Forgive. It's not all about you.* I sigh and think I don't need all this—I've already learned it. Oh really?

Sometimes His Word convicts me of what I think I've already learned. I listened to gossip. I overate or overspent or talked too much. I think, *I know, I know.* But do I really?

Do I forget that Jesus is smarter than I am? Do I act as if He doesn't know the best way for me to do life? If so, I'm behaving like a fifteen-year-old who doesn't want to listen to someone who's been driving for 50 years and has already taught four teenagers to drive, thank you very much.

Sorry, Lord. I'm listening now. —JEANETTE LEVELLIE

FAITH STEP: *If you, like me, have acted like a know-it-all teenager, ask Jesus to forgive you. Next time He tries to teach you something, listen.*

SATURDAY, SEPTEMBER 6

*Now that same day two of them were going to a village
called Emmaus, about seven miles from Jerusalem. They
were talking with each other about everything that had
happened. As they talked and discussed these things with
each other, Jesus himself came up and walked along with
them. Luke 24:13–15 (NIV)*

I WALKED ALONG BUSTLING KING STREET, head
bowed and eyes focused on the old, cracked sidewalk. People brushed by me in both directions,
and vehicles honked beside me on the narrow thor-
oughfare to Charleston Harbor. After 14 days of
leading tours, I needed a dose of encouragement to
work another week. So I prayed to the One who
could refresh my soul: "Dear Jesus, I'm completely
exhausted and a bit beat down. Please help me."

Just as I raised my head, a car passed slowly in
the congested traffic. In the back seat, two little
dark-haired girls gazed directly at me. Huge smiles
broke across their faces, and they waved as if they
had spotted their best friend. I stopped, surprised
and delighted, and waved furiously until the car
rolled out of sight.

The prayer had barely left my tongue when Jesus
sent an amazing surprise. I received the boost I desired
and the experience filled me with joy and energy to

tackle my final week of work. But even better, the smiles and waves from those girls increased my faith for a lifetime. I sought the Savior, and He heard my cry. Because Jesus walked with me on King Street, I knew He would walk with me for all my days to come. —BECKY ALEXANDER

FAITH STEP: *Do you keep a list of answered prayers? Recording them can help you celebrate your blessings from Jesus. Rereading them can strengthen your faith anew in the future.*

SUNDAY, SEPTEMBER 7

In the same way, let your light shine before others, that they may see your good deeds and glorify your Father in heaven. Matthew 5:16 (NIV)

EVERY YEAR AT THE BEGINNING of the school year, my church has a special Sunday when kids can bring in their backpacks. How proud they are to show off their new Peppa Pig or Thomas the Tank Engine or Dora the Explorer bags. They walk to the front of the church, and we pray for them—for their safety, for healthy and strong friendships, and for a year in which they will be curious and challenged in wonderful ways.

Our church staff also collects new school supplies that day to be given to local children in need. After being prayed for, our little fellow congregants open up their new backpacks filled with boxes of tissues, whiteboard markers, crayons, and pencils and transfer those items to collection baskets.

Seeing the baskets, empty just a moment before and now brimming with brand-new school supplies, calls to mind Jesus's miracle of the five loaves and two fish, where a child long ago shared what he had to feed a multitude. Helping others in need, as well as teaching children the importance and joy of sharing our blessings, feeds my body and soul…and it is a way to give praise to God. —JENNIFER GRANT

FAITH STEP: *Today, find a way to support a classroom or kids in need at the beginning of the school year and enlist young and old in your community to contribute.*

MONDAY, SEPTEMBER 8

The LORD will protect you from all danger; he will keep you safe. He will protect you as you come and go now and forever. Psalm 121:7–8 (GNT)

DELIVERY DRIVING RUNS IN MY FAMILY. My kids, husband, brother, father, grandfather, great-grandfather, and I, five generations, have provided delivery for multiple different industries using commercial trucks, vans, mail jeeps, cars, SUVs, school buses, tanker trucks, trains, semitrucks, bicycles, taxicabs, and funeral hearses. Cargos delivered include US mail, commercial uniforms, DoorDash meals, schoolchildren, pharmaceuticals, senior citizens, water, tipsy festival attendees, eyeglass frames, beauty supplies, raw milk, newspapers, taxi passengers, caskets with corpses, and bootleg hooch.

Currently, my husband, son, daughter, and brother, as well as two long-haul trucker brothers-in-law, are doing delivery driving. This line of work is not without risk. I'm constantly praying for my family's safety on the road.

When my kids were gaining their independence, able to come and go on their own, I put Psalm 121:7–8 on an index card on the doorframe where they'd see it every time they left the house. It was for my own reassurance as much as for theirs. Ten years later, and more than 600 miles away from my kids, I have that same verse taped on the inside of my back door.

Jesus comforts me in my concern for my family's continued safety in carrying out the family legacy of delivery driving by reminding me He's the Great Deliverer (2 Corinthians 1:10). My family and I deliver earthly goods and passengers, but Jesus is the Deliverer of Souls (Galatians 1:4). And when our earthly routes are fulfilled, it's Jesus who'll deliver us safely home (John 3:36). —CASSANDRA TIERSMA

FAITH STEP: *Write Psalm 121:7–8 on an index card and pray for your loved ones on the road. Thank Jesus for keeping them safe and sound in their travels.*

TUESDAY, SEPTEMBER 9

But if from there you seek the LORD your God, you will find him if you seek him with all your heart and with all your soul. Deuteronomy 4:29 (NIV)

IT'S APPARENTLY A UNIVERSAL (or nearly so) phenomenon: if a man needs to find something in the refrigerator, it will require the intervention of his wife. "Do we have any ketchup? Are we out of it?" On my best days, I walk to the refrigerator, stand beside my husband, point to the condiments shelf on the door of the fridge, and smile. On my less than best days, I add a sigh.

"Where's the leftover chicken?"

Sigh. Walk to the fridge. Move one thing—*one*—and point. "There it is."

To me, the "moving one thing" part is the definition of searching. To my husband, if he doesn't find the item where he expects it to be, he assumes it's sabotage, he needs to file a missing whatever report, or it is unfindable. It's especially humorous if he couldn't find what he was looking for because it wasn't the color, shape, or size he expected.

His inability to locate things used to bother me until I realized I'm guilty of the same attitude with Jesus far too often. If He isn't where I expect Him to be, do I move what's in the way or instead close the door and assume He's missing from the scene? Like a doctor's office? Or emergency room? Or funeral home? Or when paying bills?

How often do I assume Jesus is unfindable because my circumstances are so bleak? Just like the ketchup that could readily be found by my husband in our fridge, I'm firmly convinced of this truth: Jesus wants to and can be found, even in unexpected places. I need only look. —CYNTHIA RUCHTI

FAITH STEP: *If today you find something hiding in plain sight, remind yourself of Jesus's eagerness to be found by seekers.*

WEDNESDAY, SEPTEMBER 10

Consider the lilies of the field, how they grow: they neither toil nor spin; and yet I say to you that even Solomon in all his glory was not arrayed like one of these. Matthew 6:28–29 (NKJV)

WHEN I GO FOR A walk in our neighborhood, I head for the nature trail. Among the joys I receive

MORNINGS WITH JESUS 2025 | 349

from the trail are the different wildflowers that appear along the path during the various seasons.

I stop to admire their intricate details and lovely colors, taking pictures with my phone. In this natural area, I'm reminded that no human planted them there. Our Creator placed them where He wanted them as He designed the landscape. I imagine Him proudly appointing each flower its place like an artist does a finished work of art.

These flowers were not accidents. They were not afterthoughts. And they were no less important than any other plant or flower in the world. However, when these wildflowers show up in yards or gardens, they are often regarded as weeds, unwanted intruders into a carefully created garden plan.

I wonder who decided which flowers were weeds and which were valued. Surely the Master Gardener thought no less of one than the other. Sadly, there are times when I judge some people as having more value than others. I regard others as either wanted flowers or unwanted weeds. But Jesus sees every single person as valuable, equal to the most beautiful flower.

To Him, we are all precious "lilies of the field."
—MARILYN TURK

FAITH STEP: *Next time you take a walk, look for the beauty in the "weeds" and thank Jesus for the reminder of His love for you.*

THURSDAY, SEPTEMBER 11

Jesus wept. John 11:35 (NIV)

MOST OF US REMEMBER EXACTLY where we were and what we were doing on September 11, 2001. I was vacationing. Far from home and my loved ones, I was isolated and helpless to comfort and grieve alongside them. No matter our circumstances during those moments, the magnitude of the attacks is burned into our minds forever. The unimaginable act pulled my emotions across a spectrum of shock, confusion, and rage, then moved to grief as the horror and madness continued for weeks. The United States lost nearly three thousand people that day, with thousands more injured. In the midst of the unthinkable, the whole world wept.

When Jesus learned of the death of his closest friend, Lazarus, He wept. Because He is fully God and fully man, Jesus suffered just as we do, but with the wisdom and depth of God. In the same way His heart broke for those mourning Lazarus, He grieved along with Americans as we stood broken by this heinous act against our country.

Throughout the world and beyond today, tears will fall in remembrance and honor of the ones pointlessly martyred. This morning, I sit in my kitchen, cozy and secure. Looking back, I remember the horror of that day and the way time seemed to stand still. Again, my thoughts freeze under the great weight of sadness, until I, too, weep. —HEIDI GAUL

FAITH STEP: *Reflect on what you were doing and where you were during the attacks. Pray for healing for the families of those who perished.*

FRIDAY, SEPTEMBER 12

Though one may be overpowered, two can defend themselves. A cord of three strands is not quickly broken.
Ecclesiastes 4:12 (NIV)

MY DAUGHTER, KIM, INVITED ME to stay with her and her children for 6 weeks while her husband worked out of town. I had just signed a book contract and would need to work on my new project while I was there, so I packed various research materials in my suitcase. This, of course, made the suitcase heavy.

When I arrived at Kim's home, I parked my suitcase at the bottom of the steps that led to my bedroom. I intended to fetch it a few minutes later, but Kim got there first and began lugging it up the stairs. Her three-year-old daughter watched for a moment and then offered to help. As she reached for the handle on the side of the suitcase, she said with wisdom beyond her years, "You're much stronger with a friend."

We all need friends at the best of times because God created us to flourish in community. When life gives us a load that seems too heavy to bear, we need those friends to come alongside us even more.

Trouble is, sometimes our friends can't be there for us when we need them. They may be ill, absent, or struggling with problems of their own. But there is one friend who is always present: Jesus. We can count on Him to help us no matter what the problem is and whenever we seek His help. Nothing's too heavy for Jesus. —GRACE FOX

FAITH STEP: *Recall a time when a friend's presence, advice, or practical help strengthened you. Take a moment to write that person a note of appreciation and let her know she reflected Jesus to you.*

SATURDAY, SEPTEMBER 13

Come unto me, all ye that labour and are heavy laden, and I will give you rest. Take my yoke upon you, and learn of me; for I am meek and lowly in heart: and ye shall find rest unto your souls. Matthew 11:28–29 (KJV)

MY TO-DO LIST IS CHOCK-FULL today, but I began by doing something that didn't even make the list. I made Madeleines.

Why? Because the room temperature eggs on the counter were ready to take part in a pastry. The recipe had to be followed exactly. Soon, three bowls (one with browned butter, another with whisked flour with leavening, and the third with beaten and sweetened eggs) stood ready to be combined. And then, a surprise: the gently folded batter had to rest for at least 4 hours and as long as 20 days. That sounded important. The batter required rest. I didn't ignore that.

All too often, I resist resting. I hurry on, trying to get everything done. Washing and folding laundry. Planning and cooking dinner. And I never get it all done. Sabbath, a weekly celebration of rest, was a gift to us busy, tired humans. Jesus said it was "made to meet the needs of people, and not people to meet the requirements of the Sabbath" (Mark 2:27, NLT).

Jesus took naps in boats (Mark 4:38). He withdrew each morning to be renewed in prayer (Mark 1:35). Jesus rested. So should we.

Jesus is still calling, "Come to me." He promises to give us rest—each and every one of us. In response, I'm sitting in the recliner, my feet up, obeying Him, while the Madeleine dough chills out in the refrigerator. —SUZANNE DAVENPORT TIETJEN

FAITH STEP: *Prayerfully consider ways you could practice resting, whether daily in random moments, planned quiet times, or by attending an organized retreat.*

SUNDAY, SEPTEMBER 14

When you go through deep waters and great trouble, I will be with you. When you go through rivers of difficulty, you will not drown! Isaiah 43:2 (TLB)

VIOLENT STORMS RIPPED THROUGH OUR area recently. The wind and rain produced several tornado warnings, and one strong tornado tore a path through a nearby city, leaving significant damage to homes, schools, and businesses.

At church the next day, I asked my friend Courtney if she had any damage. I knew she lived close to the path of destruction. Her eyes lit up, and she pulled out her phone to show me a map of her city. On it, she had marked her home, her son's school, her office, and her parents' home, all within a few miles of each other. On a second map, she overlaid the path of the tornado with her marked locations. The tornado had literally zigzagged through the town like a football player dodging the defense and had missed every location she had marked. Her family had been spared, and now she was praising Jesus for His protection.

I thought of my own history with violent storms. The hurricane that destroyed our home when I was six. The tropical storm that swallowed our city for days. The ice storm that left us without power for almost a week. We hadn't always been spared, like Courtney had been, but even in the worst of those disasters, Jesus had always calmed me with His presence. Sometimes, I realized, His protection comes by sparing me from the storm. Other times, however, He simply walks with me through it. —Emily E. Ryan

FAITH STEP: *Become a biblical storm chaser by searching the word* storm *in the Bible. Write down any verses that reveal Jesus's presence, protection, or power in storms.*

MONDAY, SEPTEMBER 15

Laugh with your happy friends when they're happy; share tears when they're down. Romans 12:15 (MSG)

ONE OF MY BEST FRIENDS called. Through tears, she told me she wouldn't be able to come to my son's wedding. Of course, I understood. During the past year, she had battled non-Hodgkin's lymphoma. Her tumor had become chemoresistant, so she was given a newly approved therapy that wreaked havoc on her body. Thankfully, she's now in remission, but her body and mind are still healing from the shock of cancer and the physically intense treatment. Her doctors cautioned her about the dangers of getting a virus and the difficulty of recovery. Flying on an airplane and being in a crowded room for

356 | MORNINGS WITH JESUS 2025

the wedding felt too risky. We cried together as she grappled with having to skip another significant life event.

I knew this was the right decision, but I was sad too. My heart ached with her, knowing how disappointed she was to miss this celebration. I had the wedding and a reception with family and friends to look forward to, but she would be terribly missed.

Jesus understood and modeled being sensitive to others' emotions. When Lazarus died, He wept with those in mourning. Even though He knew He was going to raise Lazarus from the dead and a party would happen, He still shared His tears with those who were grieving (John 11:1–44).

I look forward to the time in the future when my friend can travel and join in celebrations. But for now, she is weeping and I will weep with her.
—JEANNIE BLACKMER

FAITH STEP: *Do you have a friend who is sad today? Call her to remind her Jesus is with her in her sorrow and so are you.*

TUESDAY, SEPTEMBER 16

So if you sinful people know how to give good gifts to your children, how much more will your heavenly Father give good gifts to those who ask him. Matthew 7:11 (NLT)

WHEN MY DAUGHTER MELISSA, MOTHER of two toddlers and a pre-teen, brings her brood over for Taco Tuesday, she sidles up to me, grinning, and asks, "Is Pat's Pantry open?" Melissa works in real estate and is pursuing a master's degree in counseling. She can't always get to the grocery store, and occasionally, she runs out of essentials. Whatever I have in my pantry or fridge, it's hers. The last quart of milk, the last box of cereal, the last roll of toilet paper. Anything I have, I'll gladly give to Melissa. Anything I can do for her, I'll do it. All she needs to do is ask. Giving is easy, but asking is another matter.

Why, Jesus, am I so reluctant to ask when I need something? Maybe it's too trivial. *Please, Lord, help my grandson pass his math test.* Maybe it's too huge. *Please, Jesus, heal my brother.* If I ask for anything in His name, He will do it (John 14:14). If I delight myself in the Lord, He will give me the desires of my heart (Psalm 37:4).

Maybe I don't get what I need simply because I don't ask. I think Jesus would be just as willing to grant something I requested as I am for Melissa to shop in Pat's Pantry. So during my prayer time or when the urge strikes me, I'll just go ahead and ask for that little thing. Or for that big thing. And I'll trust He will grant it. —PAT BUTLER DYSON

FAITH STEP: *Make a list of three things you desire. Ask Jesus for them.*

WEDNESDAY, SEPTEMBER 17

My God will richly fill your every need in a glorious way through Christ Jesus. Philippians 4:19 (GW)

THE INVENTORY CHANGES FREQUENTLY AT my favorite discount store, so each trip is like a treasure hunt. When I check out, the cashier usually asks, "Did you find everything you needed?" My answer is often, "Yes, and I found a couple of things I didn't know I needed!" Take, for example, the whisk I just used to stir up an exceptionally smooth sauce for homemade macaroni and cheese. I already owned three whisks, but I'd never seen one like this—with a flatter shape that easily gets into the edges of a pan. Now I use it for most stirring jobs. I didn't go to the store looking for a new kitchen tool that day, but I'm so glad I found one.

When I go to prayer each morning, I don't know what the day ahead holds. But Jesus does, and He knows exactly what I will need to get through it. I often think of asking for my material needs to be met, but how many times has Jesus equipped me for situations I didn't know would occur? A friendly stranger who entertained my fussy grandchild when I was stuck in the long line at the grocery store. An unexpected email from a friend who encouraged me when I was feeling down. The fellow driver who pulled over behind my car when the engine started smoking.

I'm glad that Jesus urges me to bring my needs to Him in prayer. I'm even more grateful that He promises to provide for the needs I don't even see coming. —DIANNE NEAL MATTHEWS

FAITH STEP: *List several ways Jesus has provided for you recently, then thank Him for being all you need.*

THURSDAY, SEPTEMBER 18

Look to the LORD and his strength; seek his face always.
Psalm 105:4 (NIV)

SEEKING THE WISDOM OF JESUS isn't a new concept for our family. I come from a long line of Jesus seekers. My parents and my grandparents consulted the Lord. I witnessed Him in the lives of aunts and uncles. My siblings and their families understand the value of inviting Jesus into our decisions.

From career paths to where to live to how to raise our children to which friendships to nurture and which to let go to problem-solving and dreaming for the future, it's, as they say, a go-to to "go to" Jesus for counsel.

When our first offer on the house we've now lived in for decades was rejected, we turned to Jesus for what to do next. My husband felt we were supposed to offer $500 more. A pittance, it seemed.

Our counteroffer was accepted instantly. That's one in a heartening string of stories of the benefits of seeking Him for wisdom.

Word meanings are a particular fascination for someone like me who works with words all day every day. So it's no surprise that scholarly comments on the original languages and biblical texts regarding the phrase "seek His face continually" captured my attention. That was, in fact, one of the interpretations. "Seek His face" in essence means to pay attention, to watch for what He's doing, and to listen to what He's saying.

Another commentator equated the phrase with watching for His smile, catching and holding the look of love in His eyes. Imagine walking through life, eyes glued to that unfathomable expression of Jesus's love. —CYNTHIA RUCHTI

FAITH STEP: *Dig a little deeper. Find a resource that explores the background behind the concept of seeking His face continually.*

FRIDAY, SEPTEMBER 19

One who has unreliable friends soon comes to ruin, but there is a friend who sticks closer than a brother.
Proverbs 18:24 (NIV)

MY COUSIN BETH IS A true friend. We are 9 months apart in age. We spent most of our summers growing up together. We attended the same college. We had our first babies the same year. We love each other.

A few months ago, I had to take a road trip from Southern California to Idaho. Beth flew down from Oregon and joined me. We feel like teenagers when we are together. We laugh a lot, eat good snacks, and sing really loud. Beth made an eighties playlist for our trip. As we made our way through the back roads of Nevada, the stereo volume was loud. The singing volume? Even louder.

We also talked a lot. We shared our hearts. We talked about the future—our hopes and dreams for our families. I trust Beth. She knows everything about me—the good and the bad. We cried a little. Sometimes that happens when we share our hearts. Beth is on my side, no matter what. And I am on hers.

Jesus is on my side too. There is nothing that He doesn't know about me. From the moment I was formed in my mother's belly to right now, He knows the ins and outs of my heart—the good and the bad. And He still loves me. I know that I can trust Him. He has forgiven my sins, healed my broken heart, and given me hope. He is a true friend.
—SUSANNA FOTH AUGHTMON

FAITH STEP: *Jesus has given you dear friends to journey through life with. Take time to pray for your close friends by name today.*

SATURDAY, SEPTEMBER 20

May my prayer be set before you like incense; may the lifting up of my hands be like the evening sacrifice.
Psalm 141:2 (NIV)

MY HUSBAND'S GRANDMOTHER RHODA DIED last year at the age of 102. But she was my grandma too, since David and I have been married for more than three decades. Although Grandma grew quieter and weaker toward the end of her life, she was still very much herself. Her main challenge was that she had become legally blind.

Her inability to see, however, didn't much slow her down. She knew her way around her small apartment and her assisted living community by heart. She listened to audiobooks. She would point out, to anyone visiting her, the pieces of art on the wall and tell them about where she'd gotten that photo or who had made that painting. Funny and talkative, she was a delight.

Being blind also didn't affect her spiritual life, and her love of Jesus shone brightly. She recited

Psalm 23 every day and prayed for each and every one of her grandchildren, great-grandchildren, and great-great grandchildren by name. She told me that every single day she listed nearly thirty names in prayer.

I'm not blind and I don't have grandchildren yet, but my memory of Grandma speaking my name and the names of her loved ones in prayer inspires me to do the same. Thank You, Jesus, for Your faithful servant Rhoda. —JENNIFER GRANT

FAITH STEP: *Jot down the names of five people whom you love before spending time in prayer. Take a few minutes to pray for each person, thanking Jesus for something you love about them and asking Him to encourage and protect them.*

SUNDAY, SEPTEMBER 21

Then the angel said to me, "Write this: Blessed are those who are invited to the wedding supper of the Lamb!"
Revelation 19:9 (NIV)

WHEN THE RESTAURANT HOSTESS SEATED our family in a private room on Sunday afternoon after church, it was an upgrade we enjoyed without ever imagining a deeper blessing behind it. All we saw in the moment was that the table was large enough to accommodate our party of nine. Never did we guess we'd be a party of eight in a few short days.

My brother-in-law's death changed the fabric of our family in many ways, but one of the most noticeable was how it affected Sunday lunches. Without warning, his chair at the table became empty. His stories unheard. His voice absent. In our grief, we avoided that particular restaurant for months, and I wondered if our family would ever heal enough to be able to enter the private room again without him.

However, many Sundays later, the day came. We gathered at the restaurant, sat at the table in the private room, and enjoyed a meal together as a party of eight. But as I absorbed the weight of the empty chair and the loss it symbolized, the Lord graciously shifted my perspective. I no longer felt that my brother-in-law was missing from our table, but rather that we were missing from his. The Lord brought to my mind the angel's words to John in the book of Revelation about feasting at the wedding supper of the Lamb and the place He is preparing for us at His eternal table. And at once I was comforted. Thank You, Jesus. —EMILY E. RYAN

FAITH STEP: *Thank Jesus for a special person in your life who has passed on and visualize the first meal you will have with them in eternity.*

MONDAY, SEPTEMBER 22

But our citizenship is in heaven. And we eagerly await a Savior from there, the Lord Jesus Christ, who, by the power that enables him to bring everything under his control, will transform our lowly bodies so that they will be like his glorious body. Philippians 3:20–21 (NIV)

As I WAS REACHING UP for something in a closet this morning, I felt a painful twinge in my lower back. *All I did was stretch my arms, for golly's sake!* I thought to myself. A while after, I couldn't bend down without wincing.

At fifty-six, this kind of thing is happening more and more. I'm a jogger, and just recently I noticed some discomfort in my knee. Not so much actual discomfort but just an awareness of something that wasn't there before. This is just the latest in a good 15 years of really noticing the effects of aging.

At forty, like clockwork, I needed reading glasses to see small print. At forty-five, I noticed I didn't recover from injuries or sickness as I used to. At fifty, well, menopause and all the side effects began to happen. I have friends who are older, and they're always saying, "Wait until you're sixty!" Or seventy! Or eighty!

Yes, these bodies of ours sure wear out over time. Yet our earthly, fragile, time-limited bodies were made to expire. They last a lifetime in their current form and then transition to another glorious form. One that won't get sick, won't wear out, won't fail us in any way. Until then, I'll look toward Jesus and heaven, grateful for the mortal body I have, aches and all. —ISABELLA CAMPOLATTARO

FAITH STEP: *Draw a figure of your body on a sheet of paper and write a prayer of thanks for each part, whether it's in peak working condition or not. If you're artistic, draw a picture of heavenly you!*

TUESDAY, SEPTEMBER 23

Carry each other's burdens, and in this way you will fulfill the law of Christ. Galatians 6:2 (NIV)

OUR RURAL HIGH SCHOOL IS not what most foreign-exchange students envision when they choose to spend a year in America. Missouri is far from the Big Apple, Hollywood, and Walt Disney World—locations that influence their cultural expectations, although we do have a few cowboys, which also make the list.

I was surprised to learn that in their preparation, the students were told when Americans ask, "How are you?" to simply answer, "Fine." I didn't realize this cultural platitude warranted special attention. Our visitors were perplexed that Americans would ask an automatic question and expect a meaningless response.

I wonder if "I'll pray for you" has also become an automatic and meaningless response. When friends share a parenting struggle, a health issue, or a complicated decision they face, I'm quick to say, "I'll pray for you." When I scroll Facebook and see a post requesting prayer, I comment, "Praying!" I'm sincere, but sometimes I forget to actually pray. How many times have I offered nothing more than an empty promise?

Instead of promising to pray when someone asks, my pastor says to stop and pray right where you are—in the Walmart parking lot or at a school sporting event. How awkward! I prefer Jesus's practice of praying in solitude. Yet when a friend was deeply troubled and confided in me, I surprised myself. I grabbed her hand, bowed my head, and prayed right then and there. Tears and appreciation filled her eyes, and Jesus filled my heart. No more meaningless or automatic prayer promises from me! —KAREN SARGENT

FAITH STEP: *Instead of telling a friend, "I'll pray for you," stop and pray where you are, even if it feels awkward. Jesus will lead.*

WEDNESDAY, SEPTEMBER 24

Come near to God and he will come near to you. Wash your hands, you sinners, and purify your hearts, you double-minded. James 4:8 (NIV)

I CLOSED MY LAPTOP, FEELING irritated. The same person in my social media feed kept appearing. Brenna often posted about her unhurried prayer time, rich Bible-reading practices, and exciting answers to prayer. Her spiritual life seemed so robust! Distracted prayers on the morning commute and Bible verses on Post-it notes were often my best efforts to connect with Jesus. I envied the vibrant spirituality I lacked in my hurried life.

My irritation and comparison kept recurring each time I saw Brenna's posts. I wondered if I was doing something wrong because I didn't have "hey, look at this!" faith experiences. I started doubting that Jesus even heard my prayers, though I had no evidence other than my feelings.

Ironically, one day at school, I was helping a fourth-grade girl who struggled with similar comparison and jealousy issues online when I had an aha experience of Jesus interacting with me. As I worked with Molly to reframe her thinking by focusing on positive things in her life, I realized the words I told her were the exact same ones I needed to hear.

I needed to stop comparing my experiences to others. Like Molly, I reframed my thinking. Instead of envying, I became mindful of Jesus's presence in positive, ordinary occurrences. With a new curiosity, I began thanking Jesus for little things—pleasant conversations, a safe commute, and enough finances to buy groceries. And I spent less time on social media. Good advice for Molly and me! —BRENDA L. YODER

FAITH STEP: *Do something to reframe your thinking. Maybe it's thanking Jesus often for simple pleasures and everyday experiences or spending less time online. Notice how this draws you closer to Jesus.*

THURSDAY, SEPTEMBER 25

He will not let your foot slip—he who watches over you will not slumber. Psalm 121:3 (NIV)

ONE OF THE MOST INTIMATELY beautiful moments a parent or grandparent can experience early in the life of a child is when the baby awakens from sleeping, makes eye contact, recognizes the face, and smiles broadly. Oh, what a wonder! The child sees, recognizes, and is pleased. If not captured in a photo, it's certainly imprinted on the mind and heart.

The Bible tells us our Lord is always watching, even while we sleep. Will His child wake screaming, eyes closed tight against the world and present circumstances? Will His child wrestle awake, squirming, unhappy, already calculating the day's workload, challenges, or miseries? Or will the child—will I—open my eyes, catch His gaze, and delight in recognizing the face of my Jesus, the One who loves me like no other?

The phrase "watches over you" appears multiple times in eight short verses of Psalm 121. He's watching, watching, watching...What will He see when I open my eyes on the new day? My attention darting everywhere else rather than locked on His face? My whole being churning, or will He see me smiling broadly because no matter what the day holds, I am held, cherished, prayed over, and watched over? This morning, may I make eye contact with the One whose gaze is already on me. —CYNTHIA RUCHTI

FAITH STEP: *If your habit is to look at the alarm clock, glance at your phone, or groan when you first awaken in the morning, build a new habit. Open your eyes slowly toward heaven, smile wide, and start the day with, "Good morning, Jesus."*

FRIDAY, SEPTEMBER 26

And be ye kind one to another, tenderhearted, forgiving one another, even as God for Christ's sake hath forgiven you. Ephesians 4:32 (KJV)

THIS MORNING I LISTENED TO the late Keith Green introduce the song "Oh Lord, You're Beautiful" by saying, "Lord, You've got to do something about my heart.... It's starting to harden up.... I wanna have skin like a baby on my heart."

That got to me.

As I grow older, my behavior may look pretty good from the outside. My sins probably aren't as obvious as they used to be. But what about my heart, Jesus—my gradually hardening heart?

I inwardly criticize people whose opinions differ from mine. I sometimes snarl at distracted drivers and find fault with those who inconvenience me. I can be mean, and sometimes irritation hides behind my smile. Could these un-Christlike traits be building calluses on my heart?

The short answer is yes. Sin wreaks havoc even when it's invisible.

Jesus warned against hardening our hearts. He said, "Love your enemies" because that's what His Father was like. "Our Father is kind; you be kind" (Luke 6:35–36, MSG). Even in our thoughts.

When someone hurts me, I can pray for them. I've started doing this when someone cuts in front of me in traffic, says something I find annoying, or maybe hurts my feelings. Both my actions and attitudes matter if I want to shed this calloused, old skin on my heart for soft, tender skin like a baby—and Jesus. —SUZANNE DAVENPORT TIETJEN

FAITH STEP: *Take a few moments to look inward. Then listen to the live version of "Oh Lord, You're Beautiful." Make a plan to get baby skin on your heart.*

Saturday, September 27

*Cleanse me with hyssop, and I will be clean; wash me, and
I will be whiter than snow. Psalm 51:7 (NIV)*

As a pickup truck passed me on the highway the
other night, I saw the strangest thing. Like a lot of
trucks, it was jacked up high, so there was a lot of
space between the tires and the frame of the truck.
However, this owner had added lights to that space
so they shone on the wheels and the underside of
the vehicle. You could actually see all the individual
parts of the truck, and they shone like the Chrysler
Building! Clearly, this guy polished the undercar-
riage of his truck, in addition to waxing the surface.

I know for a fact that the underside of my minivan
is covered in mud and rust. I never wash the surface
of it, so it's a guarantee that the underneath is a mess.
Yet glimpsing the shine of the underside of that truck
got me wondering: *What does the underside of my soul
look like?*

What bad habits have I developed that are stick-
ing to it like mud? What sins have I not confessed
that are eating away at me like rust? I don't know
that I'd ever want a bright light to illuminate the
dark places of my soul for all to see. But that shiny
truck belly reminds me to take all my wrong behaviors and sins to Jesus, confess them, and let Him
wash me clean. —Claire McGarry

FAITH STEP: *Take your car to the car wash and think about Jesus washing you clean when you bring your sins to Him.*

SUNDAY, SEPTEMBER 28

You will keep him in perfect peace, Whose mind is stayed on You, Because he trusts in You. Isaiah 26:3 (NKJV)

MY HUSBAND AND I FREQUENTLY watch the news on television while making dinner. I figure it's good to be informed about what's going on in our city, nationally, and around the world, right? After a few months of this routine, however, I discovered that knowing about every bank robbery, shooting, or family tragedy was making me lose my appetite!

I changed to reading the news in the morning. But even then I would find additional depressing news headlines or outlandish stories about famous people flash across the screen on my phone or laptop. Occasionally I've clicked a couple of links to read those unbelievable stories and pretty soon I've wasted 30 minutes. Those stories didn't uplift my spirit or help me prepare for the day ahead. More importantly, those voices stole my peace.

The internet, 24/7 news, and social media may bring advantages, but I can't hear Jesus when I'm oversaturated by mass media. So I decided to begin my day by reading Jesus's Word before I look at emails, social media, and the internet. It's only when I'm filled with Jesus's peace that I can hear Him and stomach what's happening in the world. —JENNIFER ANNE F. MESSING

FAITH STEP: *Read a chapter in God's Word today before turning on the television or reading anything online.*

MONDAY, SEPTEMBER 29

He has shown you, O mortal, what is good. And what does the LORD require of you? To act justly and to love mercy and to walk humbly with your God. Micah 6:8 (NIV)

MY FAVORITE HIKE ISN'T LONG, just a few miles. Nor is it difficult. The path remains level the entire distance. What it lacks in challenge, it makes up for in serenity. As I walk, I pass a forested area, a farmer's field, and a mellow section of the grand Willamette River. Apples from a historic orchard drop alongside the trail, and reintroduced native flowers bloom in the sunshine. The air is fresh and clean. Nothing settles my soul like this place.

I used to walk it with my German shepherd mix, Gunther. Leashes aren't always required here, so he'd traipse in and out of view, exploring and enjoying. He's gone now, but as I hike I often feel his dear presence by my side.

Since then, I've become more aware of a different presence, more constant and more powerful—Jesus. Step-by-step, He walks alongside me. Unlike the disciples who didn't recognize Jesus on the road to Emmaus (Luke 24:13–33), I am blessed to feel His presence. He shares His unshakeable peace with me, and I slow my pace, both physically and mentally. Jesus directs my eyes and ears to His magnificent creation, and I am humbled. This beautiful world in which I live turns at His pace. I gaze at the river and stop to join it in praise. —HEIDI GAUL

FAITH STEP: *Take a break from your everyday routine to visit a park or nature area. Listen to the birds, watch trees sway in the breeze, and breathe in the sweet air as you ponder Micah 6:8.*

TUESDAY, SEPTEMBER 30

For the entire law is fulfilled in keeping this one command: "Love your neighbor as yourself." Galatians 5:14 (NIV)

IN THE PREDAWN HOURS, I stood in the laundry room, yawning and stuffing towels into the washer. My mind was divided between my task and my prayer: "Lord, please help me be a better wife, a better mom, nana, daughter, sister, neighbor, stranger"—I dropped the lid with a startled jerk. *A better stranger? Where did that come from?* I wondered.

Jesus answered my question. He reminded me of a long-ago afternoon in a parking lot during my early days of following Him.

As I waited in the car, a woman exited the store pushing a shopping cart and yelling at the crying toddler inside it. My heart hurt for the little boy and for his upset mother; I felt powerless to help. Until I remembered that I could pray. So until their car faded from sight, I prayed for the little boy and his mom, lifting them up in every way I could think of.

Jesus taught that our neighbor is anyone who crosses our path. If it's in our power to do another person good, then Jesus wants us to love them as He would. After living away from family members most of my life and relocating several times, I tend to pay attention to the expressions and body language of people around me. It's often easy to spot someone who might need a friendly smile and kind words. Maybe my semiconscious prayer means I need to renew my commitment, asking Jesus to help me see each person through His eyes so I'll know how to love and pray for them. —DIANNE NEAL MATTHEWS

FAITH STEP: *As you go about your day, watch for any new "neighbors" Jesus puts in your path.*

WEDNESDAY, OCTOBER 1

Physical exercise has some value, but spiritual exercise is valuable in every way, because it promises life both for the present and for the future. 1 Timothy 4:8 (GNT)

A LITTLE GRAY MOUSE PEEKED out from under the loveseat. I saw another in the kitchen. And this morning there were two on my bed. You'd think with our resident house cat, Thomasina, this couldn't happen. But it's because of the cat that we have mice. The realistic-looking felt toy mice are her dollies, and sometimes they disappear under cabinets, couches, and armchairs. Thomasina is busy every day and night playing with her prey.

I'm grateful she has this stimulating way of entertaining herself. Active, imaginative play keeps her occupied, energized, and fit. But as a fitness instructor currently in between fitness programs, I'd much rather be reading my Bible than exercising.

I'm feeling guilty about not exercising as I watch Thomasina's robust workouts with her mice. I asked Jesus how I could incorporate fun, spontaneous, short bursts of exercise into my daily routine. Then I remembered a simple curved fitness board long ago tucked away and forgotten, like the disappearing toy mice. I promptly retrieved the brightly colored board, played a YouTube video to watch while exercising, and went to work twisting and balancing for an easy half hour.

Though using the board wasn't much compared to an exercise class, it was a start. The next time I'm exercising, whether on my curvy board or in some other way, I will thank Jesus for helping me make time for both physical and spiritual fitness.
—CASSANDRA TIERSMA

FAITH STEP: *Spend a few minutes moving your body energetically. While exercising, thank Jesus for your life. Ask Him how you can incorporate more play into your daily routine.*

THURSDAY, OCTOBER 2

However, as it is written: "What no eye has seen, what no ear has heard, and what no human mind has conceived"— the things God has prepared for those who love him—these are the things God has revealed to us by his Spirit. 1 Corinthians 2:9–10 (NIV)

MY COLLEGE GOSPEL CHOIR IS planning a fiftieth anniversary celebration of its founding for this fall. During homecoming weekend, we'll all return to our alma mater to gather once again for a concert to sing praises to God, just as we did decades ago as students. We've had numerous Zoom meetings and have been excited to see each other's faces online after all these years. I've also been thrilled to reconnect with classmates over the phone and to hear their voices. I can only imagine the squeals of joy and laughter and the hugs we'll share when we are back together on campus later this year for the big event.

As the anticipation builds for the reunion, I am also starting to think more about another reunion that's coming, one that will be more than I can envision. It will be in heaven when I'll meet Jesus face-to-face. I'll also get to see countless beloved family members—my dad, grandparents, uncles, aunts, and cousins, as well as wonderful friends who have already passed on from this world. Just thinking about the joy, laughter, and bear hugs that will take place in the presence of Jesus makes me smile. I believe we'll even get to sing! Heaven will be the place for the greatest reunion ever.
—BARBRANDA LUMPKINS WALLS

FAITH STEP: *Make a list of the things you're looking forward to in heaven. What are you doing to prepare for your heavenly reunion with loved ones and Jesus?*

FRIDAY, OCTOBER 3

You will keep in perfect peace those whose minds are steadfast, because they trust in you. Isaiah 26:3 (NIV)

MY SON ADDISON IS A junior in high school. He drives himself to school each day. The first morning that he backed out of our garage and drove away, I felt panicky. I love that he is gaining his independence, but I am nervous. He has proven himself to be a level-headed driver. I just am not sure about the folks he's driving alongside on the freeway. Are they texting? Are they paying attention? Are they following the speed limit?

I get anxious thinking about the dangers on the road. The other morning, it was snowing outside as he left for school. I felt my worry level ramp up. I envisioned giant slicks of black ice and cars spinning out. I have a terrific imagination and not always in a good way. The less control I have, the more I visualize worst-case scenarios. It's not helpful for me or my family. When my worries spin out of control, it exposes my lack of trust in the One who loves me most of all—Jesus.

Jesus invites me to fix my mind on Him. Are my thoughts ping-ponging with anxiety or are they held steadfast in the knowledge that Jesus is in control of everything, including my family? When I choose to anchor myself in Jesus and His faithfulness, my mind rests in His perfect peace.
—SUSANNA FOTH AUGHTMON

FAITH STEP: *Do your worries tend to spin out of control? Write a list of your worries and offer them to Jesus in prayer. Ask Jesus to replace your anxious thoughts with His perfect peace.*

SATURDAY, OCTOBER 4

And now, dear brothers and sisters, we want you to know what will happen to the believers who have died so you will not grieve like people who have no hope.
1 Thessalonians 4:13 (NLT)

MY MOTHER WAS DIAGNOSED WITH pancreatic cancer 4 months before her passing, and I was not prepared to lose her. I'd carted her from pillar to post hoping someone could heal her but to no avail. My heart was breaking—she was my best friend and closest confidante. *What would I do without her?* One afternoon she called me upstairs. I ran in and sat by her, concerned. She exclaimed excitedly: "Pammy, Jesus is waiting for me! I won't be with you much longer." I sobbed like a baby. *How could Jesus be waiting for you when I still need you?*

Several months later, Mom met Jesus. A wonderful nurse came to wash Mom's body and put her in her favorite frilly nightgown, awaiting the undertakers. It was surreal. Blinded by tears, Jesus gave me a special comfort that morning. I heard my mother's voice saying, "I love it here!" I had never, ever heard her speak with such incredible joy. I knew she was experiencing heaven.

Years later, each time I want to cry for her (an urge that has never really gone away), Jesus reminds me of her saying, "I love it here!" and my soul becomes peaceful. Because of that special gift, my grief turns to the hope of seeing her again, sometime soon. —PAMELA TOUSSAINT HOWARD

FAITH STEP: *If someone you've loved dearly is now with Jesus, meditate on Revelation 21, which describes heaven in all its splendor.*

SUNDAY, OCTOBER 5

Not looking to your own interests but each of you to the interests of the others. Philippians 2:4 (NIV)

I WENT TO MY DAUGHTER'S robotics state championship recently. Knowing I'd be there for 8 hours, I brought work to do. Kids were applauding and cheering for each other all day long as part of the primary pillar of robotics: gracious professionalism. Whenever Jocelyn's team wasn't actively competing, I'd put in ear plugs and work.

Suddenly, there was such a thunder of clapping and yelling I heard it through my ear plugs. Looking up, it seemed like one robot was stealing cones from the other to get more points. Jocelyn explained that that wasn't the case at all. After one team's robot fell over, the other team stopped what they were doing. Sacrificing their opportunity to rack up more points, they used their robot to pick up the other one, getting it back on its gears so it could participate. This was a competition! The point was to get as many points as possible to be the best in the state. That team didn't win in points, but they sure did in gracious professionalism. Their choice to build up the other team instead of taking advantage of their downfall drew the most praise and applause of the day.

Jesus role-modeled gracious professionalism when He came to serve instead of being served. Getting ahead and having more than others is not what His Kingdom is about. It's about stopping what we're doing to lend a hand to someone in need to help them get back on their feet so they can move forward. No doubt, serving like Jesus draws the most praise and applause from Him. —CLAIRE MCGARRY

FAITH STEP: *Take time today to help someone in need to get back on their feet.*

MONDAY, OCTOBER 6

And a highway shall be there, and it shall be called the Way of Holiness; the unclean shall not pass over it. It shall belong to those who walk on the way; even if they are fools, they shall not go astray. Isaiah 35:8 (ESV)

"JULIA, DO YOU WANT TO ride with me?" I asked my friend. "Surely we can't get lost. It's one road with no turns to Brewer High School."

We each had a child performing in the county marching band show. I picked up Julia and drove south on Highway 67. Forty minutes later, we arrived and chose seats near the 50-yard line. The show was loud and colorful and fun.

Afterward, we maneuvered through the crowded parking lot. I set the cruise control and headed for home. We chattered about the different bands, our kids, our husbands, our parents—best friends can cover a lot of topics in a short amount of time.

Suddenly, out of nowhere, a stop sign appeared. I rolled to a stop and looked at Julia. "Where in the world are we?"

"I have no idea."

"Cotaco." I pointed toward a sign. "How did we end up in Cotaco?"

Julia giggled. "Leave it to us to get lost when all we had to do was pull out of the parking lot and go left."

In my spiritual life, I get lost occasionally. I'm driving along, talking, loving Jesus, and enjoying the ride. I relax and put some things on cruise control, seeking Jesus less often and less fervently. Without even realizing it, I find myself at a stop sign in an unexpected place. I look around and wonder how I got there. But then I spot Jesus. He patiently opens a map and gets me back on track. —BECKY ALEXANDER

FAITH STEP: *Are you on the right path? Seek Jesus to adjust your spiritual route.*

TUESDAY, OCTOBER 7

People will come from east and west and north and south, and will take their places at the feast in the kingdom of God. Luke 13:29 (NIV)

I'VE LIVED NEAR RAILROAD TRACKS all my adult life. My farming community is considered a train town, or "hub city," which is made apparent by the large railway yard just off our main street. I've never been bothered by the clanking of cars coupling on the sidetracks or the sounds of those lonesome whistles blowing. When I'm awakened from a troubled sleep, the rhythmic *clack-clack* of engines chugging past comforts me. My thoughts turn to the passengers whizzing by inside those railroad cars. Where did their journeys begin and where will they end up? I think of the children's author Dr. Seuss's words, "Oh, the places you'll go! You'll be seeing great sights!" and I nod back to sleep.

My faith journey with Jesus reminds me of train travel. Most of the time, I have no inkling of what lies just ahead, whether it will be a detour through badlands or a scenic panorama. But I love this trip and trust Jesus to keep me on the right track. I know where I've come from, and I understand that as a Christian, I'll ride every mile with Jesus by my side.

Fellow believers are also on their way, learning and growing in Jesus just as I am. We're gathering from every corner of the earth and will meet at the last stop, our eternal final destination—the Kingdom of God—beautiful beyond anything imaginable. The glorious end of the line. —HEIDI GAUL

FAITH STEP: *Visit a nearby train station and take in the contagious excitement of the travelers as they embark and disembark. Consider your journey with Jesus and the incredible destination that lies ahead.*

WEDNESDAY, OCTOBER 8

The desert and the parched land will be glad; the wilderness will rejoice and blossom. Isaiah 35:1 (NIV)

A DECADE AGO, MY HUSBAND and I lived near an industrial area with pipelines, storage tanks, towers, and ever-present flares burning off excess gases. The proximity of this view made the bits of nature in our golf course subdivision even more precious, especially the small wooded area along the main entrance. One weekend, we returned from a trip to find this area bulldozed. Uprooted trees lay among huge clumps of earth; not a single living plant remained.

I adopted a new route for my morning walk to avoid the devastation. Over the next 2 years, the scheduled construction of new homes never happened. Then on a beautiful October morning, I walked down that end of the sidewalk and found the area full of color and life. Masses of small yellow, purple, and pink wildflowers. Tall grasses in all shades of green. Here and there a sapling rose up. It didn't look the same as before, but it was breathtaking.

Isaiah wrote poetic passages predicting a future time in Israel's history when the Messiah will return to reign. These images also apply to the lives of anyone who follows Jesus today. Sudden life changes have made me feel uprooted or barren. Sometimes my spiritual journey resembles wandering in the wilderness. But Jesus won't leave me that way. As I draw close to Him and wait for His timing, He will cause my life to bloom. And His presence will make it breathtaking. —DIANNE NEAL MATTHEWS

FAITH STEP: *Go for a walk and look at the flowers and plants around you. Invite Jesus to help every area of your life bloom.*

THURSDAY, OCTOBER 9

And a woman was there who had been subject to bleeding for twelve years. She had suffered a great deal under the care of many doctors and had spent all she had, yet instead of getting better she grew worse. Mark 5:25–26 (NIV)

MY HEART HURT FOR MY oldest daughter as she described the chronic pain she'd endured for a decade. Other than walking this journey with medical professionals and her husband, she'd suffered in silence. But no more. Her dad and I now knew about her situation, and we committed to seek Jesus's compassion and healing on her behalf through prayer.

We've kept our word through several years of highs and lows. The biblical account of the woman healed after suffering a dozen years inspires us to persevere.

This woman's pain was not only physical. She suffered emotional and mental anguish too. Within the cultural context of her day, she contaminated anyone she touched, any chair or bed on which she sat, and any dish she used. Twelve years under those circumstances must have felt like a very long time, but she did not surrender hope. She braved her circumstances and sought Jesus, and He rewarded her faith in Him.

My daughter's journey feels like a very long time for her and her husband too. Chronic pain takes a toll. Some days are brighter than others, but even in the dark, we cling to hope. Jesus knows our daughter's situation, and He hears our cries for help. We will continue to seek His face and trust Him for a good outcome in His time. —GRACE FOX

FAITH STEP: *Send a text, email, or greeting card to someone who suffers from chronic pain. Make it a sweet reminder of Jesus's love.*

FRIDAY, OCTOBER 10

And let us not neglect our meeting together, as some people do, but encourage one another, especially now that the day of his return is drawing near. Hebrews 10:25 (NLT)

WHEN I FIRST STARTED MY online small group several years ago, I did it mainly as a favor to my husband. He is our online pastor at church, so I wanted to show my support for his ministry by volunteering to help. Plus, my schedule has always prevented me from joining an in-person Bible study group, so I thought I'd "settle" for an online group instead. Now, dozens of Tuesday nights later, I've realized what a blessing online ministry can be. It reminds me of the spiritual community of the early church, when believers would meet in homes as well as temple courts. They had a level of intimacy with each other that is hard to replicate if our day-to-day lives never intersect.

The women in my online group see me as I really am. Not made up and neatly pressed for Sunday church services, but worn out at the end of a long day, a little frazzled, and leaning on Jesus for every ounce of strength I have. Our weekly appointment allows us to walk through life's highs and lows together, pray for the specifics of our day-to-day needs, and hold each other accountable as we get to know Jesus more intimately through His Word.

The group has also helped me to see the potential and need for a greater emphasis in online ministry. Never before could we reach the unreachable in such an easy way. Now, every time I go online, I see the internet as my own personal mission field.
—EMILY E. RYAN

FAITH STEP: *Think of one way you use technology to connect with other believers or introduce others to Jesus. Do it today.*

SATURDAY, OCTOBER 11

And I pray that Christ will be more and more at home in your hearts, living within you as you trust in him. May your roots go down deep into the soil of God's marvelous love.
Ephesians 3:17 (TLB)

AFTER PULLING OFF A SUCCESSFUL out-of-town event, my friend CJ and I went back to the house we'd rented to relax a bit before meeting others for a celebratory dinner. While chatting, we heard someone coming through the front door. We flew out of our seats, ran to the door, and positioned ourselves to attack. Before we could do anything, CJ yelled, "Stop." She recognized the voice of the person talking on the other side of the door. It was the owner of the house.

Upset and confused, CJ reminded the owner that we were paying to stay in his home during our trip. It was not right for him to walk in on us unannounced. He apologized profusely and explained that the rental agreement we signed was for a shared space. As it turned out, he had every right to be there. If we had read the contract thoroughly, we would not have been surprised to hear him coming in.

When I accepted Jesus, I agreed to open up my heart to Him and let Him live inside of me. I am no longer on my own. Hearing His voice call out to me should not come as a surprise. After all, my heart is a shared space. —ERICKA LOYNES

FAITH STEP: *Make Jesus feel at home in your heart. Spend 2 minutes in silence this week actively listening to Him.*

SUNDAY, OCTOBER 12

---

*Sweet friendships refresh the soul and awaken
our hearts with joy.* Proverbs 27:9 *(TPT)*

I PUSHED MY SPADE INTO the ground and slowly lifted a clump of irises. I'd received these plants over the past two decades, but last spring only a handful of them bloomed. They'd become overcrowded. I needed to divide them again.

Irises are special to me because they've all found their way to my flower beds from friends and family. Double-blooming purple ones from Grandma Marge. Statuesque white beauties from Mariann, my mom's best friend. Bonnie, the mother of my ex-boss, gave me a petite lavender variety. Nana, my husband's grandmother, contributed bearded golden blossoms. And a coworker, Jennie, offered me some Superstition bearded iris—such a dark purple that they almost look black.

Each spring when they bloom, I remember with fondness the friends who shared their tubers with me. I marvel that these flowers have thrived in my flower beds as a living tribute to the women who gave them to me, even though all but one of these women have passed away. The simple gift of friendship in the form of flowers outlived their bodies— beautiful reminders of them and how each of us lives on through the legacy of our actions.

Recently, Jan, a friend from church, wanted some rhizomes. In the coming years, the gifts from my long-ago friends will bloom in the flower bed of a person they never met. A sweet reminder that Jesus sends me friendships that never die. —STEPHANIE THOMPSON

FAITH STEP: *As you thin out your flower bed or vegetable garden, thank Jesus for the friends He has placed in your life. Find a few rhizomes, seeds, or cuttings you've received from others to share with a friend.*

MONDAY, OCTOBER 13

Now finish the work, so that your eager willingness to do it may be matched by your completion of it, according to your means. 2 Corinthians 8:11 (NIV)

ONE TINY BEDROOM IN OUR home is my studio. It holds my loom, two spinning wheels, and a sewing machine. Bins of handspun and commercial yarn are stacked in the closet along with unspun wool. One basket holds supplies for teaching children to spin, while another tiny basket holds a hand spindle, which I use for spinning in the car. Last summer's flax dries in the barn, destined to become linen. One bin among these fiber riches bothers me though. It's my bin of UFOs (unfinished objects). It's just one plastic bin of half-finished projects I began with anticipation but, for one reason or another, abandoned. Maybe we moved (that happened a lot), or I put an item down to "try out a new stitch" and never came back.

All too often, I fail to finish what I started.

I prayed about the problem raised by my UFO bin and discovered a lack of discipline in my spiritual life too. I need to look to Jesus, whose food was to do His Father's will and accomplish it. Jesus finished what He started (John 4:34). If anyone could help me, it was Him!

My UFO bin is also an Ultra Fabulous Opportunity for me to be more like Jesus. With His help, I decided to finish those items I started before beginning anything new. —SUZANNE DAVENPORT TIETJEN

FAITH STEP: *Turn your unfinished objects into ultra fabulous opportunities. Pray for Jesus's help to finish something you've been putting off.*

TUESDAY, OCTOBER 14

I praise you because I am fearfully and wonderfully made; your works are wonderful, I know that full well.
Psalm 139:14 (NIV)

I HAVE TWO DIFFERENT-COLORED EYES, one brown and one green. I've always felt self-conscious about this, especially when I see photos of myself because my green eye often shows up red in pictures. Most people compliment me when they notice my eyes, but I refuse to believe it. Recently, I had a professional photo taken and I asked the photographer to make both eyes brown.

I've fallen into the trap of self-criticism. In our culture, many women feel pressure to measure up to strict and unrealistic social and cultural beauty ideals. It's easy to forget that I am "fearfully and wonderfully made." Especially when I think negatively about features I cannot change. Not only do I have two different-colored eyes, but also my hair is turning gray, I'm shorter than I'd like...the list goes on. I go to all sorts of lengths to change aspects of my appearance, such as touching up photos, coloring my hair, and wearing high-heeled, uncomfortable shoes.

The Word says Jesus loves me unconditionally and He rejoices over me with singing (Zephaniah 3:17). It's remarkable Jesus has created billions of human beings, each one uniquely beautiful in His eyes. Criticizing myself is really an insult to God because He created me.

I'm working on accepting what I think of as flaws. I'm not touching up photos anymore or wearing uncomfortable high-heeled shoes, but I am still coloring my hair. Instead of seeing two imperfect eyes when I look in the mirror, I want to see myself through the eyes of Jesus, who loves me and created me just as I am. —JEANNIE BLACKMER

FAITH STEP: *Write down three things about yourself you wish you could change but can't. Then tear up that list, throw it in the trash, and tape Psalm 139:14 to your mirror.*

WEDNESDAY, OCTOBER 15

And after the earthquake there was a fire, but the LORD was not in the fire. And after the fire there was the sound of a gentle whisper. 1 Kings 19:12 (NLT)

MONTHS AGO, I JOINED A weight-loss group. In 6 weeks, I was able to lose 12 pounds. Thankfully, I've kept most of it off, but I still needed to lose another 20 pounds to be at my healthiest weight.

I worked on shedding the additional fat on my own but hadn't made a dent. I complained that it was because I no longer had the support of the group to push me past my comfort zone. No one was waiting for that picture of my toes on the scale every Saturday morning, and no more text buddy was there to nudge me forward.

Working from home one afternoon, I'd bent over the computer for hours without stopping to eat properly. Stomach growling, I went to the kitchen to grab something quick. An opened bag of my husband's blue corn chips called to me. I'd eaten a few handfuls before I realized how much those empty calories would count against me. I cried out to Jesus for supernatural strength—I could not go on this way! I was already working out as hard as my middle-aged body could tolerate. Something had to give.

Later that evening when the house was quiet (and my emotions were too), I heard His simple instructions: "Fast one day a week. You'll lose weight and we can spend more time together too." Wow. Yes! I could do that. Jesus's gentle voice was the support I needed to help me achieve my goal. —PAMELA TOUSSAINT HOWARD

FAITH STEP: *Do you have a hard-to-kick habit? Ask Jesus for a tailor-made word of support to help you make a plan and get to work.*

THURSDAY, OCTOBER 16

You will go out in joy and be led forth in peace; the mountains and hills will burst into song before you, and all the trees of the field will clap their hands.
Isaiah 55:12 (NIV)

I GOT UP CRANKY. Plagued by anxiety, I hadn't slept well, and I had a headache. I grouched over to the couch, where my husband, Jeff, and I devote 30 precious minutes each morning to devotions and prayer with our coffee. I spent 27 minutes indulging in what *Jesus Calling* author Sarah Young calls "those sister sins of criticizing and complaining." When I had run out of gripes, I told Jeff I was ready to do our devotions.

"Sorry, Pat, I need to get to work. We've talked through our time," Jeff said. He could have said, "You *whined* through our time," but he was too nice.

I told Jeff I was sorry and moped back to the couch to read devotions on my own. I looked up the scripture Jeff had underlined in our devotional book, Isaiah 55:12, about hills singing and trees clapping their hands. We don't have any hills, vocal or otherwise, in flat little Beaumont, Texas. But we have trees. I stepped out on our porch and gazed at the large oak in our backyard, imagining it clapping its hands. And I laughed out loud! *A tree clapping its hands, Jesus!* So much joy in my world, so much to be grateful for. How could I be troubled when trees clapped their hands?

I decided on the spot to give my problems to Jesus and to choose joy for myself! Joy was a choice. The right choice. —PAT BUTLER DYSON

FAITH STEP: *Draw a picture of a tree clapping its hands or of hills singing. Are you smiling?*

FRIDAY, OCTOBER 17

The third time he said to him, "Simon son of John, do you love me?" Peter was hurt because Jesus asked him the third time, "Do you love me?" He said, "Lord, you know all things; you know that I love you." Jesus said, "Feed my sheep." John 21:17 (NIV)

MACARONI AND CHEESE IS MY soul food of choice. As I spooned an ample serving into my bowl, I wondered how such a simple combination of pasta, cheese, and a few extra ingredients could feed my heart as well as fill my belly. This dish is like a warm hug.

My daughter responds in the same way to chicken and dumplings, and my husband gets all cozy inside over hot dogs. Many of us have memories tied up in these dishes, recollections of times gone by when we felt safe, loved, and completely satisfied.

Three times Simon Peter mouthed the words "I love you" to Jesus, but Jesus wanted more. He wanted Peter to feed His sheep, to take the extra step and share the Bread of Life with those starving for the assurance of eternity.

I enjoy offering love in a dish to old friends and new ones, be it ooey-gooey pasta or a cup of home-made soup. I'm hoping sweet memories will fill the person's heart the next time they enjoy the same food, wherever they are.

But more than feeding them tasty carbs, my goal is to satisfy their hunger with the original, true soul food. And I pray that I honor Jesus's request to feed His flock in both body and soul. —HEIDI GAUL

FAITH STEP: *Next time you entertain, pray for your guests as you prepare the food. Be ready to offer a serving of the Bread of Life along with the meal.*

SATURDAY, OCTOBER 18

And my God will meet all your needs according to the riches of his glory in Christ Jesus. Philippians 4:19 (NIV)

AS A PROFESSIONAL WRITER, it's easy for me to become consumed with the idea of success. Sometimes I think my worth as a writer is tied to the number of books I sell or the accolades I receive. I must remember that my value and purpose are not found in achievements but in my obedience to Jesus. When I consider Jesus's view of success, I remember He gave me the desire to write. My writing is not just a hobby or a way to make money but rather a way for me to use the gifts and skills He's given me to glorify Him and share His love with others.

This truth isn't just for me—it's also for my family. When I work for the glory of Jesus, I'm an example to my family. By prioritizing my time and energy in a way that honors Him, I can show my family what it looks like to live a life of faithfulness and obedience.

As you consider your God-given gifts, remember these truths: Jesus gave us skills and talents for a reason. Our job isn't to rise to what society tells us is great success. Instead, our greatest desire should be to draw closer to Jesus by doing His will. Only when we do that will we find true success. —Tricia Goyer

FAITH STEP: *What's one skill or hobby you enjoy but have yet to make time to pursue? How can you honor Jesus with your talent?*

SUNDAY, OCTOBER 19

Keep your heart with all vigilance, for from it flow the springs of life. Proverbs 4:23 (ESV)

ON OUR WAY TO CHURCH, we pass a quaint little shop with a for sale sign in the window. This is the third time in 2 years the building has been emptied of its contents and put on the market.

The curious thing is all three failed businesses were women's boutiques. The location seems ideal at a busy downtown intersection. The glass store-front is perfect for displaying trendy merchandise on mannequins. Even more puzzling, when one boutique failed, another opened and failed, then a third took its place. Now the building is barren again. A pattern has emerged. This shop is not ideal for a successful women's boutique. I pray the next owner has a different plan.

Peering into the vacant storefront, I'm reminded of empty seasons in my life. I filled my days with family, teaching, church, and a little recreation when I could. I didn't make time to attend a Bible study or read the Bible on my own. My prayers sounded like an order at a drive-through—I want, I want, I want, and please supersize it. My life was stuffed with trendy things, but if you peered inside, you'd see emptiness. Longing to be filled, I realized I could not keep repeating the same patterns.

A few friends and I started our own Bible study so we could flex our meetings around our busy schedules. I found a mentor who taught me to take a deep dive into scripture, how to walk it out, and how to talk with Jesus. I changed how I do business, and now my life is full. —KAREN SARGENT

FAITH STEP: *Pray for a small business owner in your community. Skip the chain store and shop small.*

Monday, October 20

The words of the Lord are pure words, like silver tried in a furnace of earth, purified seven times. Psalm 12:6 (NKJV)

I HIRE A FAVORITE ARTIST, my daughter, Cassie, to paint canvases as gifts for family and friends. For birthdays last year, I came up with the idea of "words to live by" pieces. I asked Aunt Gail and my sister, Cindy, to select three biblical words that held special meaning to them, along with three colors that matched their home décor.

For my aunt, Cassie brushed "Trust," "Joy," and "Peace" with gold paint across a mingled background of hunter green and deep purple. Now, the striking artwork hangs above Aunt Gail's nightstand. It reminds her to trust in the One who is trustworthy, choose the joy of Jesus on happy days and hard days, and seek the kind of peace that passes all understanding.

Cindy's painting turned out beautifully also. Cassie used a different font for each of the words "Salt," "Light," and "Truth." Bright yellow lettering popped on a turquoise and mint backdrop. Today, the cheerful canvas in Cindy's office keeps her goals before her: be salt and light in a troubled world and share the Truth—Jesus—with others.

I rely on Jesus's words from the Bible for daily inspiration too. His words are pure and refined like silver.

They encourage me to pursue my best life within His plans and purposes. They offer help and direction in every situation I face. How can I possibly narrow them down to only three for a canvas of my own?
—BECKY ALEXANDER

FAITH STEP: *Select three words to live by. Display them in a place where you'll see them often, such as on the refrigerator, your computer background, or maybe even in a painting.*

TUESDAY, OCTOBER 21

He who sits on the throne will shelter them with his presence. Revelation 7:15 (NIV)

DESPITE THE CRISP FALL AIR TODAY, I sat outside, wrapped in a blanket, trying to pray. As the wind blew through the trees, my eyes were caught by the twirling leaves showering down like pixie dust. It was mesmerizing.

My appreciation of it became my prayer. I praised Jesus for the elaborate detail He's woven through nature. Then it occurred to me that all those falling leaves were covering the garden I'd just cleared out and put to bed. As frustration began to take hold, I had to remind myself that God is always working for my good.

I could see the falling leaves as a complication, or I could see them as God's perfect plan to shelter and protect my garden from the upcoming winter. I chose the latter and welcomed the array of colorful leaves that enveloped my garden like an intricate quilt. It seems there's always another way to look at what life sends me. When things don't go my way, I need to stop and look at them from a different angle. Jesus is always sending His love to protect and prosper me, even amidst the difficulties. Every time I recognize His hand in the events of my life, I see how He stitches yet another square into the protective quilt He wraps me in. —CLAIRE MCGARRY

FAITH STEP: *Is there something that isn't going right at the moment? See if you can look at the situation through Jesus's loving eyes and identify the good it may hold.*

WEDNESDAY, OCTOBER 22

O LORD, our Lord, how majestic is your name in all the earth! Psalm 8:1, 9 (ESV)

WHEN MY HUSBAND AND I moved to Tennessee last year, I found myself startled by the beauty of the sunsets in our new state. I frequently rushed outside in the evenings to take photos, even though my phone's camera seemed unable to capture the incredible blend of colors. One day I realized that our previous location likely had beautiful sunsets too, but with a house situated in the middle of the subdivision, my view had been obstructed.

Whenever I read Psalm 8, I feel a kinship with King David. What he saw in the sky inspired him to write down beautiful expressions of praise and worship (Psalm 8:3). David shared his amazement that the God who reveals His power and majesty to us through His creation wants to have a personal relationship with us. In fact, he began and ended Psalm 8 with the exact same sentence.

Our Creator begins and ends each day with a display of His power and presence, so I have a new goal. As my husband and I search for a home to purchase, I'm hoping for one that offers views of both the sunrise *and* sunset. But even if that doesn't work out, I plan to begin and end each day with a statement of praise and thanks to Jesus. —DIANNE NEAL MATTHEWS

FAITH STEP: *Practice beginning and ending your daily prayer time with a statement about Jesus's character or His importance in your life.*

THURSDAY, OCTOBER 23

My intercessor is my friend as my eyes pour out tears to God; on behalf of a man he pleads with God as one pleads for a friend. Job 16:20–21 (NIV)

I'D TOLD MY FRIEND ABIGAIL what a difficult year it had been. I'd helped move my mother into a memory care facility after she had a serious fall, broke her hip, and was diagnosed with severe dementia. The facility was excellent on every level, but Mom wanted to be back at home.

My mother's sadness about her changed life circumstances took a toll on me. As I told Abigail, I longed for a sense that my family and I were doing the right thing for Mom. But my mom's ongoing resistance and sadness left me feeling discouraged and weary. Every day, I'd speak to her on the phone or visit, and every day, she would plead with me to take her home.

Abigail is a good listener and a loving person. She often sent me short texts or encouraging notes in the mail. One day, she texted me a picture of a lit candle. She was traveling and visiting a small chapel where parishioners were invited to light candles in prayer.

"Lit a candle for your mom," she wrote.

This small act of kindness brought light to my heavy, burdened heart. The situation with my mother didn't change, but knowing Abigail was bringing my plight to Jesus, for Him to work out in His perfect way, encouraged me. —JENNIFER GRANT

FAITH STEP: *Think of someone who is in need of a strong sense of Jesus's presence. Light a candle before asking Him to bring them comfort. Afterward, let that person know you lit a candle and prayed for them.*

FRIDAY, OCTOBER 24

The LORD hears his people when they call to him for help. He rescues them from all their troubles.
Psalm 34:17 (NLT)

MY TODDLER GRANDSON, JOSHUA, IS learning to verbalize his wants and needs. He knows how to ask for milk or water and his favorite foods. He communicates his desire to be held, to go outside, or to play with a specific toy. He even knows to ask for help when playing with an object that doesn't do what he wants it to do.

For instance, Joshua has a little bus that holds four passengers designed to bend at the waist so they can sit in their seats. He hasn't yet mastered the skill of putting the passengers into a sitting position, and failed attempts frustrate him. He comes to me with the problem passenger in hand and says, "Fix it."

I see myself in my grandson: I have problems too, and failed attempts to fix them bring frustration. And so I seek Jesus's help. Sometimes words fail, so I express myself in the best way I know. Two simple words say it all: "Fix it." My request is not eloquent, but I know Jesus understands.

Josh comes to Grandma with childlike faith, expecting to find help. I go to Jesus with the same confident expectation. I know He hears me

because Scripture declares this to be true. And I know Jesus will help me because He loves me.
—GRACE FOX

FAITH STEP: *Identify one problem in your life that needs help beyond your capability. Pause now and ask Jesus to fix it, and thank Him (in advance) for doing so because He loves you.*

SATURDAY, OCTOBER 25

I love those who love me, and those who seek me find me.
Proverbs 8:17 (NIV)

I DO THIS SILLY THING with my kids where I hide random objects for them to find in unexpected places. It comes from my mission training decades ago. Before being sent overseas, a group of us spent our weekdays together in Maryland studying peace and justice issues, cultural norms, foreign languages, and other things. On the weekends, we went into Washington, DC, to explore the sights. On one excursion, Margaret found the plastic leg of a superhero action figure on the lawn of the Washington Monument. Unsuccessful in finding its owner, she slipped it into her pocket. The next morning, when Bridget poured her cereal, out came the plastic leg right into her bowl! So began the game of "hide the leg." If you found it, you hid it for the next person. It always seemed to show up in the most random and unexpected places, bringing the finder surprise and lighthearted joy.

Just as I hide objects for my kids, Jesus tucks grace into my life with the hopes I'll find it. When I do, it's then my turn to pay it forward, looping other people into the exchange by taking some action that leads them to Him. Whether it's holding the door for someone at the grocery store, paying for coffee for the person in line behind me, or dropping a special treat on the doorstep of someone in need, I pray the receiver finds the real source of surprise and joy in Jesus. —CLAIRE McGARRY

FAITH STEP: *Perform an act of kindness in secret so when it's discovered, the finder is led to Jesus.*

SUNDAY, OCTOBER 26

Not that I have now attained [this ideal], or have already been made perfect, but I press on to lay hold of (grasp) and make my own, that for which Christ Jesus (the Messiah) has laid hold of me and made me His own. Philippians 3:12 (AMPC)

As a neonatal nurse practitioner, I performed a thorough exam on babies admitted to the neonatal ICU. This included their palmar grasp reflex. Grasping begins in the womb as early as 16 weeks gestational age and is one of the earliest reflexes to manifest. Simply put, when anything brushes against the palm of a baby's hand, the fingers curl inward to grab whatever touched it. We are born grasping— holding on. This reflexive grasp is strong enough to hold the baby's weight. (Getting the baby to release his grip is *not* reflexive, as any mother whose little one tangled his fist in her hair knows all too well.)

Reflexive grasping fades away when the baby is about four months old after blazing a nerve pathway from the hand to the brain so that the baby can now hold and cling to people and things on purpose.

A baby's palmar grasp reflex is spiritually significant for me. I read the Bible daily. I believe it and want to understand and obey. Even more, I want to take hold of faith like a lifeline thrown. I want to wrap my fingers around the rope of it—that vital connection with Jesus on the other end. I want to grasp it on purpose, hold on to it in faith, and never let go. —Suzanne Davenport Tietjen

---

Faith Step: *Watch your hands as you go about your day, especially noticing grasping. Imagine your faith in Jesus taking similar actions.*

MONDAY, OCTOBER 27

. . . how much more will your Father in heaven give good gifts to those who ask him! Matthew 7:11 (NIV)

MY DAUGHTER RANDI WAS CREATED to love all of God's creatures, great and small. Dogs, cats, turtles, fish, lizards, and even pet mice have been residents in our home. When she was seven, I tucked her into bed one night and she announced, "I don't know why you won't let me have a baby giraffe." I asked where she would keep a baby giraffe. In her room, of course. When I explained the giraffe would grow too tall, she gave a simple solution: cut a hole in the roof. She was so serious I tried not to laugh.

I bet Jesus tries not to laugh at some of the creative ways I negotiate my requests. Like my daughter, I tell Him, "I don't know why You won't let me have (fill in the blank)." And then I proceed to cut a hole in my roof. I may see blue skies and sparkling stars for a while, but inevitably the rains come and that hole doesn't seem like a good idea anymore. Have you cut holes in your roof too?

Often Jesus doesn't give me what I think I need or want because He knows things I don't understand. Instead, if I align my desires with His will, Jesus has gifts for me that are beyond anything I could request for myself. I'm thankful He wants blessings to pour down on me, not rain. I'm thankful, too, that a guinea pig was a good substitute for a baby giraffe. —KAREN SARGENT

FAITH STEP: *What are you asking Jesus for today? Read John 14:14 and James 4:3 with Matthew 7:11. Journal how these verses clarify your understanding of petitioning Jesus.*

TUESDAY, OCTOBER 28

Now faith is confidence in what we hope for and assurance about what we do not see. This is what the ancients were commended for. By faith we understand that the universe was formed at God's command, so that what is seen was not made out of what was visible. Hebrews 11:1–3 (NIV)

ONE OF THE TOTALLY UNEXPECTED perks of aging is that my vision has improved—really. I've been wearing glasses for distance since I was fifteen, but the normal consequences of aging that cause most people to need reading glasses have resulted in my distance vision improving. When I updated my driver's license recently, I passed the eye test without my glasses for the first time in 40 years, and I still don't need readers either. Amazing!

I believe my spiritual vision has gotten sharper over the years too. I have navigated all manner of highs and lows, including the deaths of my brother and both parents, attaining two degrees with nursing babies at home, moving to a new state, starting a successful business and surviving its failure, enduring a challenging marriage and divorce…the list goes on.

As I've often desperately sought Jesus through all of it, I've learned more about His character, methods, correction, provision, and faithfulness. Jesus has seen me through it all, and in the process, I have gained greater assurance about His unseen workings and more confidence in the hope we have here and hereafter. —ISABELLA CAMPOLATTARO

FAITH STEP: *Take a few minutes to reflect on the way you saw family, friends, work, faith, and challenges 10, 20, and 30 years ago versus today. How has it changed?*

WEDNESDAY, OCTOBER 29

Yet for us there is but one God, the Father, from whom all things came and for whom we live; and there is but one Lord, Jesus Christ, through whom all things came and through whom we live. 1 Corinthians 8:6 (NIV)

I KNOW SOMEONE WHO IS a diabetic. Being in her company a lot, I've learned why it's so important for her to prick her finger and test her blood multiple times throughout the day. As her sugar levels rise and fall based on her food intake, the amount of insulin she needs to balance that out rises and falls too. When I recently heard about continuous glucose monitors (CGM), I was curious. Looking into it, I learned that each CGM has a sensor that's permanently inserted under the skin in the upper arm. It monitors blood sugar levels 24/7 and consistently releases insulin to keep balance in the body. I was telling my friend about it and how it has revolutionized lives. Those who use them wonder how they ever lived without them.

What a CGM does for a diabetic's body is what Jesus does for my soul. If I stay connected to Him, He consistently pushes grace into my veins so it flows throughout my life. On the days when chaos reigns and the pressure of it all threatens to topple me, He injects a higher dose to keep me balanced and in His protective grip. I often wonder how I'd ever survive if I didn't have faith and His love in my life. Jesus revolutionized me. —CLAIRE MCGARRY

FAITH STEP: *Each time you take a sip of water today, imagine it's Jesus sustaining you for whatever lies ahead.*

THURSDAY, OCTOBER 30

But you are a chosen people, a royal priesthood, a holy nation, God's special possession, that you may declare the praises of him who called you out of darkness into his wonderful light. 1 Peter 2:9 (NIV)

"You ARE A STINKY WINKY," I scolded my kitten, Princess, stroking her shiny black fur. She didn't even acknowledge me. Just closed her eyes and gave me a smug smile.

Every morning for weeks, Princess had awakened me at four or five, crying piteously for breakfast. In spite of these shenanigans, I continued to feed her, pet her, and talk baby talk to her. "Maybe I need to rename you Stinky Winky instead of Princess," I said. Then I remembered Jesus. And how He views me, even when I act stinky.

The minute I made Him the Lord of my life, Jesus gave me a new identity. He now calls me God's Chosen, Holy, and Dearly Loved (Colossians 3:12). Just as I continued to love Princess based on who she is, Jesus loves me based on who I am and not on my behavior.

I finally cured Princess of her early-morning habit by flicking a bit of water in her face. It took 3 days for her to let me sleep in until six. If only I could overcome all *my* bad habits in 3 days. But even when I act like a stinky kitten, Jesus never changes my name. My identity in Him remains intact. I'll always and forever be His princess.

—JEANETTE LEVELLIE

FAITH STEP: *Go to a mirror and read 1 Peter 2:9 aloud. Insert your name instead of saying "you" while reading.*

FRIDAY, OCTOBER 31

Is not my power to help myself nothing, and has not every resource been driven from me? Job 6:13 (NET)

WHEN MY CELL PHONE SERVICE provider upgraded its network, my old device became obsolete. The company sent me a new phone that was supposed to be good-to-go straight out of the box. But no matter how many times I tried charging it, it would *not* take a charge. Beyond frustrated, I resigned myself to visiting the closest cell phone store more than 40 miles away. Once there, I explained the problem to the technician, took the phone from the box, and handed him the device.

"It's so light," he said in surprise. Producing a special tool, he deftly opened the battery compartment to find it empty.

Having thoroughly searched the box it came in, I knew there was no battery in the box. Nevertheless, the technician did his own search whereupon he discovered a thin, flat compartment under the bottom floor of the box that held a slim battery. Nothing in the packaging or instruction booklet had mentioned anything about the battery being hidden in this secret compartment—without which the device was useless. Strange that something so basic and necessary was such a mystery.

I'm sometimes in a similar predicament when I don't take time to read my Bible and pray. Without my spiritual battery—God's Word—I, too, am lightweight and useless. Time spent with Jesus and His Word is basic and necessary so I can be fully charged for my daily affairs. It's no mystery that I need Jesus to be fully workable and good-to-go. —CASSANDRA TIERSMA

FAITH STEP: *Recharge your spiritual battery today by taking more time than usual to read the Bible and pray.*

SATURDAY, NOVEMBER 1

If any of you lacks wisdom, you should ask God, who gives generously to all without finding fault, and it will be given to you. James 1:5 (NIV)

A FREQUENT PRAYER IS "JESUS, please help me find my [fill in the blank]." On any given day, it could be my keys, an important note, a phone number, or the item I bought at the grocery store that seems to have disappeared. That happened with 5 pounds of frozen cod one time, but that's another story.

Not long ago, I hunted high and low for an item I knew had slid off the passenger seat when I took a corner a little abruptly. Errands kept me busy, so it wasn't until the next day that I took time to look for it.

How many minutes was it before I realized I was looking in the wrong vehicle? I'd driven our other car the day before.

It wasn't lost to me, pardon the pun, that I've sometimes looked for Jesus where He wasn't. If I want to find Him, I need to go where He is.

I don't think I'm alone in this. Culture often attempts to pull together the pieces that will help form and inform my faith. But when I'm looking to influencers or popular opinion or human theories, I'll be disappointed. I need to look where Jesus is in His Word, His stories, His life—the threads of

Jesus truth woven through both biblical and historical reports.

Searching in the wrong car reminded me that seeking Jesus only brings results if I'm looking where He is. —CYNTHIA RUCHTI

FAITH STEP: *Where do you most clearly find Jesus? Creation? The Bible? Praise songs? Spend extra time there today.*

SUNDAY, NOVEMBER 2

He taught them many things by parables. Mark 4:2 (NIV)

LIVING IN A COLLEGE TOWN, I've had the opportunity to mentor college-aged girls. Born in the mid 1990s to early 2010s, this generation is known as Gen Z and also dubbed the "anxious generation."

One girl I mentor couldn't sleep for a week after reading a story on the internet about an attack on college women. Another student called me to talk about her anxiety about her uncertain future. She was looking for a job, dealing with roommate issues, and having questions about her boyfriend, who wasn't sure if he was ready for marriage. She felt panicky and could not stop her mind from racing.

The American Psychological Association reported that 90 percent of Gen Z experienced psychological or physical symptoms due to stress in the last year. This generation has little or no memory of a life without smartphones and access to the internet. And they have grown up in a world where social media, political polarization, racial unrest, and shootings are realities.

I don't have the answers to all their questions. I can't quell their anxiety. But I can meet with them and tell them encouraging stories. I can tell them about Jesus, who told parables to His disciples. I can share stories from my life. I tell them how God brought Zane and me together, how He provided great job opportunities for me, and how He answered prayers for my sons. I think it's working because they keep coming back for more, and this gives me opportunities to delve deeper into scripture with them. I pray they discover peace and will have stories of their own to tell future generations. —JEANNIE BLACKMER

FAITH STEP: *Find a younger woman who needs encouragement and share stories about your relationship with Jesus with her.*

MONDAY, NOVEMBER 3

Jesus answered him, "Truly I tell you, today you will be with me in paradise." Luke 23:43 (NIV)

IN 2009, MY HUSBAND AND I celebrated our thirty-fifth anniversary with a trip to Hawaii, although we delayed it from June until November because of a work project. We landed on Oahu late at night, so I didn't see our surroundings until the next morning. After breakfast, we hiked up to a lookout point at Diamond Head State Monument. Then we finally reached the top of the 760-foot-high peak and my jaw dropped. Every thought melted away except the beauty of the Pacific stretching out before me: deep turquoise water sparkling in the sun against a backdrop of bright sky and puffy white clouds. I had seen the Atlantic Ocean a few times, but never had I gazed at a view like this. I did not want to leave.

Now that I've reached the age when the loss of family members and friends happen more frequently, I find that memory especially comforting. We think of death as something dark and ugly, but when we close our eyes on this world for the last time, we open them to the bright presence of our Savior. Earthly troubles, worries, fear, sadness, and pain will melt away. Will our jaws drop open at the beauty of His face and the place He's prepared for us? Those who follow Jesus can look forward to being greeted with a view that makes the most beautiful sights on earth pale in comparison. And we'll be grateful we never have to leave.
—DIANNE NEAL MATTHEWS

FAITH STEP: *Have you lost a loved one recently? Take comfort in imagining what their first moment in heaven must have been like as they stepped into the waiting arms of Jesus.*

TUESDAY, NOVEMBER 4

All who heard the shepherds' story were astonished, but Mary kept all these things in her heart and thought about them often. Luke 2:18–19 (NLT)

I WAS UNMARRIED, APPROACHING MIDDLE age, and living in New York City when I attended a friend's wedding in Atlanta. Afterward, I had 2 days of downtime before my flight home. Bored, I looked out of the guesthouse window, admiring the greenery bursting from everywhere. Then I asked Jesus an interesting question: "What am I still doing here, Lord?" Immediately, I heard this in my spirit: "I have something for you here." Wait, what was He saying? Did He actually mean for me to *move* here? Me? A big-city Northern girl move down South? Hmm.

As an only child, I would not easily leave my elderly, widowed mother behind in New York. Yet as I pondered His words, a peacefulness and excitement began to emerge. Before long, an opportunity to enroll in a biblical studies program at a college in Atlanta surfaced. It was a great fit. More pieces fell into place: an affordable, nearby apartment with another student became available. I decided to trust Jesus and make the move.

Two years later, I graduated and was able to buy a townhome (with grass!), and Mom came to live with me. I found a job as a safety instructor, and the hours allowed me to continue writing. Two years after that, I met my wonderful husband, Andrew, at a work event.

Me, move down South? Yes, ma'am! So glad I trusted in the words Jesus spoke to me one boring day. —PAMELA TOUSSAINT HOWARD

FAITH STEP: *Think of a question you can ask Jesus. Wait for an answer and ponder it in your heart until He directs you to take action.*

WEDNESDAY, NOVEMBER 5

Satisfy us in the morning with your unfailing love, that we may sing for joy and be glad all our days.
Psalm 90:14 (NIV)

RON AND I SAT ACROSS from each other in our kitchen, frustrated with ourselves and each other. The same argument repeated itself, even after 30 years of marriage. I came across as critical. He got defensive. You'd think we would have grown past such behaviors.

As a counselor, I coach clients to speak up for their needs. When I shared my needs with Ron, they came across as disappointment or unmet expectations. He shut down, and I felt unheard. We both felt stuck.

I was embarrassed that I felt so needy. Why couldn't I do for myself what I help others with? I knew Ron loved me. Wasn't that enough?

One day, I heard a song that described God's unfailing love. I remembered a Bible verse about being satisfied by God's love. I realized I expected Ron to satisfy intimate longings I'd had since childhood—being understood, heard, and validated. I expected him to meet a need only Jesus could.

I asked Jesus to satisfy me with His unfailing love rather than putting those expectations on Ron. Ron forgave me when I shared my realization. We attended a marriage retreat to learn better patterns of relating. We started sharing what we appreciate about one another. Ron was more intentional in listening and validating my feelings. I was more thoughtful in how I expressed things. We laughed more.

We're still growing these skills. But knowing Jesus's love is the only love that satisfies the unmet expectations we put on each other. —BRENDA L. YODER

FAITH STEP: *Tell your spouse or loved ones daily what you appreciate about them while asking Jesus to satisfy you with His unfailing love.*

THURSDAY, NOVEMBER 6

This is what the LORD says—your Redeemer, the Holy One of Israel: "I am the LORD your God, who teaches you what is best for you, who directs you in the way you should go." Isaiah 48:17 (NIV)

MODERN TECHNOLOGY REALLY BLOWS MY mind. We've got coffee pots that start themselves in the morning so we can have a hot cup of java as soon as we get out of bed. Navigation devices tell us how to get to where we need to go. Cars can start and drive themselves. Lights flick on automatically in our homes before we enter. But the one tech tool I truly love is my smartwatch, which can seemingly do everything.

My watch tells me when I've sat too long and need to get up and move. It even tells me when I'm in an environment that is too loud. One day after receiving an alert from my watch, I thought, *Wouldn't it be nice if Jesus alerted me to things I needed to pay attention to?* But then He reminded me that He does! It's through that still, small voice inside me that says this is the way, now walk in it (Isaiah 30:21). Sometimes it's the voice of a friend or a stranger that speaks directly to a problem I'm facing that they know nothing about. And other times it's through His words that seem to leap off the page as I read Bible passages. Indeed, Jesus speaks to me in various ways. I just need to be smart enough to listen for Him as He sends His alerts. —BARBRANDA LUMPKINS WALLS

FAITH STEP: *Be on the lookout today for Jesus's voice. Is He speaking to you through the Bible? Through conversations with family or friends? Or in some other way?*

FRIDAY, NOVEMBER 7

Do you not know that your body is a house of God where the Holy Spirit lives? God gave you His Holy Spirit. Now you belong to God. You do not belong to yourselves.
1 Corinthians 6:19 (NLV)

I'M ADDICTED TO SUGAR. You wouldn't know to look at me because I have a fast metabolism. Even though I went 7 years without eating sugar after failing a pre-diabetes questionnaire, I've let it creep back into my life. I'm paying for that with irritability and headaches whenever I go without sugar for more than a few hours. Eating protein with sugary treats dampens the sugar high, but now that I keep chocolate-coated ice cream cones with caramel centers in the freezer, I'm feeling convicted about where I turn for comfort.

When I'm worried, afraid, or sad, I find myself reaching for an ice cream cone or something—anything—sweet. During the years that sugar was out of my system, I reached for my Bible instead and looked for the red letters highlighting the words of Jesus. I found answers and real comfort there as I listened to what Jesus had to say.

My battle with eating too many sweets goes better when I leave the treats at the store. I'm avoiding anything with added sugar and eating more fiber and protein and keeping my red-letter Bible close at hand. "How sweet are your words to my taste, sweeter than honey to my mouth!" (Psalm 119:103, NIV). Jesus—not sugar—provides all the comfort I need. —SUZANNE DAVENPORT TIETJEN

FAITH STEP: *Call to mind whatever you love too much and bring it to Jesus in prayer. Look to Jesus, not food, when seeking comfort.*

SATURDAY, NOVEMBER 8

"Come," he said. Then Peter got down out of the boat, walked on the water and came toward Jesus. But when he saw the wind, he was afraid and, beginning to sink, cried out, "Lord, save me!" Matthew 14:29–30 (NIV)

THERE ARE TIMES WHEN I feel a tug from the Holy Spirit to speak an encouraging word to a family member, check in on a distant relative, send a prayer to a friend, or give money to a stranger. When these actions fit nicely into the box that is my way of doing things, I find moving according to the Spirit's leading easy to do. And although I know Jesus wants to use me as a vessel to bless others, I am still humbled at the thought that He does.

Other times, when an action seems too extravagant, audacious, or difficult to achieve, I question if Jesus is impressing these ideas on my heart or if it's the voice inside my head talking. I overanalyze the situation and the focus slowly turns toward me. I wonder what people will think and how they will respond, and I am no longer listening or looking to Jesus for direction. Inevitably, the opportunity passes, and I miss out on being a blessing or being blessed.

Just as Jesus asked Peter to have faith to walk on the water, Jesus is asking me to have that same faith to do both ordinary and extraordinary things. In both situations, I won't falter if I remove the focus off of me and keep my eyes on Him. —ERICKA LOYNES

FAITH STEP: *What out-of-the-ordinary action have you been avoiding? Don't second-guess yourself. Stay focused on the eyes and voice of Jesus.*

SUNDAY, NOVEMBER 9

You make known to me the path of life; you will fill me with joy in your presence, with eternal pleasures at your right hand. Psalm 16:11 (NIV)

I WENT TO A WAKE recently where I didn't know the deceased well. Her name was Ruth. I was there to support her daughter, Sue, my cousin's wife. As I stood in the receiving line, I looked at the poster boards along the wall filled with memorabilia and photos of Ruth through the years. The one that really caught my eye was an article from the local newspaper about her and her husband's sixty-fifth wedding anniversary. In the photo, her husband was dressed in his fireman's uniform and Ruth held a gallon of ice cream and a scoop. It was clear what her husband did for work. But the line moved forward before I could read why Ruth held the ice cream.

I asked a relative of hers about it. She explained that Ruth got to know every neighborhood kid's favorite ice cream flavor. Then she stocked them all in her freezer. Whenever a child came to visit, she was at the ready to give them the ice cream flavor that pleased them the most.

On the ride home, I had an image of Jesus holding a gallon of ice cream and a scoop in His hands. He knows me individually and intimately. He knows exactly what brings me joy. When I visit Him in my prayer time, He's at the ready to give me what pleases me most. —CLAIRE MCGARRY

FAITH STEP: *Discover the "favorites" of each person who comes to your home. Stock up on them so you have them at the ready for the next time they visit.*

MONDAY, NOVEMBER 10

This is the message we have heard from him and declare to you: God is light; in him there is no darkness at all. 1 John 1:5 (NIV)

I SAT IN OUR DARK DEN, my eyes focused on the flames flickering in the fireplace. At this moment, I wasn't proud of myself. I'd snapped to judgment about someone's situation. Though I'd kept my opinion to myself, it was still wrong. Acknowledging that sin burned hot as embers.

An eye for detail and a critical eye are two very different things. One is a gift often used to protect, especially in the medical and scientific fields. The other can be a trait used to scrutinize situations or people harshly. I possess both qualities. Though I try not to judge, at times I slip into that mindset. If allowed, it can become a black hole of negativity. Left unchecked, it can lead to depression.

When I reflect on Jesus, I'm resolved to change. It may take time, and there might be the occasional slipup. That's OK. I'm human. But I can't allow the light of God inside me to be quenched. Like a lamp on a stand, I need to shine (Matthew 5:15) for others to see His glory. Responding to Jesus's love and acceptance brings me closer to Him. I gaze at the fire.

Like Him, I am not a part of the darkness. Because of Jesus, I am the light. Because of Jesus, I am the flame. —HEIDI GAUL

FAITH STEP: *Watch a flame, be it in a candle or fireplace. Its light glows and warms, drawing people to its light. Emulate that fire—and Jesus.*

VETERANS DAY, TUESDAY, NOVEMBER 11

He consoles us as we endure the pain and hardship of life so that we may draw from His comfort and share it with others in their own struggles. 2 Corinthians 1:4 (VOICE)

DRIVING PAST THE ORANGE COUNTY Vietnam War Memorial, I thanked Jesus for Jerry Gatch, the man who'd built it. Jerry, my high school classmate, known for his zany behavior and outrageous schemes, had been drafted by the Army and had served in Vietnam. He'd come home physically intact but bearing a deep wound inside for his brothers who'd returned in flag-draped coffins. He grieved they hadn't been properly honored.

"I'm going to write a book about the soldiers from Orange County, Pat," he told me. "And then I'll build them a memorial." I smiled. *Same old Jerry and his outrageous schemes.*

Through research, Jerry discovered that twenty-eight men from Orange County had died in Vietnam. One by one, he visited the families of these men. After so many years, family members who'd thought their soldier had been forgotten wept as they reminisced, Jerry's tears mingling with theirs. Compiling information and photographs provided by family members, Jerry created a book, *28 Men Fell,* honoring the heroes from Orange County.

But Jerry wasn't finished. He raised money, partly from sales of his book; found a location; assembled volunteers, including homeless veterans; procured donated materials; and a year later, dedicated the Orange Country Vietnam War Memorial. There, the names, images, and service records of every man are etched into granite. Jerry's efforts had honored the fallen and had brought healing to the families and to himself. *I was wrong to doubt, Jesus. Jerry said he'd do it, and with Your help, he did!*
—PAT BUTLER DYSON

FAITH STEP: *Visit a veteran. Ask him to tell you his story.*

WEDNESDAY, NOVEMBER 12

I urge, then, first of all, that petitions, prayers,
intercession and thanksgiving be made for all people.
1 Timothy 2:1 (NIV)

I CALL IT THE "LITTLE GIRL RUN." It happens Monday through Friday, morning and afternoon. My niece, Sophi, gets transported to and from the middle school. My granddaughter Sadie gets dropped off and picked up at the elementary school. My preschool granddaughter Chloe arrives and departs at a church childcare center. The run requires coordination and energy from our whole family to make sure everybody is where they should be and on time.

But we don't mind it at all. We love those girls, take care of them, and most importantly, pray for them without ceasing.

I recently did a scripture study about seeking Jesus on behalf of other people. In 1 Timothy 2:1, I learned there are four key words that represent a different part of prayer. "Petitions" are to fight against evil. "Prayers" are to ask for good. "Intercession" is to lay the needs of others before the Savior. And "thanksgiving" is to recognize the blessings we've received.

Now I use that pattern when praying for our girls. I petition Jesus to protect Sophi, Sadie, and Chloe from any harm, naming my concerns one by one.

I lift prayers for their good—that their hearts will open wide to Jesus's voice and that their lights will illuminate a dark world. My intercessions request help in their challenges, even spelling tests and friend spats. Then, thanksgiving flows from deep inside for the joy the three of them bring to our family.

It's two forty. I better hit the road. Time to do the Little Girl Run again. —BECKY ALEXANDER

FAITH STEP: *Write a prayer for someone using the pattern in 1 Timothy 2:1.*

THURSDAY, NOVEMBER 13

If any of you lacks wisdom, you should ask God, who gives generously to all without finding fault, and it will be given to you. James 1:5 (NIV)

I'LL ADMIT IT—I LIKE TO SLEEP. But most mornings, I'm awake before everyone in the house to read my Bible, pray, and seek direction for my day. With my husband and four kids still at home—and my mom and grandma living with us too—early mornings are my only guaranteed quiet time. With so many people to care for and an abundance of projects and activities, it's a real struggle not to pull the covers up to my neck and stay in bed to get rested up for whatever the day may throw at me.

But I don't. I know it's essential to make time to seek direction that only Jesus can provide.

Drawing closer to Jesus is worth losing a little sleep. My day improves when I turn my thoughts to Jesus's will for me, my family, and the world first thing in the morning. My hours go better when I look at my to-do list and serve in light of His example. When I feel overwhelmed, I turn to Jesus for direction and clarity. His Spirit stirs me to the needs of those around me and gives me the strength to graciously be His hands and feet.

When I seek Him first, my family members awaken to a wife, mom, daughter, and granddaughter who looks forward to living the day by serving them with joy, peace, and confidence. As much as I like to sleep, I better like who I am after spending the morning with Jesus. —TRICIA GOYER

FAITH STEP: *If you don't have an early-morning habit, set an alarm and give yourself time with Jesus before you do anything else. Try this for a week and see the difference it makes.*

FRIDAY, NOVEMBER 14

I am the Alpha and the Omega, the Beginning and the End, the First and the Last. Revelation 22:13 (NKJV)

LAST YEAR WHEN MY DAUGHTER and son-in-law were expecting a new baby boy, they asked their other four kids for name suggestions. Three-year-old Leo offered Chicken Nugget as a possibility. I knew my daughter and her husband would wait until after the birth to share the chosen name, so I began referring to my grandson as Chicken Nugget. At least it was more personal than "the new baby" when we talked about anything baby-related, even though saying it made me hungry at first. Several months later, my relationship with Chicken Nugget became more up-close and personal. I then came to know him as Jordan.

I love that the Bible uses many names to refer to Jesus. He is the Beginning, the End, the First, and the Last. His name is Wonderful, Counselor, Mighty God, Eternal Father, Prince of Peace (Isaiah 9:6). Although He never changes (Hebrews 13:8), my circumstances, emotions, and needs frequently do. As my personal relationship with Jesus has deepened, I've come to know Him in different ways. I felt overjoyed to meet Jesus as the Savior who paid for my sins (1 Peter 2:24). I soon came to know Him as the Good Shepherd who guides, protects, and provides for me (John 10:11). As I studied the Word, I understood the seriousness of obeying Him as Lord (Luke 6:46); when I failed in this area, He mercifully revealed Himself as Faithful and True (Revelation 19:11). No matter which of His names

I use, I'm so grateful to know Him as my Jesus.
—DIANNE NEAL MATTHEWS

FAITH STEP: *List the different ways you have come to know Jesus through the years. Thank Him for how each facet of His character or role impacts your life.*

SATURDAY, NOVEMBER 15

He said, "Throw your net on the right side of the boat and you will find some." When they did, they were unable to haul the net in because of the large number of fish. John 21:6 (NIV)

SEVERAL YEARS AGO, I SENSED Jesus nudging me to start a faith-based one-day women's conference in Canada. Drawing from lessons learned from colleagues about the power of partnerships, I asked another speaker and a worship leader to join me. They were innovative, enterprising women. I wanted them on my team.

Together we launched "Radiant." For 3 years, we collaborated with churches to host unique conferences that drew women from all denominations. Teamwork enabled us to accomplish more than we could have done on our own. Our gifts complemented one another's abilities, and we enjoyed planning and praying together. But the ultimate key to our effectiveness was partnering with Jesus. We always asked for His wisdom and guidance, and we followed His lead. His presence and power brought results we wouldn't have experienced otherwise.

The disciples partnered with Jesus too. They'd fished all night and caught nothing, but everything changed when Jesus stepped into their situation. They worked and He worked, and together they saw amazing results.

This principle of partnership is woven throughout scripture. I'm learning to apply it more within the context of my writing and speaking ministry, but I'm also making it a daily priority in my relationship with Jesus. I don't want to do life on my own—ever. I want Jesus to be my partner from the moment I wake up until I close my eyes to sleep. No matter what work I do, I want Him on my team. —GRACE FOX

FAITH STEP: *Write your name in the blank: Jesus +* _____ *= the best possible partnership.*

SUNDAY, NOVEMBER 16

Seek him that maketh the seven stars and Orion, and turneth the shadow of death into the morning, and maketh the day dark with night: that calleth for the waters of the sea, and poureth them out upon the face of the earth: The LORD is his name. Amos 5:8 (KJV)

I LIVE WAY OUT IN the country in the Ozark Mountains of Arkansas. There is no Starbucks, but there are stars. Millions of stars. On a clear night, we can lie on a blanket in our front yard and feel like the only people on earth, underneath a sky of black velvet—the backdrop for celestial diamonds of all sizes, from the big ones in Orion's Belt to the dust flung outward in spirals from the Milky Way.

When my son was little, we used to do that a lot. We learned to identify constellations. I used stargazing to teach him about the mystery of a Savior powerful enough to create such beauty and personal enough to live in our hearts.

My son is grown now. He has gone to college and we don't get to stare at the sky much together anymore. But every time I look up at the stars at night I am reminded that Jesus is big enough to have created the universe and close enough to meet all of my needs as if I were the only person on earth. —GWEN FORD FAULKENBERRY

FAITH STEP: *Tonight after dark, go outside and look into the night sky. If you can, take someone with you. Remember that the One who made the stars lives in you.*

MONDAY, NOVEMBER 17

A generous person will prosper; whoever refreshes others will be refreshed. Proverbs 11:25 (NIV)

WHILE I WAS IN NEW ORLEANS recently for a conference, I reconnected with a former colleague who took me to brunch at a famous restaurant in the city. Jerry is friends with one of the restaurant's owners, and we received the royal treatment from the moment we stepped through the door. At the end of the meal, we were stunned when servers presented us with five—yes, five—desserts, compliments of the restaurant's co-owner. Bread pudding, strawberry shortcake, cheesecake, an ice cream parfait, and bananas foster—a generous table of treats!

As the waiter prepared the bananas foster at our table, I overheard a young couple seated next to us say they wanted to order it. After the flaming dessert was served, I asked if they would like to have some of ours. "Yes!" the man said without hesitation. They enjoyed it, even before their entrees arrived. It was wonderful to share our sweet abundance with others.

Jesus generously gave of Himself to bless others. He fed hungry crowds who came to hear Him speak (Luke 9:16). He washed the dirty feet of His disciples (John 13:5). And He gave His life to pay for the sins of the world, and that includes mine (Galatians 1:4).

Jesus's generosity blesses me, and I believe I'm blessed to be a blessing to others. So why not share Him—even if it's through a tasty dessert? —BARBRANDA LUMPKINS WALLS

FAITH STEP: *It doesn't take much to brighten someone's day. What will you do to bless a family, friend, or even a stranger today?*

TUESDAY, NOVEMBER 18

The clean of hand and pure of heart, who has not given his soul to useless things, what is vain. He will receive blessings from the LORD, and justice from his saving God. Psalm 24:4–5 (NABRE)

TOWEL ON THE BATHROOM FLOOR. Half-full mug of tea on the table. Empty orange juice carton on the counter. Such is life in a house with two active teens and a husband who works full-time and is in school earning a degree. Usually it's not this bad, but on days like today, I find myself playing the role of sweeper, following grumpily behind as I collect discarded items after my family members rush out the door.

Keeping house while keeping my sanity can be difficult. Checking the fridge before I depart myself, I blanch at the rotten pepper in the vegetable drawer. Hidden underneath fresher items, it was so far gone that I needed a few deep breaths and a few extra minutes to clean that mess too.

The same can be said of my prayer life sometimes. Failing to pause for regular times in prayer often leaves larger messes in my heart for Jesus. I never intended for Him to become my sweeper, cleaning up my careless words and thoughtless deeds. But because of His sacrifice, I'm clean.

With Jesus, I begin anew, trying once more to happily support my busy family without grumbling. I just hope I don't find more rotten peppers.
—GLORIA JOYCE

FAITH STEP: *During your usual routine today, secretly tidy for someone else. Take the time they may not have had. Ask Jesus to bless them in their haste.*

WEDNESDAY, NOVEMBER 19

Everything in the Scriptures is God's Word. All of it is useful for teaching and helping people and for correcting them and showing them how to live.
2 Timothy 3:16 (CEV)

I LIKE TO PEEK INTO people's houses but not in a weird, creepy way. My hubby and I are converting a 40-foot school bus into a custom motorhome, so we watch "van life" and "skoolie" video tours on YouTube. I look in closets, bathrooms, kitchens, and bedrooms. I see what's in people's drawers and cupboards. I welcome others' creative ideas and completed projects.

But I'm disinterested in those that resemble pristine model homes. I want to see all the colorful chaos of real-life living on the road, surrounded by all the stuff of life—books, plants, pets, and assorted daily use items. These videos provide a visual how-to for the particular way of life my hubby and I are planning. And, hopefully watching them will help us avoid making unnecessary mistakes.

Similarly, when I first became a follower of Jesus, I was astonished to discover the book of Proverbs was a practical guide to life. *Why hadn't I known about that? Where had this wisdom been all my life? If only I could've learned these teachings earlier, I could have avoided unnecessary mistakes.*

Just as I like watching realistic virtual tour videos, I want life advice from people whose lives are not perfect. I need how-to advice from God's Word with practical real-life instruction on how to live more like Jesus from a book about colorful, messy, imperfect people I can relate to. —CASSANDRA TIERSMA

FAITH STEP: *Starting today, read a chapter a day from Proverbs. Discover a favorite verse with real-life advice, write it on a note card, and put it in a place where you will see it often.*

THURSDAY, NOVEMBER 20

*One thing I ask from the L*ORD*, this only do I seek: that I may dwell in the house of the L*ORD *all the days of my life, to gaze on the beauty of the L*ORD *and to seek him in his temple. Psalm 27:4 (NIV)*

"THIS IS THE FIRST TIME I was ever in a city where you couldn't throw a brick without breaking a church window," Mark Twain said. He visited Montreal in 1881 and dubbed it "the city of a hundred bell towers."

During that period in history, the many bell towers in Montreal played major roles in people's lives. Churches not only offered spiritual inspiration but also sponsored hospitals, schools, and social services. Some historians believe 90 percent of the residents attended religious services regularly. Sadly, through the decades, the percentage dropped drastically and now sits at just 10 percent.

My tour director job took me to Montreal several times, and I got to see a few of the more than six hundred remaining churches. Red doors and green entryways. Tall steeples and tiny chapels. Rock exteriors and white-painted wood. Stained glass and paned windows. All the structures represented Jesus's touch on the Canadian town and on those who sought Him there.

I paused to pray in front of the churches, sensing the presence of Jesus at the sacred spots. I wondered what miracles might have taken place within the walls. Like Mark Twain, I marveled at the stunning bell towers, stretching upward, decorating an empty sky. Those rooftop beacons of hope invited me—and everybody in Montreal—to come to Jesus and dwell in the house of the Lord. —BECKY ALEXANDER

FAITH STEP: *Notice the bell towers atop churches this week. Stop by one of them for a closer look. Thank Jesus for His presence in your city or town.*

FRIDAY, NOVEMBER 21

Cheerfully share your home with those who need a meal or a place to stay. God has given each of you a gift from his great variety of spiritual gifts. Use them well to serve one another. 1 Peter 4:9–10 (NLT)

OUR RECENT THANKSGIVING CELEBRATION WASN'T traditional. Instead, our three adult children, son-in-law, three grandsons, and two couples who are our daughters' friends shared a delicious potluck meal together in our home.

I hesitated to welcome guests. Two of our dining room chairs don't match the rest, some of our furnishings and accessories are out of date, and our kitchen floor is rather old. I tried to be thankful for what I had, but deep down I sometimes wished for more. Nevertheless, my husband and I were agreeable to hosting the two couples, one pair recent newlyweds and the other pair who are still dating, who are not believers in Jesus. When my husband prayed a blessing on our meal, everyone bowed their heads with us briefly and mouthed a quiet "amen" at the end.

After dinner, we gathered in our front room and listened to our son Gabriel play a piano piece while we ate dessert. Lively conversation and laughter filled our home. Our daughter's friend Shira and her boyfriend thanked us several times for including them, and the recent bride Uaulani even complimented how I decorated.

Funny thing, no one mentioned our mismatched dining chairs or our old kitchen floor. All that seemed to matter is that they were included and accepted. That's something I can be thankful for! —JENNIFER ANNE F. MESSING

FAITH STEP: *At your next holiday gathering, invite a few people over who might otherwise celebrate alone.*

SATURDAY, NOVEMBER 22

A gentle answer turns away wrath, but a harsh word stirs up anger. Proverbs 15:1 (NIV)

I WAS EXCITED WHEN I saw the note taped to our front door that Saturday. Maybe it was an invitation to a party! Hardly. It was a note of complaint from a customer who'd visited our family's hardware store that morning. From the time they'd walked in, they'd found fault with the employees, the products, the service. Further, they'd said that since they could get batteries anyplace, they would take their business elsewhere. By the time I'd finished reading the sarcastic missive, I was fuming. I called my husband, Jeff, at the hardware store and read the note to him, knowing he'd be as mad as I was.

"Did they give a phone number?" Jeff asked me.

"Yes," I said. "And I hope you'll tell them you'd be delighted for them to shop elsewhere."

Instead, Jeff told me he'd call and listen to their complaints, apologize, refund their money for the purchase, and send them a gift card. "Maybe they were just having a bad day," he said.

Not what I'd have done, but it's what Jesus would have done. When someone attacks me, my impulse is to strike back, but that's not what Jesus taught. He preached turning the other cheek, loving my neighbor as myself, spreading peace, not discord. Jeff responded cordially because he didn't want to lose the customer. But beyond that, he recognized that the individual might have been experiencing difficulties in their life. Sadly, the milk of human kindness had curdled in my veins. I apologized to Jesus and thanked Him for my compassionate husband. —PAT BUTLER DYSON

FAITH STEP: *Recall a time when Jesus prompted you to return someone's meanness with kindness. How did the person react?*

SUNDAY, NOVEMBER 23

The thief comes only to steal and kill and destroy; I have come that they may have life, and have it to the full. John 10:10 (NIV)

I LIKE PLANNING MY MEALS for the week and shopping accordingly. But this last week, I had a tight schedule. I knew I wouldn't have time to run to the store before dinner last night. I hopped on my computer and placed my grocery order. I wanted to make burrito bowls with fresh pico de gallo salsa. My recipe called for four jalapeño peppers, but they were only sold by the pound. So I ordered a pound.

When I picked up my order from the grocery store, I found I had grossly miscalculated how much peppers weigh. They had given me twenty-one jalapeños. I texted my neighbors to see if they wanted any. I had zero takers. What I did have was an abundance of peppers—more than I expected or hoped for.

It is like that with Jesus. I have an idea of what I think my life should look like. I tend to go small. I want enough of Him to get me through the week. But His plan is different. He works in different quantities than I do. He offers me complete joy (John 15:11) and peace that passes all understanding (Philippians 4:7). He gives me love as wide as the heavens, justice that is ocean deep, and faithfulness that reaches the sky (Psalm 36:5–6). He came so that I could have abundant life and live it to the fullest. Jesus gives me more than I expected or hoped for. —SUSANNA FOTH AUGHTMON

FAITH STEP: *Think how Jesus has given you abundant life. List the ways He's given you more than you expected or hoped for.*

MONDAY, NOVEMBER 24

We demolish arguments and every pretension that sets itself up against the knowledge of God, and we take captive every thought to make it obedient to Christ.
2 Corinthians 10:5 (NIV)

WHEN I FIRST TRANSITIONED TO a new career as a teacher, one of the hardest adjustments for me to overcome was the perpetually fragmented schedule.

My previous job had allowed for long periods of uninterrupted work with plenty of margin for deep thinking. Now, with classes switching every 45 minutes and constant movement all around me, it felt as if I rarely had time to gather my thoughts, much less deepen them. It took time, patience, and a lot of trial and error, but slowly I learned how to make the most of those bite-sized moments.

The skill also helped me in my relationship with Jesus. I used to think that the only way for me to grow spiritually was through long, focused periods of silence and solitude. Unfortunately, this mindset meant that if I couldn't think deeply about Jesus, I wouldn't think about Him at all. He either got all of my attention or none of it.

Then a Bible teacher reminded me that every thought, no matter how fleeting or superficial, could be claimed for Christ. Paul describes it as "taking our thoughts captive" so that everything we think falls under the command of Jesus. I found that when I began including Jesus in my thoughts, my relationship with Him naturally grew deeper and sweeter over time. My inner monologue turned into a conversation with my best friend. —EMILY E. RYAN

FAITH STEP: *Share your thoughts with Jesus by talking to Him as if you're sending Him brief text messages throughout the day.*

TUESDAY, NOVEMBER 25

O God, thou art my God; early will I seek thee: my soul thirsteth for thee, my flesh longeth for thee in a dry and thirsty land, where no water is. Psalm 63:1 (KJV)

TWO YEARS AGO, I JOINED an online challenge designed for content creators—professionals who make educational, entertaining, or informative online materials. Usually, I ignore the competition for prizes in a challenge and focus solely on the virtual training that's offered. This time was different. From simply doing the weekly assignments, I jumped into the top twenty on the leaderboard. At the end of the challenge, the top ten would win a prize. The night before the challenge ended, I didn't sleep. I sat up in bed and stayed on my phone, engaging in every possible task to secure a top spot. When the winners were announced, I just made it at number ten. As promised, the top three winners received fabulous prize bundles. The rest of us won the coveted company-branded mug.

The prize was more than a mug for me. It represented what I could achieve by pushing past obstacles and ignoring limiting beliefs. It also symbolized the longing I had for Jesus to fill me up, so I could regain the strength, energy, and joy that was necessary to continue serving in the purpose He has given me.

Going after what Jesus has for me may require extra time and effort, but the sacrifice will be worth the work. Unlike my mug that is inanimate, fragile, and temporal, the rewards Jesus has for me are life-giving, incorruptible, and eternal. —ERICKA LOYNES

FAITH STEP: *How hard are you going after things that have everlasting value? If you're noticing most of your pursuits have temporal value, ask Jesus to help you increase your pursuit after Him.*

WEDNESDAY, NOVEMBER 26

But be sure to fear the LORD and serve him faithfully with all your heart; consider what great things he has done for you. 1 Samuel 12:24 (NIV)

WHEN OUR KIDS WERE YOUNG, we'd take a 10-hour road trip to celebrate Thanksgiving with dear friends. Every year, we'd do a gratitude exercise on Thanksgiving Day. Labeling paper leaves with the names of people or things we were grateful for, we would glue them to a gratitude tree.

Some years the kids listed their favorite foods, dramatically claiming that they couldn't *imagine* a world without macaroni and cheese or Nutella. Other years, the conversation centered on favorite animals, from our pet dogs to the mere existence of creatures such as dolphins, horses, and sloths.

As the kids grew older, the responses got deeper, and we'd often express gratitude for the way prayers had been answered. One year, a child expressed his thanks after healing from a painful broken leg. Another said how grateful she was that her grandma had survived a health scare. After weightier words of thanks, we'd sit in silence until someone broke the somber mood, listing his favorite TV characters or her favorite desserts. Not surprisingly, year after year, these conversations left us feeling *truly* thankful.

By taking time to express our thanks for all that Jesus had done for us, we not only came to know one another better but also were able to thank God, in very specific terms, for all He had done in our families' lives. —JENNIFER GRANT

FAITH STEP: *Write down one specific thing Jesus has done for you, and then share your thoughts with someone you love.*

THANKSGIVING DAY, THURSDAY, NOVEMBER 27

Give thanks in all circumstances; for this is God's will for you in Christ Jesus. 1 Thessalonians 5:18 (NIV)

THANKSGIVING DAY DIDN'T GO AS expected when a storm knocked out the electricity. Besides making it impossible to cook a festive meal, it turned roads into a slippery mess that created chaos for everyone trying to join family or friends for dinner. Like countless others, my husband and I chose to avoid unnecessary risks on the highway and hunkered down at home instead.

Bad weather squelched our plans to enjoy time and a traditional meal with my in-laws, but it couldn't dampen our attitude of gratitude for the gifts Jesus had given us: health, employment, a boat-home that provided shelter, clean drinking water, food, friends, and freedom to worship. We named our blessings one by one and added the changed plans to our list.

Thanksgiving came as a much-needed, guilt-free pause amidst a busy season. It provided a focused and unhurried opportunity for us to ponder and appreciate the many gifts that Jesus had lavished on us. It also gave us time to acknowledge life's disappointments and pain in a positive light. Sad and hurtful things over which we'd had no control had happened in the previous months, but we never lacked Jesus's loving presence. Day after day, He'd encouraged us through His promises and through praying friends who walked alongside us.

A storm stopped our plans, but it gave us a Thanksgiving Day filled with thanksgiving. For that we were grateful. —GRACE FOX

FAITH STEP: *Today might turn out just as you hoped, or it might turn out much differently than expected. Either way, say thank You to Jesus for at least three things.*

FRIDAY, NOVEMBER 28

The Spirit himself testifies with our spirit that we are God's children. Romans 8:16 (NIV)

MY CLOSET IS FILLED WITH T-shirts from my favorite coffee shops, vacation spots, and sports teams. Others proclaim important ideas such as "Choose Joy!" I once heard we wear what we love or believe. My wardrobe is evidence of that. Except for one shirt I bought recently.

"Daughter of the King" is printed in script on the front. I struggle to believe that title is more than a catchy phrase. Like some women, I'm uncertain how it feels to be a beloved daughter.

My biological father died when I was a baby. I know he existed and adored me, but my heart never experienced him. My stepfather was a provider and disciplinarian, critical and impossible to please. I learned an unhealthy respect for him and to keep a safe emotional distance. These experiences shaped how I saw myself as a daughter.

So here I am in the midst of an identity crisis. Beneath my crooked crown, my head knows I'm a daughter of the Most High King. My heart is the problem. So I've been working hard to convince it.

I list what I know about Jesus: He is present tense, not past tense like my father. Unlike my stepfather, Jesus is loving, patient, kind, gentle, and good. I read Scripture and ask the Holy Spirit to remind me *whose* I am. And I wear a T-shirt declaring my birthright, not to others but to myself, to help me believe I am truly a daughter of the King. —KAREN SARGENT

FAITH STEP: *Rewrite Romans 8:16 by replacing the pronouns our/we with my/I to make it personal.*

SATURDAY, NOVEMBER 29

On the day I called, you answered me; my strength of soul you increased. Psalm 138:3 (ESV)

QUESTIONS ARE NOT ALWAYS WELCOMED. Parents can get tired of what seems like an endless string of queries from a toddler. When the child gets older, the questions may make a parent uncomfortable or embarrassed. Politicians sometimes react to reasonable questions by acting offended, giving a vague or irrelevant response, or simply walking away.

Jesus never seemed bothered by questions. He was ready when Nicodemus, a prominent Jewish leader, came at night to query about His teaching (John 3:1–21). He waited by a well in Samaria to answer a troubled woman's questions (John 4:4–30). Since Jesus knew people's hearts, He sometimes answered their unasked questions (Luke 5:21–26). As John the Baptist languished in prison expecting to be executed, he had a moment of doubt. John sent two of his disciples to ask Jesus if He were truly the Messiah. Jesus lovingly sent back an assuring message (Matthew 11:2–6).

I've always been full of questions. Sometimes it's my natural curiosity kicking in, but much of the time I'm wondering about the meaning of a scripture passage, wanting guidance about an important decision, or needing insights into a tough relationship problem. I'm thankful for resources like Bible study tools, pastors, teachers, and wise friends who are strong in their faith. Most importantly, I'm grateful to Jesus for the Holy Spirit living inside me who can reveal anything He wants me to know and who is never annoyed at questions.
—DIANNE NEAL MATTHEWS

FAITH STEP: *Imagine Jesus sitting by your side right now. What is the one question you most want to ask Him? Talk to Him about it and commit to watching for His answer.*

First Sunday of Advent, November 30

The virgin will conceive and give birth to a son, and they will call him Immanuel (which means "God with us").
Matthew 1:23 (NIV)

ADVENT IS TYPICALLY A BLUR for me. The Christmas story is familiar background noise to the hustle and bustle of the season. As a mom who has worked in a school system for years, I think of Advent Sundays as days to mark off on an incredibly full calendar.

However, Jesus invited me to see parts of His story differently this past holiday. It was as if I heard elements of the Christmas narrative for the first time. During their annual Christmas program, the men's chorus at our church sang a lyric about God being held by human hands. I marveled with wonder. *God wrapped Himself in a human body to have a relationship with us. Imagine!*

That idea stayed with me for days. Jesus showed me that His skin contained the God of the universe. That He, the same God, also now lives in me. Jesus communes with me in a space so private as my heart, mind, and soul. The idea of this personal intimacy overwhelmed me. How could I have taken this for granted?

This revelation gave me additional curiosity throughout the holiday season. Rather than overlooking Advent's significance with its regular rhythms and traditions, I was more inquisitive about the life-changing magnitude of Jesus Emmanuel, God with us and in our innermost being. —BRENDA L. YODER

FAITH STEP: *Be curious and intentional about understanding the Advent season differently. Read the Christmas story in various versions of the Bible or read the text of familiar Christmas hymns, asking Jesus to show you the new dynamics of His story.*

MONDAY, DECEMBER 1

We had to celebrate this happy day. . . . He was lost, but now he is found! Luke 15:32 (NLT)

'TWAS A TINY MINI-CRISIS AT church last winter. As the congregation decorated the sanctuary before Advent, the children were tasked with displaying the handmade ceramic Nativity set. They arranged all the figurines (except baby Jesus) "just so." To keep the wee figurine from getting lost or broken before Christmas Day, when the children laid it in the manger, baby Jesus typically gets tucked away for safekeeping, swaddled in bubble wrap. I showed the children the hiding place so they could put baby Jesus in the manger on Christmas morning.

Weeks later, housebound with winter colds, hubby and I missed the Christmas morning service. Responding to a church elder's email afterward, I said I hoped the kids remembered where the baby Jesus was for their Nativity display. "They didn't remember. The baby is still hidden," he replied. Reading that, I burst into laughter. Contrasted with "the reason for the season," the triviality of this minor fiasco was so comical that I could do nothing but laugh.

Later, my friend Corinna described how, on Christmas morning, everyone searched for the figurine to no avail, and Pastor declared baby Jesus missing. The following Sunday, upon retrieval of baby Jesus from its hiding place, eleven-year-old Pearl laid the figurine in the manger. Our pianist good-naturedly joked, "In this church, baby Jesus isn't born until Cassandra gets here."

That ceramic baby might not have made it into the Nativity on cue, but thanks to Jesus, I'm no longer lost. —CASSANDRA TIERSMA

FAITH STEP: *Whenever you see a Nativity display this winter, prayerfully thank Jesus that with Him you are never lost.*

TUESDAY, DECEMBER 2

For the word of God is alive and active. Sharper than any double-edged sword, it penetrates even to dividing soul and spirit, joints and marrow; it judges the thoughts and attitudes of the heart. Hebrews 4:12 (NIV)

THE BUZZ AT A GATHERING of English teachers recently was the release of the latest chatbot software that uses artificial intelligence to write almost anything. A colleague demonstrated its capabilities, and my jaw dropped as I watched multi-paragraph essays, short stories, and poems materialize in moments. *I cannot show this to the students!* I knew they'd never write anything on their own if they discovered they could click a button and have coherent words appear on the screen for them.

Sure enough, I watched in dismay as one of my students refused to write during an assignment the following week. When I gently reminded him the paper was due the next day, he said with a smirk he'd get it done at home in less than 5 minutes on his computer. It was the first, but certainly not the last, time I fought against the power of computer-generated writing. "No one but you can tell your stories," I said with conviction. "A robot hasn't had your experiences. A computer can't feel what you've felt. Only *you* can breathe life into your words!"

Immediately, I thought about the connection between Jesus and my Bible. Because of Him, the written Word of God is "alive and active." It's not a sterile collection of impersonal maxims and rules written by a machine. It's a living document that pulses with the heartbeat of my Savior. I paused and thanked Jesus for the intimacy I have with Him through His Word. —EMILY E. RYAN

FAITH STEP: *Reread your favorite Bible passage. Talk candidly with Jesus about what you read.*

WEDNESDAY, DECEMBER 3

Therefore we do not lose heart. Though outwardly we are wasting away, yet inwardly we are being renewed day by day. 2 Corinthians 4:16 (NIV)

AUTUMN IS MY LEAST FAVORITE season. While friends rave about the vibrant leaves as they change and the return of pumpkin spice lattes, sadness settles in my soul.

Summer is *my* season. Hot temperatures, lots of sunlight, yellow hibiscus, red begonias, and pink geraniums in full bloom. From April to October, I'm able to enjoy time outside in the pool or sitting on the back porch. I awake early and work from home to wrap up my workday by 4 p.m. and stay outside until dark. Every day feels like a celebration!

This year, I'm taking the passing of summer hard. I had a birthday that ended in a zero in mid-September. If my lifetime were divided into seasons, this birthday would put me on the cusp of winter, the final season of my life. But I don't want summer to end. I don't want to grow older. Logically, I know nothing I say or do can stop time. My vanity about aging cannot alter the seasons. That's why I'm in mourning.

So on this December morning, I throw on a robe and take the dog outside. Daylight slowly illuminates the darkened sky. It grows into a fiery red-orange sunrise, the likes of which I've never seen in my beloved summer. It's so magnificent that I snap a photo and post it on social media. My emotional darkness brightens as I watch the sun rise in the sky.

Thank You, Jesus, for showing me that this season has much to offer too. —STEPHANIE THOMPSON

FAITH STEP: *What is one thing about December that you can celebrate today?*

THURSDAY, DECEMBER 4

When Jesus spoke again to the people, he said, "I am the light of the world. Whoever follows me will never walk in darkness, but will have the light of life." John 8:12 (NIV)

STANDING IN THE FRONT YARD, I squinted. The sky was overcast, a glaring slate blanket hiding even the sun from sight. In some ways, the gray day matched my mood. It was as if difficult times, like the panoramic gloom overhead, had come to define my days.

How different from the stars I'd viewed the previous evening. Glimmering and glittering, they put on a show for all who cared to watch. The longer I gazed up into the darkness, the more shimmering lights I saw. Layer after layer of our incredible heavens opened up to me, discernible to my naked eye. Simple wonder filled my soul. I recognized Jesus, the Creator's (John 1:1–3) presence as He shared this magnificence, and I gloried in His company.

When morning arrived, cold and dreary, the joy I'd experienced only the night before seemed to slip away. But soon, the haze burned off, and the sun shone warm and bright. Though the darkness had masked the light, it had been there all along. And beyond the sun, stars continued twinkling, hidden by the greater light but still present. I sensed an unspoken message.

Jesus is here with us, even in the midst of dark times. His light is ever-present and eternal, bright enough for the whole world. We can trust in it. We need never walk in darkness. —HEIDI GAUL

FAITH STEP: *Next time you feel down, make time for stargazing. Whether you spot a falling star or a simple constellation, know that you see Jesus in one of His grandest shows.*

FRIDAY, DECEMBER 5

Call to me, and I will answer you. I will tell you great and mysterious things that you do not know. Jeremiah 33:3 (GW)

SHE'S A RUBY-RED BEAUTY, my 1950s rotary-dial telephone. With a vintage ringtone that is louder than any cordless or cellular phone, she's played a supporting role in a comedic skit I performed at church. She's also been requested for a photo shoot by a local photographer. My old-fashioned landline that doesn't require batteries or electricity mostly collects dust, patiently waiting on standby in case the power goes out and I need to make an emergency call.

Her faithful reliability is reassuring. Unfortunately, she can't elicit the phone calls I want. Wishing one of my kids would call, there sat my red rotary hotline—silent. Jesus promptly reminded me of the verse dubbed "God's Phone Number" in Jeremiah 33:3: "Call to me, and I will answer you."

How disappointed Jesus must feel when I don't call Him. I have a 24/7 direct line to Him, but, like my red rotary just sitting there, I'm sometimes silent. Knowing the joy hearing my kids' voices brings me, I feel remiss in not calling on Jesus more often.

When I miss hearing from my kids, my red rotary will be an ever-present reminder for me to call Jesus. I have His phone number. It's Jeremiah 33:3.

—CASSANDRA TIERSMA

FAITH STEP: *Write the words in Jeremiah 33:3—Jesus's phone number—on a Post-it note near your landline or cell phone charger. Call on Him; He loves to hear from you.*

SATURDAY, DECEMBER 6

On coming to the house, they saw the child with his mother Mary, and they bowed down and worshiped him. Then they opened their treasures and presented him with gifts of gold, frankincense and myrrh. Matthew 2:11 (NIV)

MY FAVORITE NATIVITY SET IS made of banana leaves. Aunt Joyce, a world traveler, purchased it for my family when I was a girl many decades ago. Mom never liked it, so she gave it to me when I married Kevin. I've unpacked those wrinkled brown figures for forty-eight Christmases and lovingly placed them in a prominent spot in the living room.

I've tried to repair the hut with packing tape. I've lost a little lamb. One of the camel's blankets is always falling off. And over the years, the tallest wise man's neck has weakened. It causes his head to bend nearly to his chest. In my estimation, he's the wisest man of the three.

I can't imagine that those magi, after traveling hundreds of miles and finally arriving at Mary and Joseph's home in Bethlehem, jumped and danced and shouted when they saw the infant Messiah.

I believe the hearts of those magi stirred with the awe that only comes from being in the presence of God Almighty. Although rich and powerful, they presented to Jesus far more than the treasures in their camel bags. With humble hearts, knees on the dirt floor, and faces bent, they gave Him the gift He most deserved: worship.

This is why I love this crèche and the wise man with his head bowed. It reminds me exactly how to approach Jesus, my King. —JEANETTE LEVELLIE

FAITH STEP: *No matter how many gifts you have for Jesus, it's your heart He wants the most. Bow in prayer and give it anew to Him.*

SECOND SUNDAY OF ADVENT, DECEMBER 7

Because Joseph her husband was faithful to the law, and yet did not want to expose her to public disgrace, he had in mind to divorce her quietly. Matthew 1:19 (NIV)

I READ THE FAMILIAR STORY of Joseph being told about Mary's impending pregnancy. So often, I've minimized this portion of Scripture compared to the miraculous virgin birth. This Advent Sunday, Jesus drew my attention to the disgraceful aspect of His story.

I often correlate Jesus's life with suffering but not disgrace. Scandal swirled around the Son of God even before He was born. I was curious why God chose this manner for the beginning of Jesus's life.

I talked with Jesus about this for days. He showed me how humanity had disgraced itself with sin since Eden (Genesis 3). Though sinless, Jesus entered our shameful, unworthy condition at conception.

Disgrace is a different perspective of Advent. I think of Christmas as a wonder-filled experience of a baby transforming the world. Instead, Jesus becoming man was an act of humiliation as He dwelled in the world filled with shame. Jesus's disgrace gave me a deeper understanding of God's plan to connect with and meet us where we are. His amazing conception and birth can lead us to marvel at His glory even in His humiliation. —BRENDA L. YODER

FAITH STEP: *Bring Jesus into the hidden place of your heart, mind, and soul. Prayerfully invite Him to enter the areas you've been trying to hide. He's already there, without shame or condemnation.*

MONDAY, DECEMBER 8

The LORD is God, and he has made his light shine on us. With boughs in hand, join in the festal procession up to the horns of the altar. Psalm 118:27 (NIV)

I LOVE IT WHEN MY neighbors or the shop owners in my community put up holiday lights. It's even better when they keep their lights up all year long. In the middle of a gray Midwestern winter, tiny white lights twinkling from hedges or big, fat, colorful bulbs blinking from inside an apartment window lift my mood.

I also love learning the origin of different customs, and I recently learned that the first Christmas lights were candles that were attached to Christmas trees by pins in the sixteenth century. They were placed on the tree branches to light up and show off cherished ornaments. It was later, in 1882 in New York City, when the first Christmas tree was lit with electric lights. In time, electric lights became safer to use and less expensive to buy than candles, so more and more people adopted the practice of using them.

Some might complain about gaudy lights or Christmas lights being up year-round, but Jesus described Himself as the "light of the world" (John 8:12). Seeing all the lights, shining bright at night, I can't help but be reminded of the light Jesus brings, a gift no matter the season. —JENNIFER GRANT

FAITH STEP: *As you walk or drive around your community, pay special attention to the festive, twinkling lights and say a prayer of praise to Jesus that He is the light of the world.*

TUESDAY, DECEMBER 9

What good will it be for someone to gain the whole world, yet forfeit their soul? Or what can anyone give in exchange for their soul? Matthew 16:26 (NIV)

I LOVE EVERYTHING LEADING UP to Christmas: the shopping and decorating, the Christmas programs and candlelight services. Yet these same things can leave me feeling overwhelmed and stressed. As I celebrate Jesus's birth, it's important for me to seek Jesus's presence to find heart happiness and peace amidst the chaos of the season. While things are busy for me, I have friends who find Christmas the loneliest day of the year. Maybe it is due to the death of family members or perhaps because they never married or had children, even though that was a great desire.

No matter where you fall, a truly happy heart comes by connecting with Jesus during this holiday season. Seeking Jesus transforms our attitude and soul. A happy heart that's in the process of being transformed by Jesus changes the view of our circumstances.

Christmas may be full or empty, but the greatest gift we could give ourselves is to connect with Jesus through prayer, reading the Bible, or simply sitting in quiet reflection. Happiness and peace can be found, even amidst the chaos of Christmas, when we remember Jesus is the reason for the season. —TRICIA GOYER

FAITH STEP: *Ask Jesus to bring to mind someone who doesn't know Him or who may be sad this holiday. Reach out with a small token that proclaims Jesus is the reason for this season.*

WEDNESDAY, DECEMBER 10

Jesus replied, "Truly I tell you, the Son is not able to do anything on his own, but only what he sees the Father doing. For whatever the Father does, the Son likewise does these things." John 5:19 (CSB)

THE TIME HAD COME TO STOP. I was doing too much, feeling overwhelmed, burned out, and stressed. My capacity level was well past its limit, yet my superwoman tendencies were in high gear. A peer needed a document proofread. *No problem.* A leader needed assistance with a presentation. *Done.* My original project deadline moved up a week. *I had it handled.* An urgent email needed writing. *You got it.* A can't-miss event was happening over the weekend. *I was there.* And, I kept going.

In contrast to Shonda Rhimes's book *Year of Yes*, I decided to enact a year of no. To ensure I kept this commitment to myself, I informed key people in my life whom I knew would keep me accountable. I declined any more work that year and kept only the things I had already committed to doing. My load became lighter and, therefore, more manageable.

However, I had gone from one extreme, piling on numerous tasks and getting overburdened, to another, saying no and possibly missing out on a number of good opportunities. What I needed was balance.

When Jesus walked on the earth, He had no problem saying yes or no to the people around Him. Ultimately, He made His decisions based on the will of His Father. That's when it hit me—if I prayed over my activities and opportunities, Jesus could balance them out. I no longer needed to be a superwoman if the ultimate Superhero was calling the shots. —ERICKA LOYNES

FAITH STEP: *Are you doing too much or too little? Invite Jesus to evaluate your workload and discover what's self-led and what's Savior-led.*

THURSDAY, DECEMBER 11

But seek ye first the kingdom of God, and his righteousness; and all these things shall be added unto you. Matthew 6:33 (KJV)

I RAN FOR OFFICE IN a local election and lost. It was a devastating experience because I felt like it was something Jesus was leading me to do. I really wanted to help people. I poured my whole heart into the campaign, and believed I would win. I had plans to do great things.

Those plans shriveled up in my heart when I was not chosen. I sank into sadness, bordering on depression. I couldn't get out of the funk I felt, and it seemed impossible just to ease back into my normal life, returning to the person I had been and the routine I'd followed before spending a year working to be elected.

I ended up going to therapy. Jesus used the counselor to help me see how to turn my disappointment into action by seeking other outlets to help my community and doing some of the work I had hoped to accomplish in different ways. I prayed and asked for help finding opportunities to glorify Him. One by one, chances came along to serve with my writing, advocacy, training, and teaching.

These other opportunities have become such a blessing. I suspect Jesus was leading me there all along. —GWEN FORD FAULKENBERRY

FAITH STEP: *Is there something you have tried or hoped for that did not work out as you planned? Write down how you could seek His face to accomplish this, even if you have to look in new places.*

FRIDAY, DECEMBER 12

"For this child I prayed, and the LORD has granted me my petition which I asked of Him. Therefore I also have lent him to the LORD; as long as he lives he shall be lent to the LORD." So they worshiped the LORD there. 1 Samuel 1:27–28 (NKJV)

I FOLLOWED THE CLUES AS our young adult son, AJ, stacked a bunch of microwaveable meals on his shelf in the freezer. Then a canvas lunch bag and Thermos arrived for him from Amazon. Finally, a shiny blue Welcome folder from a new job appeared at my place at the dinner table. The Holy Spirit whispered, "He's telling you what he's doing."

I'd done my stepmotherly best to steer AJ toward college right after high school. I wanted him to have a career, not just a job. But his mind was made up: he wanted to work full-time for a year. I felt disappointed, even betrayed, and scared for his future. I admit, we didn't speak for weeks. At night I cried to Jesus, but I stayed frozen by day. It put a considerable strain on our relationship. When the Lord reminded me that AJ is *His* son too, my hardened heart began to melt, and I bowed to the truth Jesus whispered to me: He was in charge of AJ's future. It was not my burden. We parents are caretakers who train them up (Proverbs 22:6) and let them go.

The next time I saw AJ, I hugged him. Whether he is in college or working, I know Jesus has great things in store for him. —PAMELA TOUSSAINT HOWARD

FAITH STEP: *Are your expectations for someone else causing hard feelings? Write that person's name in the margin of this book or in your journal. Pray until you have released them to Jesus.*

SATURDAY, DECEMBER 13

… "Where is the one who has been born king of the Jews? We saw his star when it rose and have come to worship him." Matthew 2:2 (NIV)

EVERY YEAR WE WATCH THE Christmas classic *It's a Wonderful Life* with Jimmy Stewart and Donna Reed. With each viewing, a different scene hits me in a new way. This year it was the scene where George Bailey and Mary walk home from the school dance. As George talks about all the grand plans he has for leaving Bedford Falls and finding happiness elsewhere, Mary grabs a rock, tosses it at a window in the old Granville house, and makes a wish. When she refuses to tell him what she wished for, George asks Mary what she wants. If she wants the moon, he'll lasso it and pull it down so she can swallow it. Then the moonbeams will shoot out of her fingers, toes, and the ends of her hair. Later, we learn all Mary wished for was that George stay in Bedford Falls and love her forever.

That scene inspires me to lasso the Christmas star to pull me closer to what it shines upon: the newborn King. I shouldn't be distracted by grand plans for the season or going elsewhere to find happiness. It's all right here, within my grasp when I recognize that the One to come loves me forever, to the cross and beyond. When I ingest that fact, I live a life where His grace radiates out from my fingers and toes and my actions. As I spend time worshipping Him, I can't help but feel I'm living a wonderful life! —CLAIRE MCGARRY

FAITH STEP: *Watch the movie* It's a Wonderful Life. *Identify the scene through which Jesus wants to speak to you.*

THIRD SUNDAY OF ADVENT, DECEMBER 14

---

*The people walking in darkness have seen a great light;
on those living in the land of deep darkness a light has
dawned. Isaiah 9:2 (NIV)*

ADVENT SHOULD BE A TIME of joyful anticipation. For me, it evokes the dread of a long, gloomy winter. I combat the darkness with indoor lights on my fireplace and windowsills from October through March. The soft glow provides comfort and peace.

December's darkness mirrors other things, like evils I see when scrolling social media or watching the news. My work as an elementary school counselor is cumbersome in December as kids' negative behaviors increase before the holidays. Many live in chaotic, harsh environments and don't want to be away from the caring adults at school.

I complained to Jesus about the weight of all the darkness on a morning commute. I didn't seem to make a dent in the world's ills. Jesus whispered that it wasn't my job to face the darkness. He overcame evil at the cross (Colossians 2:15), and it's His burden to carry. I am to be His light (Matthew 5:16).

Jesus reminded me that everyone without Him walks daily in darkness, no matter the time of year. He showed me that I'm overwhelmed by darkness when I focus on it. Instead, He asked me to shine

His love, peace, and restoration into it like a light in the darkness. —Brenda L. Yoder

---

Faith Step: *Consider areas of influence at work or in your community where Jesus asks you to be a caring, peaceful presence this holiday season. Make a list of the ways you can bring light.*

Monday, December 15

Glory to God in the highest heaven, and on earth peace to those on whom his favor rests. Luke 2:14 (NIV)

Instead of traditional Christmas cards, my husband, Kevin, and I write poems and print them on Christmas stationery for friends and family.

A few years ago, I felt uninspired. I told Kev to recycle one of my former poems.

He was horrified. "That's like cheating," he said. "People want to receive a new poem each year."

But I had nothing. Kevin agreed to recycle one of my poems. Even though we decided to do that, I had no peace about it.

Maybe it was the spirit of Christmas, but 2 days later, I had an idea for a new poem:

"As we read from the angels' announcement at His birth,

Jesus brought peace from God to the earth.

Peace. More than the absence of war. Peace. More than silence, stillness, or tranquility.

The peace that Jesus gave was a restoration of our relationship with God.

The peace that we lost when we listened to the serpent and ate forbidden fruit.

And became enemies of God. Banished from our garden of fellowship.

Because of Jesus, we are once again friends with God.

Jesus bought our place in God's throne room and God's heart.

He made peace between God and us."

Thankfully, Jesus, the true Spirit of Christmas, comes through when I can't. And that gives me real peace. —JEANETTE LEVELLIE

FAITH STEP: *Look up the synonyms for* peace *in a thesaurus. Pick a favorite and write it on a sheet of paper to remember Jesus's peace this Christmas season.*

TUESDAY, DECEMBER 16

"I am the Lord's servant," Mary answered. "May your word to me be fulfilled." Then the angel left her. Luke 1:38 (NIV)

I AM A DOER AND a fixer and have a full set of power tools to prove it. As things in our home break down, I see them as personal challenges. I love to be the one to repair them. When four appliances all died after Thanksgiving, though, I knew I was in over my head. I'm not an electrician or a technician. It was agony not being able to solve the problems myself. I was frustrated and irritable, focusing more on my issues than on preparing for Christmas. Then I looked at my Nativity set and I understood. This was exactly where I needed to be: in a position where I had no control, with the need to depend on others.

This season isn't just an invitation to say yes, as Mary did, so God's plan can be birthed within me. It's also an invitation to say yes, as Jesus did, so God can take me back to infancy—that place of vulnerability where I have no control and no choice but to depend on others and on Him.

Yes, I'm meant to participate in solving a lot of the troubles in my life. If and when I start to confuse "participate" with "control" and "complete independence," I need to remember that God is the One in charge. It's His plan I need to follow, not my own. To do so, I need to continue to say yes, as Mary and Jesus did, and turn the control (and my power tools) over to Him.
—CLAIRE MCGARRY

FAITH STEP: *Sit quietly with your Nativity set, reflecting on where Jesus is asking you to say yes.*

WEDNESDAY, DECEMBER 17

Your eyes saw my unformed body; all the days ordained for me were written in your book before one of them came to be. Psalm 139:16 (NIV)

MY MOM IS EIGHTY-EIGHT YEARS OLD. She has no interest in eating or drinking, and hospice is involved in her care due to her recent weight loss. She is confined to her bed or recliner. She doesn't know my sisters and me anymore, although we visit frequently. And today I learned that she has pneumonia.

I don't know how or what to pray as I sit, bundled up, on my deck and watch the snow fall. It is gently blanketing the remnants of my garden. Mom's quality of life is poor, but is she ready for her life on earth to end? I don't know.

I find myself contemplating God's creation of flowers. What a beautiful plan He designed, with annuals completing their life cycles in one season and perennials returning year after year.

Our lives on earth are like flowering plants. When we complete our life cycle, our seeds—our souls—remain, ready to sprout again in heaven. Once we get to heaven, our life cycle never ends. I don't know Jesus's plan for the remainder of Mom's earthly life cycle. And I still don't know how or what to pray for

Mom, but it doesn't matter. Jesus knows the plan.
—Kristy Dewberry

Faith Step: *Today, when you pray, try to imagine the cycles of your life and recognize that Jesus is working out His plan for you.*

THURSDAY, DECEMBER 18

How precious to me are your thoughts, God! How vast is the sum of them! Were I to count them, they would outnumber the grains of sand—when I awake, I am still with you. Psalm 139:17–18 (NIV)

My husband, Scott, is an idea generator. As a teaching team pastor and a marketing strategist, he is constantly coming up with new thoughts and ideas. He loves finding ways to solve problems. At work, he has the gift of being able to connect with people and help brainstorm strategies for their teams. When he is preparing for a sermon, he is constantly running his notions by me. One idea sparks another. He loves to teach people what he has learned.

Scott is always learning. Right now, there are at least fifteen books on his bedside table. He has a big brain. He is beyond creative. And he uses his idea generator to help me every day. He helps me think through problems. He has ideas about how I can run my business better. And I am wiser when I listen to him.

Jesus has millions of thoughts about me and my life. His creativity is unparalleled. He thinks of me so often that His thoughts outnumber the grains of sand. I can't fathom that. He is the original idea generator and the ultimate problem solver. And He transforms my life with His wisdom. —SUSANNA FOTH AUGHTMON

FAITH STEP: *What problems are you trying to solve right now? Ask Jesus to speak to you through His Holy Spirit and His Word to give you ideas and thoughts.*

FRIDAY, DECEMBER 19

Your word is a lamp for my feet, a light on my path.
Psalm 119:105 (NIV)

"WHAT I MISS MOST ABOUT being younger is my vision," I announced to my husband. He replied, "What? Yoga helps you make decisions?" Obviously, not only is my ability to see on the decline but so is his hearing. I do miss having twenty-twenty vision, especially at night.

Night blindness has become a problem for me. According to Google, as I age my pupils are getting smaller, which decreases the incoming light required for good vision at night. I live in a rural area where roads twist up and around Ozark Mountains. There are no streetlights to illuminate the dark. Yellow lines keep me on my side of the road, and white lines keep me out of the ditch.

Driving on dark roads can be tricky. So can walking in a dark world with crooked paths. But I walk in faith because Jesus illuminates the way. He not only lights my path, but He also calls me the light of the world (Matthew 5:14). He wants His light to shine within me so I can help push back the darkness for others (Matthew 5:16). Even as a child, I learned what to do with this little light of mine. Let it shine!

While I may be white-knuckled behind the wheel at night, I'm not anxious in this dark world. The Word will brighten the space between the lines where I am to walk. Jesus's light shines in me. —KAREN SARGENT

FAITH STEP: *Recall the words to "This Little Light of Mine." Write the meaning of each line as it pertains to you as an adult.*

SATURDAY, DECEMBER 20

After they had heard the king, they went on their way, and the star they had seen when it rose went ahead of them until it stopped over the place where the child was. Matthew 2:9 (NIV)

WHEN I WAS A KID, the electric company ran commercials with "Lester Lightbulb." He was a cartoon lightbulb who encouraged the public to conserve energy by turning off lights when no one was in a room. Both my husband and I try to convey the same message to our kids so as not to be wasteful. The one lamp that still gets left on, however, is in our front foyer, where there's a cathedral ceiling. All night long, it illuminates upstairs and down so my kids can find their way to the bathroom or come into our room to be comforted after a bad dream. Come morning, as sunlight streams into the foyer and overpowers the light, we don't even notice it's still on.

The Christ Child is like that light. When things are darkest in my own life, my need for Jesus becomes so illuminated, everything else recedes into the shadows. I follow His light and find comfort in His arms.

The tricky part is when the busyness of the holiday season streams in and I allow it to overpower me. That's when I need to recognize that the Light of the World still burns bright for me all hours of the day, calling me out of the shadow of chaos and back into His loving embrace. —CLAIRE MCGARRY

FAITH STEP: *As you turn lights on and off in your home today, reflect on the coming of Jesus as the Light of the World and give thanks.*

FOURTH SUNDAY OF ADVENT, DECEMBER 21

And it will be said: "Build up, build up, prepare the road!
Remove the obstacles out of the way of my people."
Isaiah 57:14 (NIV)

"YOU SEEM STRESSED," MY SON said that December. He was right. It was the first holiday season with each of our four children living in their own homes, some several hours away. Gathering for the holidays felt more like a cataclysmic event to me than a low-key homecoming. Our family had grown to include new grandchildren, new spouses, and new dating partners, all coming together for the first time.

I wanted our house to feel warm and welcoming so everyone felt comfortable. I worried about food, arrival times, and conversations. During my devotional time, I read Isaiah 57:14 as part of my Advent readings. It talked about removing obstacles out of the way of God's people for the coming of Jesus. I felt Jesus draw my attention away from worrisome obstacles like holiday details. He invited me to consider how to make coming home like a pathway to Him.

I wanted Jesus's love to reign during the holidays rather than my obsession over details. *Throw it around like confetti,* I heard Him whisper. Let love be carefree and light, trusting Him to do a work I couldn't orchestrate on my own.

I began praying for Jesus to carry my worries. As the time approached for everyone to arrive, I felt Jesus remove my stress and anxiety. The path was clear for a calm, joyful celebration, just as Jesus had planned. —BRENDA L. YODER

FAITH STEP: *Give your holiday anxieties to Jesus. Focus on simplified preparations and expectations rather than stressful obstacles for your peace and others'.*

MONDAY, DECEMBER 22

The kingdom of heaven is like treasure hidden in a field. When a man found it, he hid it again, and then in his joy went and sold all he had and bought that field.
Matthew 13:44 (NIV)

A GIANT BULLETIN BOARD HANGS in a prominent spot in my home office. An outer frame holds nine square sections—one pegboard, two whiteboards, and six corkboards covered with various fabrics. The design is mine, but the handiwork belongs to my husband.

The board triggers joyful moments through-out the day. Family and friends smile at me from pictures, and small souvenirs remind me of interesting destinations I've visited.

The board also infuses faith into my workday. A ceramic cross displays the word "love," and a wooden ornament proclaims the word "joy." Bible verses and song lyrics fill the whiteboards in multicolor. And a curious canvas cap, hanging on a top corner, connects my thoughts to Jesus's parables of the treasure hidden in a field.

A few years ago, I stumbled upon the kitschy hat hidden behind a collection of blue mason jars at a yard sale. The khaki cap has an oversized bill trimmed in yellow. An enormous flower attached to the right side gives it a modern-day Minnie Pearl feel. I couldn't look goofier in it, and I couldn't love it more. My yard-sale cap inspires me to think about Jesus's story and the best treasure of all—the Kingdom of God. I'm so glad I've found that, and Him. —BECKY ALEXANDER

FAITH STEP: *What do you gaze at during your week? Put a few things in your view that take you to happy places and help you focus on Jesus.*

TUESDAY, DECEMBER 23

The lions may grow weak and hungry, but those who seek the LORD lack no good thing. Psalm 34:10 (NIV)

I WAS SORTING THROUGH SOME old papers and notes recently, when I found a spiral-bound notebook from more than 20 years ago that I had used as a journal. It was in that notebook where I had written to the Lord and shared what was in my heart and on my mind.

I sat and read about the fears and anxieties I experienced at that time and how I pleaded with Jesus to provide and see me through. I asked Him questions about the future. I was worried about my job, finances, world events, the health of family and friends, being a good wife, and so much more. I was also desperately seeking to draw closer to Jesus.

It dawned on me that many of my concerns decades ago are still some of the concerns that I have today. But the difference is I have learned to trust and depend more on the Lord. Now that I am on the other side of those old concerns and struggles, I see how Jesus was indeed Jehovah Jireh, Jehovah Rapha, and Jehovah Shalom—God my Provider, Healer, and Peace. Sometimes it's good to look back so that I can continue to move forward.
—BARBRANDA LUMPKINS WALLS

FAITH STEP: *Take time today to look back on your life and jot down some of the prayers that Jesus has answered over the years. Stop and give Him thanks and praise for what He has done.*

CHRISTMAS EVE, WEDNESDAY, DECEMBER 24

But the angel said to them, "Do not be afraid. I bring you good news that will cause great joy for all the people."
Luke 2:10 (NIV)

I IMAGINE THOSE SHEPHERDS, regular guys, huddled around a desert fire, shooting the breeze while the sheep slept in the stillness of a starry night. Maybe they were talking about their planned route, their families, the prospect of getting home, or some conflict with a friend. They were simple men doing their jobs. Just another night at work.

Then suddenly, God interrupted, dispatching an angel, a notoriously terrifying being. Evidently, the angel knew this because he reassured them that his message was good news. I can only imagine the shepherds' heart-stopping terror and wonder. *What's this all about?* They would soon learn and then see for themselves that what the angel said was true. Jesus is really good news.

Just as He did with the shepherds, God has sometimes interrupted my life with something that seemed scary at first. When I learned I was having a baby with Down syndrome, I was utterly terrified and devastated. I sought the Lord desperately for

comfort and strength. Jesus responded and continues to respond with love.

Just like Jesus's arrival, the arrival of my son Isaac
15 years ago heralded a new beginning, brimming
with healing, valuable growth opportunities, and
above all, love.

This Christmas Eve, I pray we can all reclaim
the awesome wonder of the lowly baby Jesus, an
unexpected Savior, and embrace His good news.
—ISABELLA CAMPOLATTARO

FAITH STEP: *Are you burdened with an unexpected
development and unknown outcome? Take a Christmas card
and write a prayer to Jesus, then place it in your Nativity near
baby Jesus.*

CHRISTMAS DAY, THURSDAY, DECEMBER 25

Now eagerly desire the greater gifts.
1 Corinthians 12:31 (NIV)

ON THE PIANO AT THE church we pastor sits a
purple velvet box topped with a thick gold ribbon.
The tag attached to the ribbon tells us to use the
empty box as a reminder that Father God emptied

His heart to send Jesus to earth, a gift for every one of us.

Last Christmas, instead of using it as a decoration, our congregation started a new tradition. On the two Sundays leading up to Christmas, I handed out 3x5 cards before worship. "Please write on these cards what you plan to give Jesus for Christmas," I said. "It could be anything from shoveling snow for a neighbor to increasing your missions giving to smiling more often." I didn't limit how many cards each person could take. But I told them not to sign their names. Only Jesus would know the giver of each gift.

After the service, we placed our birthday gift note cards for Jesus in the velvet box. At our Christmas Eve service, I opened the box—fuller than I expected—and read each promise out loud. To give more compliments. To read my Bible every day. To pray for our nation. To quit complaining (that was mine, and, girlfriend, it's not been easy!).

I like to imagine how on Christmas morning, when we opened brightly wrapped gifts surrounded by our families, Jesus was there among us. He held those cards in His nail-scarred hands and said to every person, "Thank you for the birthday presents."

Happy birthday, Jesus. —JEANETTE LEVELLIE

FAITH STEP: *Next time you pray, ask Jesus what He wants for Christmas.*

FRIDAY, DECEMBER 26

Each of you must bring a gift in proportion to the way the LORD your God has blessed you. Deuteronomy 16:17 (NIV)

WHEN MY SON GIDEON WAS sixteen, he got a job sacking groceries and collecting shopping carts at the Kroger store in our neighborhood. He liked having extra spending money and began dropping hints that he'd be using some of his spoils to buy us Christmas gifts that year.

True to his word, packages appeared under the tree after his last holiday shift at the store. The presents I'd wrapped were color- coordinated in red-and-white paper with matching ribbon and bows. Gideon's contributions to the pile were plain brown boxes with names written in bold, black Sharpie. When we opened Gideon's gifts on Christmas morning, we discovered that every gift came from the produce aisle at Kroger: ten bell peppers, five pineapples, five bunches of bananas, twenty oranges, and forty limes. Every time we unboxed a new crop, Gideon's smile grew wider and wider.

At first, I wasn't sure what to make of my son's first official act of generosity, but my husband helped me see what was happening under the surface. Jesus had blessed Gideon with a little money, a goofy personality, and a desire to make his family laugh. The gifts he'd given were in direct proportion to how Jesus had blessed him. I thought of how my own gifts to Jesus and others had changed over time. As a child, I gave pennies, drawings, and skits as gifts. Now I give tithes, time, and words. I thanked Jesus that He accepts every gift given from a gracious heart. —EMILY E. RYAN

FAITH STEP: *Are the gifts you give to Jesus and others proportional to the blessings you have received? If not, what adjustments need to be made?*

SATURDAY, DECEMBER 27

You will seek me and find me when you seek me with all your heart. Jeremiah 29:13 (NIV)

MY THREE-YEAR-OLD GRANDDAUGHTER, LEXI, enjoys playing a game called "Find the Treasure." I played it with her on a recent visit to her home. She explained the rules: Grandma would hide the treasure, 3-inch-tall figurines of Anna and Olaf, characters from the movie *Frozen*, and she would search until she found it. She used a simple hand-sketched map and a healthy dose of imagination to conquer the task.

I assumed that Lexi would play only a couple of times before shifting her attention to another activity, but I was wrong. She enjoyed the game so much that we repeated it at least a dozen times that day and the next.

Lexi's enthusiasm about searching for her toy treasure challenges me to consider my enthusiasm about seeking Jesus. In Jeremiah 29:13, the first usage of the word *seek* is translated from the Hebrew word *baqash*, which implies trying to obtain someone's presence. The second usage is *darash*, which denotes searching for Him by honoring, studying, and obeying His Word.

Jesus is the ultimate treasure, and He invites us to seek Him because He wants to be found. We search for Him by taking intentional actions such as studying His Word and walking in obedience to His directives. When we do these things with our whole hearts, He fulfills His promise to let us find Him.

Seeking Jesus isn't a child's game, but neither is it complicated. Jeremiah 29:13 is our map, and following it leads us to the greatest treasure of all.
—GRACE FOX

FAITH STEP: *Make a timeline map and note when you were seeking Jesus most. What patterns did you find?*

SUNDAY, DECEMBER 28

Do not be anxious about anything, but in every situation, by prayer and petition, with thanksgiving, present your requests to God. And the peace of God, which transcends all understanding, will guard your hearts and your minds in Christ Jesus. Philippians 4:6–7 (NIV)

WHEN I STARTED HOMESCHOOLING, I had a chart scheduling our day into 15-minute increments. There was time for Bible study, math, reading, play, and more. Looking back, I can see now that my desire for control stemmed from my anxiousness. As a young mom, I worried I wouldn't be able to give my children the education they truly needed, so I tried to cram in as much as possible. I wish I could say that homeschooling was the only area that I overplanned, but it wasn't.

For many years, I worked hard to control every part of my life instead of turning over my anxiousness and worries to my Savior. As I spent time with Jesus, I learned that only His peace could help my days go smoother.

The truth is, no matter how much I try, I will never be able to control everything. Peace and contentment only come from lifting my eyes to Jesus and understanding that He can take away every anxiety. Bringing my worries and fears to God in prayer works much better than scheduling my days into 15-minute increments. A peaceful heart is worth more than any well-planned day. —TRICIA GOYER

FAITH STEP: *Write out an area of your life that you want to control. Talk to Jesus and ask Him to replace your overplanning with peace.*

MONDAY, DECEMBER 29

Remember the days of old; consider the generations long past. Ask your father and he will tell you, your elders, and they will explain to you. Deuteronomy 32:7 (NIV)

I PUT THE UNFINISHED HEIRLOOM quilt into its wooden frame. I was determined to finish quilting over the holiday break. With little free time, I hadn't worked on it for months.

I started the project for our grandson, Luca, during the pandemic. I'd collected fabric for years, thinking someday I'd be creative with old clothing worn by grandparents, parents, and even my children. As a new grandma, I loved cutting and hand-sewing squares together during the lockdown.

But life had changed since then: a wedding, more grandbabies, a new job, my husband Ron's near-fatal accident, and my dad's death. I avoided finishing the quilt. Mixed emotions were attached to each fabric square. Dad's shirt still smelled like him. The pinstriped overalls—how could my baby now be a father? The jeans of Ron's mom, Lois, last worn baking cookies with our kids.

Bittersweet memories continued. Dad's immigrant beginning. Lois's prayers for her grandchildren she didn't get to see grow up. Gratitude, tears, and prayers intertwined as each person's legacy became a tangible thread that held the quilt together.

I finished Luca's quilt, but I got the real gift. I didn't realize how much grief I carried until the memories entered a physical space. Jesus used each stitch to heal my heart. The quilt encompassed change but also celebration. The legacy of loved ones, in the form of fabric, would cover Luca for years to come—a heritage he would surely treasure. —BRENDA L. YODER

FAITH STEP: *Use a creative outlet to make meaning from memories. Whether sewing, drawing, writing, or woodworking, allow Jesus to heal your heart as you work with your hands.*

TUESDAY, DECEMBER 30

Then he opened their minds so they could understand the Scriptures. Luke 24:45 (NIV)

CHOOSING NOT TO HAVE A television has afforded me a lot of free time. Usually, I spend those extra hours out in the garden or curled up with a magazine or good book. Long walks and thrift shopping fill in the gap. But today I'm indulging in one of my favorite hobbies. Working puzzles, or puzzling, slows my thoughts and lends me focus. It's as if somewhere in the background my mind can concentrate on solving a problem as my main attention is centered on finding that elusive missing piece. Seeing a picture come together bit by bit helps me to understand how the different aspects of my life fit together.

When I first came to Jesus, reading the Bible seemed like struggling against a puzzle with no interlocking pieces. The unfamiliar names and places, cultures, and history confused me. How could one piece of fruit cause so much trouble (Genesis 3:6–7)? Why did Jesus die for us—for me (John 3:16)? What exactly is redemption (Colossians 1:13–14)?

But as my faith matured, more of Jesus's story became clear to me. A parable of Jesus connected with a tenet of Jewish faith (Luke 10:27–37; Deuteronomy 6:5). One passage led me to a manger in Bethlehem (Luke 2:4–8), another to a cross at Golgotha (Mark 15:22), and a third to an empty tomb (John 20:1–18). My heart and mind engaged, and at last I understood the depth of love and goodness contained in our Lord (Ephesians 3:17–19).

No longer puzzled, every blessed piece fits.
—HEIDI GAUL

FAITH STEP: *Set aside a block of time daily to read the Bible. Find connections between the characters and the parables and the way they fit into your life.*

NEW YEAR'S EVE, WEDNESDAY, DECEMBER 31

But as for me, I watch in hope for the LORD, I wait for God my Savior; my God will hear me. Micah 7:7 (NIV)

WHEN I WAS IN MY TWENTIES, I looked forward to getting together with friends or going out to celebrate as one year ended and another one began. But now I love gathering with fellow believers at my church for what we call Watch Night Service, a time to look back and to look forward.

It's a spirit-filled occasion as we pack the sanctuary to share testimonies of God's goodness, mercy, and grace. We offer prayers and sing glorious praises to Him for another year's journey. History tells me that enslaved African Americans, some of them my ancestors, did the same more than 150 years ago. With hope and anticipation, they assembled on December 31, 1862, to await news of the Emancipation Proclamation and celebrate their coming freedom.

So once again on New Year's Eve, I will look back and think about how I got through trials and tribulations as well as dangers seen and unseen. I will joyfully lift my voice and my hands to thank Jesus for His many blessings, past and present. I will remember how He has shown me His glory in large and small ways. And I will look forward with great expectation for what lies ahead. You can say I will praise Jesus, coming and going. —BARBRANDA LUMPKINS WALLS

FAITH STEP: *List as many blessings as you can think of that Jesus has bestowed on you this year and your hopes for the new year. Hold that list in your hand as you pray and give thanks to Him before midnight strikes.*

ABOUT THE AUTHORS

 BECKY ALEXANDER teaches for the International Guide Academy, leading tours to many destinations. She even works on cruise ships from time to time. Before her travel adventures, she was a children's minister for 25 years. Now, she invests in kids by volunteering year-round with Operation Christmas Child, a ministry of Samaritan's Purse.

Besides *Mornings with Jesus*, Becky's devotions also appear in Guideposts' *Pray a Word a Day*. Her story "Connected by Kindness" in *Chicken Soup for the Soul: Miracles & Divine Intervention* received first-place awards from the Carolina Christian Writers Conference and Southern Christian Writers Conference.

Becky loves to write about the colorful wildflowers and singing warblers on her family's farm in Decatur, Alabama. She collaborated with her biologist brother and teacher sister to create *Clover's Wildflower Field Trip*, an award-winning children's book that supports elementary science units on plants and natural habitats. You can meet Clover, the book's character, and say hi to Becky at happychairbooks.com.

 SUSANNA FOTH AUGHTMON is an author/speaker who loves to use humor, scripture, and personal stories to explore how God's grace and truth intersect with our daily lives. Susanna lives in Idaho with

her funny, creative husband, marketer and pastor Scott Aughtmon. She is mom to three fantastic young men, Jack, Will, and Addison, who bring her a whole lot of joy. Susanna likes to connect with her readers through her blog, *Confessions of a Tired Supergirl*, and her *Good Things Newsletter*. You can catch up with her on Facebook and her website, sfaughtmon.com.

JEANNIE BLACKMER lives in Boulder, Colorado. Her most recent books include *Talking to Jesus: A Fresh Perspective on Prayer* and *MomSense: A Common Sense Guide to Confident Mothering*. She's been a freelance writer for more than 30 years and has worked in the publishing industry with a variety of authors on more than twenty-five books. She's also written numerous articles for print and online magazines and blogs. She's passionate about using written words to encourage women in their relationships with Jesus. She loves chocolate (probably too much), scuba diving, beekeeping, a good inspirational story, her family, and being outside as much as possible. She and her husband, Zane, have three adult sons. Find out more about Jeannie at jeannieblackmer.com.

ISABELLA CAMPOLATTARO cherishes opportunities to share how Jesus has transformed her mayhem into messages of encouragement. She has been writing for *Mornings with Jesus* since 2018 and contributed to *Guideposts One-Minute Daily Devotional, Pray a Word a Day, Every Day with Jesus, Daily Guideposts*

for Recovery, God's Comforting Ways, and the *Witnessing Heaven* series. A ghostwriter, editor, blogger, and speaker, Isabella is also author of *Embracing Life: Letting God Determine Your Destiny,* a Bible study aimed at helping women navigate challenging transitions. Holding an MS in public relations and management, Isabella formerly worked in corporate communications. She lives on Florida's fabulous Suncoast with her two sons, Pierce and Isaac. She enjoys travel, cooking, watching her sons participate in sports, writing, reading, running, arts and culture, random adventures, deep conversation, the beach, dancing, and music.

KRISTY DEWBERRY is a freelance writer. She is a winner of the 2020 Guideposts Writers Workshop contest and was recognized by *Guideposts* as one of five women to celebrate on International Women's Day for her articles on Alzheimer's disease. She is also a contributor to *Strength & Grace,* a bimonthly devotional magazine for caregivers. Kristy has a passion for writing about her experiences in the hopes it will help and inspire others. When not writing, Kristy runs her eBay business and loves to travel with her husband. She has six delightful grandchildren, a faithful dog, and a cranky Quaker parrot who will probably outlive them all.

PAT BUTLER DYSON lives and writes from her home in Beaumont, Texas. She shares life with Jeff, her good-natured husband of 42 years, who hammers out a living in the family hardware business.

Pat, having only recently learned to tell a wrench from a ratchet, has been discouraged from working in the family business, which is fine with her. She'd rather write about Jesus or play with her four toddler grandchildren. Formerly an English and special education teacher, Pat has contributed to Guideposts publications for 28 years. She enjoys writing devotions for *Strength & Grace*, Guideposts' magazine for caregivers, and has been published on the website prayerideas.org. Pat feels privileged to share her walk with Jesus and the heart and humor in her life with *Mornings with Jesus* readers; connect with her on Facebook.

GWEN FORD FAULKENBERRY is a mother, teacher, newspaper columnist, and director of Arkansas Strong, a nonprofit, nonpartisan organization that tells stories of everyday Arkansans doing good things and seeks to bring people together to benefit the community. She lives in the Ozark Mountains on a family ranch accessible only by a rough dirt road. Gwen figures she is the only Southerner who hates sweet tea but admits she loves writing and talking about Jesus. When she's not chasing her kids, teaching, or writing, she bakes artisan bread and takes long walks with Jesus and her bulldog, Mugsy.

GRACE FOX lives on a sailboat with her husband near Vancouver, British Columbia. She's the author of fourteen books, including the first in a three-part series, *Names of God: Living Unafraid.* She's also a devotional blogger, a member of the First 5 writing team (Proverbs 31 Ministries), and cohost of the podcast *Your Daily Bible Verse*. Through her writing and Bible teaching, she inspires hope and courage—with a dash of adventure.

Grace is also codirector of International Messengers Canada, a missionary sending agency with a staff of nearly three hundred in thirty-one countries. She and her husband lead short-term mission teams to Eastern Europe annually. In her spare time, Grace enjoys sailing, spending time with her kids and thirteen grandchildren, taking long walks with Jesus, and snapping photos of flowers and seaside scenes. Learn more about her at gracefox.com and fb.com/gracefox.author.

HEIDI GAUL lives in a historic home with her husband and furry family in Oregon's Willamette Valley. She loves to garden, hike, and repurpose damaged items to new life as beautiful art pieces. Travel—whether around the block or the world—is her passion, and she thrives on experiencing new adventures. An ex-Bible Study Fellowship group leader, she has contributed to twelve Guideposts books, including *Every Day with Jesus, Mornings with Jesus, Guideposts One-Minute Daily Devotional, Pray a Word a Day, Exploring God's Promises: Hope,* and *Pray a Word for Strength.*

A Cascade Award winner for devotions, many of her pieces have also appeared in *The Upper Room*, and her stories are included in twelve *Chicken Soup for the Soul* anthologies. She has served as a finals judge for many major Christian writing competitions. Heidi enjoys sharing her journey to hope in Jesus through life's broken dreams and detours. She leads writing and Bible workshops and mentors writers' groups. She'd love to hear from you at heidigaul.com or on Facebook.

TRICIA GOYER is an acclaimed author known for her captivating storytelling. With more than eighty published books, she's a prolific writer of historical and contemporary fiction and nonfiction. As a wife, mother of ten, and former teen mom, her writing resonates with authenticity and hope. Tricia's works tackle themes of faith, family, and redemption. She's also a speaker and mentor, sharing her wisdom with aspiring writers. You can connect with Tricia at triciagoyer.com.

JENNIFER GRANT is a writer, editorial consultant, and author of books for both children and adults. She has written for many print publications, including *Woman's Day* and *Chicago Parent*. For more than a decade, she wrote features, restaurant profiles, and general interest columns for *Sun-Times Media* newspapers and was a health and family columnist for the *Chicago Tribune*. Jennifer's most well-known work for kids is *Maybe God Is Like That Too*, which won multiple awards for excellence in children's literature. Her most recent book for adults is *Dimming the Day: Evening Reflections for Quiet Wonder*, and her most recent book for kids is *What If I Can't Explain God?* Jennifer lives in Chicago with her husband.

PAMELA TOUSSAINT HOWARD is a native New Yorker who currently lives and works in Atlanta, Georgia. She developed a love for writing and the confidence to become a writer and editor from her dad, a printing plant supervisor. Pamela pursued a degree in journalism from Fordham University and won a coveted summer internship at *Essence* magazine. She went on to become the magazine's associate editor and subsequently a trade newspaper reporter, nonprofit media spokeswoman, and coauthor of eight published books, including *His Rules* (Waterbrook/ Penguin Random House). Also a licensed minister, Pamela enjoys opportunities to teach at women's conferences, Bible studies, and occasionally on local television.

She and her husband, Andrew, love to travel and also to minister to the homeless and the formerly incarcerated through their informal backpack outreach. Visit her at pamink.com

JENNIE IVEY lives and writes in Tennessee. She was selected to attend the Guideposts Writers Workshop in 2008 and has been writing for Guideposts publications ever since. She's also a weekly columnist for the *Cookeville Herald-Citizen* newspaper and the author of three books: *Tennessee Tales the Textbooks Don't Tell, E Is for Elvis,* and *Soldiers, Spies & Spartans: Civil War Stories from Tennessee.*

GLORIA JOYCE, a longtime reader of *Guideposts* magazine, won a spot in the 2022 Guideposts Writers Workshop contest. "I am honored for the opportunity to share my heart in *Mornings with Jesus* and to encourage readers in the same way that Guideposts has always encouraged me." Gloria hopes to inspire others on their journey with Jesus, using the little moments of life to bring them greater reward in their relationship with Him.

Gloria lives in Pennsylvania with her husband and two daughters whom she has been homeschooling for 13 years. She has a degree in human resources management and marketing, and while she has used that experience to train many corporate employees and executives, Gloria says training her children in the aspects of education, life, and our Lord has been her most rewarding position.

JEANETTE LEVELLIE and her pastor husband, Kevin, make their home in Paris, Illinois. They love feeding birds outside their dining room window, watching the sunset in a smog-free sky, and thanking their helpful neighbors who rescue their cats from under the garage eaves (don't ask).

Jeanette is the author of six humor and inspirational books and hundreds of published articles, stories, and devotionals. She is also an ordained minister who preaches and teaches about Jesus with enthusiasm and laughter. Her favorite book of the Bible is Colossians because it resonates with the deity of Jesus and assures us of our right standing with God.

When she's not reading or writing, you'll find Jeanette watching a black-and-white movie with Kevin or talking baby talk to one of her four cats, Pokey, Dr. Phibes, Wally, and Princess Di.

 ERICKA LOYNES first fell in love with words as a child in Chicago, performing speeches under the guidance of her mentor, civil rights activist Mamie Till Mobley, the mother of Emmett Till. Seeing her own mother publish works for a Christian company sparked the idea in Ericka that she, too, could be a writer. Ericka has written in spaces ranging from college journals to corporate training. She contributed to the book *Blessed Is She: The Transforming Prayer Journeys of 30 African American Women* by Victoria Saunders McAfee and is a coauthor of *The Ashes Have Voices: Stories to Motivate, Inspire and Ignite Healing.* Ericka is also one of the 2018 Guideposts Writers Workshop contest winners.

Currently, Ericka is a director of organizational development and design. She enjoys encouraging others through career and Enneagram coaching, motivational speaking, and, of course, inspirational writing. Born and raised in Chicago, Ericka lives in Memphis with her husband and young adult son.

 ERIN KEELEY MARSHALL has enjoyed writing for Guideposts books for many years and counts her opportunities to contribute to *Mornings with Jesus* among her favorite career blessings. Her work

spans numerous genres as an editor, and she is published in both fiction and nonfiction. Visit her at erinkeeleymarshall.com and on Facebook @ErinKeeleyMarshall-Author and Instagram @erinkeeleymarshall.

 DIANNE NEAL MATTHEWS attended her first writers' conference in 1999 after fantasizing about being an author since first grade. Since then, she has written, cowritten, or contributed to twenty-five books. Her five daily devotionals include *The One Year Women of the Bible* and *Designed for Devotion: A 365-Day Journey from Genesis to Revelation* (a Selah Award winner). Dianne has also published hundreds of articles, guest blog posts, newspaper features, stories for compilation books, Bible studies, and one poem. Since 2012, her favorite writing project each year has been sharing her faith journey with some of her favorite people in the world, the wonderful readers of *Mornings with Jesus*. Dianne and her husband, Richard, live in west Tennessee. When she's not writing, Dianne enjoys volunteering at her church, trying new recipes, reading, soaking up nature, and FaceTiming with her three children and five grandchildren, who all live too far away. Connect with Dianne through her Facebook author page or diannenealmatthews.com.

 CLAIRE MCGARRY feels blessed to be contributing to *Mornings with Jesus* again this year. She is a maker of lists, mistakes, brownies, and soups. Dirty laundry is her nemesis as she tries to focus

more on creating a loving home, rather than cleaning it. She's the author of *Grace in Tension: Discover Peace with Martha and Mary* and the family Lenten devotionals *Abundant Mercy* and *With Our Savior*. A regular contributor to *Living Faith* and catholicmom.com, her stories have appeared in various Guideposts publications, *Chicken Soup for the Soul* books, and numerous devotionals. A former lay missionary and founder of MOSAIC of Faith, she endeavors to fish for more people to bring to Jesus through her speaking engagements, women's groups, and writing. Claire lives in New Hampshire with her husband and three kids, who always keep her laughing and humble. Connect with her via her Facebook author page and her blog, shiftingmyperspective.com.

JENNIFER ANNE F. MESSING is the author of four books, including American Fiction Award–winner *Love's Faithful Promise: Heart-Stirring Short Stories and Poems of Romance and Faith*. A Cascade Writing Contest two-time winner ("published short story"), she's a poet, speaker, graphic designer, worship leader, and past president of Cascade Christian Writers. Jennifer Anne has had numerous articles, short stories, and poems published in various online magazines and books, including *The Proverbs 31 Woman*, *Woman's World*, *Bible Advocate*, *LIVE*, *Purpose*, *Standard*, and more.

Originally from the Philippines, Jennifer Anne and her husband, Michael, are the parents of three grown children, grandparents of three young boys, and reside in Oregon. Connect with her on Facebook @jenniferannemessing.

author, on X (formerly Twitter) at @JennyAnnMessing, and on her website, jenniferannemessing.com.

 CYNTHIA RUCHTI is perhaps best known throughout the writing world for telling stories hemmed in hope. Her tagline is "I can't unravel. I'm hemmed in hope." She enjoys paying attention to people's needs and the Word of God to watch where they intersect, and then expressing the life-giving connection through story. Cynthia is the author of forty books (fiction and nonfiction), serves on the worship team at her church, speaks often at women's groups and writing conferences, and serves as a literary agent with Books & Such Literary Management. She and her husband first met in grade school and have been devoted to each other and the Lord ever since. Their three children and six grandchildren live close enough to share a row at church or bump into each other at the grocery store. You can learn more about Cynthia and her pursuits at cynthiaruchti.com.

 EMILY E. RYAN is a minister's wife, mother of four, and English teacher who first dedicated her writing life to Jesus when she was a child. Most of her devotions begin as prayers on the way to work when Jesus reminds her of His infinite love and amazing grace as she drives toward the sunrise. In this season of life—full of teens, tweens, and all the beautiful noise and chaos that comes with them—Emily is familiar with the

struggle to find those rare quiet moments and claim them for Jesus. She writes about this struggle in her latest book, *Guilt-Free Quiet Times*, and encourages women with practical creativity to ditch guilt and embrace grace. A writer and speaker for more than 20 years, Emily sees contributing to *Mornings with Jesus* as one of the highlights of her ministry.

Emily and her family live Texas. She loves hearing how God is working in the lives of her readers; connect with her at emilyeryan.com.

KAREN SARGENT's first submission to Guideposts was published in *Angels on Earth* in 2017. Since then, she has enjoyed writing devotions for *Strength & Grace*, *Pray a Word a Day*, *Mornings with Jesus*, and more. Karen is the award-winning author of *Waiting for Butterflies* and leads book launches for authors. She and her husband enjoy retirement in beautiful Southeast Missouri, where they are growing into their new roles as Mimi and Pops.

STEPHANIE THOMPSON seeks Jesus's face as she petitions Him to protect and guide her loved ones from the Greatest Generation to iGen, including her twenty-year-old daughter, who is at college; her octogenarian widowed mother, who has had a couple of falls; her ninety-five-year-old grandmother-in-law, who lives at their house; and her hardworking husband, Michael, who makes life an adventure.

A former TV news reporter, syndicated newspaper columnist, radio talk show host, and public relations director, Stephanie began writing for Guideposts after winning the Writers Workshop contest in 2004. She is a contributing editor for *Guideposts* and *Angels on Earth* and has contributed to *Witnessing Heaven*, *Walking in Grace*, *All God's Creatures*, *A Grateful Heart*, *Strength & Grace,* and *Mornings with Jesus*. Stephanie lives in Edmond, Oklahoma, and invites readers to connect with her on Facebook and Instagram.

 CASSANDRA TIERSMA is a self-confessed messy-a.n.i.c. (messy, absentminded, normal-ish, imperfect, creative) woman of faith. Her articles, photography, and poetry have been published in multiple newspapers. Her book *Come In, Lord, Please Excuse the Mess!* is a guide for spiritual healing and recovery for messy-a.n.i.c. women who struggle with clutter bondage. With a colorful history as a performance artist, writer, speaker, workshop presenter, and ministry leader, it is Cassandra's mission to bless and encourage women in their faith so they can become the full expression of who God created them to be.

Cassandra and her husband, John, are currently building a "skoolie" rolling tiny home. Cassandra also plays autoharp and serves as women's ministry director at the historic little stone chapel that is their church home. Connect with Cassandra by sending an email to cassandra@cassandratiersma.com.

 SUZANNE DAVENPORT TIETJEN is the author of *The Sheep of His Hand* and *40 Days to Your Best Life for Nurses*, in addition to writing for *Mornings with Jesus*. She and her husband, Mike, have lived on his family farm in Illinois, in a cabin deep in the Hiawatha Forest of Michigan, and now on the High Plains of Wyoming. Suzanne was a longtime shepherd and currently keeps bees. She is a retired neonatal nurse practitioner who cared for sick and tiny newborns in ambulances, helicopters, and hospitals of four states for more than 25 years.

 Award-winning author MARILYN TURK writes historical and contemporary novels seasoned with suspense and romance. Marilyn considers herself blessed to be a Guideposts contributor to its various publications, including *Walking in Grace*. Marilyn and her husband are lighthouse enthusiasts and have visited over 100 lighthouses, even serving as volunteer lighthouse caretakers at Little River Light off the coast of Maine.

She is a member of American Christian Fiction Writers; Faith, Hope and Love Christian Writers; Advanced Writers and Speakers Association; Word Weavers International; and the United States Lighthouse Society.

Marilyn and her husband, Chuck, live in Florida, where they have fun playing tennis, walking their golden retriever, Dolly, and spending time on the water kayaking and fishing. Find her at marilynturk.com.

BARBRANDA LUMPKINS WALLS is a writer and editor in northern Virginia, where she fights traffic and gets inspiration daily for connecting God's Word to everyday life. Barbranda served as the writer for the book *My Sunday Best: Pearls of Wisdom, Wit, Grace, and Style* and the lead essayist for the photography book *Soul Sanctuary: Images of the African American Worship Experience.* The former newspaper reporter and magazine editor has written for a number of national publications, including *Guideposts, Cooking Light,* and *Washingtonian.* Besides appearing in *Mornings with Jesus,* her devotions can be found in *Voices.*

Barbranda and her husband, Hal, enjoy spending time with friends and family, especially their adult son and daughter, son-in-law, and beloved grandson. Connect with her on X (formerly Twitter) at @Barbrandaw and on Instagram at barbl427.

BRENDA L. YODER is a licensed mental health counselor, elementary school counselor, former history teacher, and lover of antiques, gardens, front-porch rockers, and her grandkids. She and her husband, Ron, raised four children on their family dairy farm in northern Indiana, where they currently raise Bernese mountain dogs, goats, chickens, and cattle and host an Airbnb. They love camping and visiting their grandchildren and adult children throughout the country.

A passionate educator, Brenda twice won the Touchstone Award for teachers. She has authored *Uncomplicated:*

Simple Secrets for a Compelling Life; Fledge: Launching Your Kids Without Losing Your Mind; and *Balance, Busyness, and Not Doing It All.* She has been featured in Guideposts' *Evenings with Jesus; Chicken Soup for the Soul* books; and *The Washington Post.* She hosts the *Midlife Moms* and *Life Beyond the Picket Fence* podcasts and the Midlife Moms Facebook Group. Connect with Brenda at brendayoder.com.

Author Index

AUTHOR INDEX | 521

Acknowledgments

Every attempt has been made to credit the sources of copyrighted material used in this book. If any such acknowledgment has been inadvertently omitted or miscredited, receipt of such information would be appreciated.

Scripture quotations marked (AMP) are taken from the *Amplified Bible*. Copyright © 2015 by The Lockman Foundation, La Habra, California. All rights reserved.

Scripture quotations marked (AMPC) are taken from the *Amplified Bible, Classic Edition*. Copyright © 1954, 1958, 1962, 1964, 1965, 1987 by The Lockman Foundation.

Scripture quotations marked (CEV) are taken from *Holy Bible: Contemporary English Version*. Copyright © 1995 by American Bible Society.

Scripture quotations marked (CJB) are taken from the *Complete Jewish Bible* by David H. Stern. Copyright © 1998. All rights reserved. Used by permission of Messianic Jewish Publishers, 6120 Day Long Lane, Clarksville, MD 21029. messianicjewish.net

Scripture quotations marked (CSB) are taken from *The Christian Standard Bible*. Copyright © 2017 by Holman Bible Publishers. Used by permission.

Scripture quotations marked (ESV) are taken from the *Holy Bible, English Standard Version*. Copyright © 2001 by Crossway Bibles, a division of Good News Publishers. Used by permission. All rights reserved.

Scripture quotations marked (GNT) are taken from the *Holy Bible, Good News Translation*. Copyright © 1992 by American Bible Society.

Scripture quotations marked (GW) are taken from *God's Word Translation*. Copyright © 1995 by God's Word to the Nations. Used by permission of Baker Publishing Group.

Scripture quotations marked (HCSB) are taken from the *Holman Christian Standard Bible*. Copyright © 1999, 2000, 2002, 2003, 2009 by Holman Bible Publishers, Nashville, Tennessee. All rights reserved.

Scripture quotations marked (KJV) are taken from the *King James Version of the Bible*.

Scripture quotations marked (MSG) are taken from *The Message*. Copyright © 1993, 1994, 1995, 1996, 2000, 2001, 2002 by Eugene H. Peterson.

Scripture quotations marked (NABRE) are taken from the *New American Bible*, revised edition, © 2010, 1991, 1986, 1970 Confraternity of Christian Doctrine, Inc., Washington, DC. All rights reserved.

Scripture quotations marked (NASB and NASB1995) are taken from the *New American Standard Bible*. Copyright © 1960, 1962, 1963, 1968, 1971, 1972, 1973, 1975, 1977, 1995 by The Lockman Foundation, La Habra, California. Used by permission.

Scripture quotations marked (NCV) are taken from the *New Century Version*. Copyright © 2005 by Thomas Nelson.

Scripture quotations marked (NET) are taken from the *NET Bible*® (New English Translation). Copyright © 1996–2017 by Biblical Studies Press, L.L.C.; http://netbible.com. All rights reserved.

Scripture quotations marked (NIV) are taken from *The Holy Bible, New International Version*. Copyright © 1973, 1978, 1984, 2011 by Biblica, Inc. Used by permission of Zondervan. All rights reserved worldwide. zondervan.com

Scripture quotations marked (NKJV) are taken from *The Holy Bible, New King James Version*. Copyright © 1982 by Thomas Nelson.

Scripture quotations marked (NLT) are taken from the *Holy Bible, New Living Translation*. Copyright © 1996, 2004, 2007 by Tyndale House Foundation. Used by permission of Tyndale House Publishers Inc., Carol Stream, Illinois. All rights reserved.

Scripture quotations marked (TLB) are taken from *The Living Bible*. Copyright © 1971 by Tyndale House Publishers, Inc., Carol Stream, Illinois. All rights reserved.

Scripture quotations marked (TPT) are taken from *The Passion Translation*. Copyright © 2016 by Broadstreet Publishing Group, Savage, Minnesota. All rights reserved.

Scripture quotations marked (VOICE) are taken from *The Voice Bible*, copyright © 2012 Thomas Nelson, Inc. The Voice™ translation copyright © 2012 Ecclesia Bible Society. All rights reserved.

A NOTE FROM THE EDITORS

WE HOPE YOU ENJOYED *Mornings with Jesus 2025*, published by Guideposts. For over 75 years, Guideposts, a nonprofit organization, has been driven by a vision of a world filled with hope. We aspire to be the voice of a trusted friend, a friend who makes you feel more hopeful and connected.

By making a purchase from Guideposts, you join our community in touching millions of lives, inspiring them to believe that all things are possible through faith, hope, and prayer. Your continued support allows us to provide uplifting resources to those in need. Whether through our communities, websites, apps, or publications, we inspire our audiences, bring them together, and comfort, uplift, entertain, and guide them. Visit us at guideposts.org to learn more.

We would love to hear from you. Write us at Guideposts, P.O. Box 5815, Harlan, Iowa 51593 or call us at (800) 932-2145. Did you love *Mornings with Jesus 2025*? Leave a review for this product on guideposts.org/shop. Your feedback helps others in our community find relevant products.

Find inspiration, find faith, find Guideposts.

Shop our best sellers and favorites at
guideposts.org/shop
Or scan the QR code to go directly
to our Shop

Made in the USA
Columbia, SC
29 November 2024

47862360R00289